Calvin Wiley

Scriptural views of national trials

The true road to the independence and peace of the Confederate States of America

Calvin Wiley

Scriptural views of national trials
The true road to the independence and peace of the Confederate States of America

ISBN/EAN: 9783337223632

Printed in Europe, USA, Canada, Australia, Japan

Cover: Foto ©Suzi / pixelio.de

More available books at **www.hansebooks.com**

SCRIPTURAL VIEWS

OF

NATIONAL TRIALS:

OR

THE TRUE ROAD

TO

THE INDEPENDENCE AND PEACE

OF THE

CONFEDERATE STATES OF AMERICA

BY

REV. C. H. WILEY,

SUPERINTENDENT OF PUBLIC SCHOOLS OF NORTH CAROLINA.

"As for us, our eyes as yet failed for our vain help: in our watching we have watched for a nation *that* could not save *us*."—*Lam. IV: 17*.

'Come, let us return unto the Lord: for He hath torn, and He will heal us; He hath smitten, and He will bind us up."—*Hosea, VI: 1*.

GREENSBORO, N. C.:
STERLING, CAMPBELL & ALBRIGHT.
1863.

PREFACE.

The author of the following work has been prompted to its preparation by a single motive, a stern and increasing sense of duty to God and to his country.

From the commencement of the American crisis he has looked to see the Church or some of its most distinguished members lead the public mind to the consideration and application of those great Truths by which alone the convulsions and trials of time are to be correctly accounted for ; and this expectation was not unreasonable in a community long enjoying the services of such a ministry as that found in the Confederate States of America, learned in the Scriptures, godly and sound in the faith.

But while the christian element of society has very generally recognized the doctrines which control the revolution through which the country is passing, it has not embodied them in any permanent, solemn deliverance, nor given to them that prominence which their paramount importance deserves ; and this has been owing not to any want of knowledge or of religious zeal, but to the intense and absorbing interest which all have felt in the immediate issues and the passing phazes of a terrible struggle for national existence and independence forced upon the country by an ambitious and cruel power.

Every patriotic member of the community has felt a burning desire to contribute something to the safety of the state so unjustly and fiercely assailed—a desire in which the writer has largely shared and which has induced him to wish that he could, by some invention or discovery, arm his suffering and devoted countrymen with such weapons of war as would render their courage as triumphant as it is invincible.

But while such thoughts have occupied his mind, he has still felt sure conviction that he, in common with his fellow christians, did know of a still more certain means of sucess; and he was equally certain that if the Holy Scriptures are the Word of God, this means only could be made effectual to the deliverance of the nation.

But he had an insuparable repugnance to the position of a leader in spiritual things; and while he was ever ready to follow, with his whole soul, the Church or any of its great lights in the direction to which his conscience pointed, he was very anxious not to have to unfurl the standard himself.

He hopes the public will do justice to his motives—but whatever may occur, he feels bound to pursue the course he has entered on, by considerations that over-ride all scruples of delicacy and all fears of worldly criticism.

His purpose has been to embody, in as brief a form as is consistent with utility, the great principles of revealed Truth which explain all national troubles, and which furnish an infallible remedy —to apply these to the circumstances of his beloved country, and to enforce them by such suggestions and appeals as the exigency of the times, and the state of public opinion seemed to require

He expressly repudiates the idea of wishing to be considered a leader in any sense; the charge which will most profoundly mortify him will be that of being "a setter forth" of new and strange doctrines, whatever be the spirit which may prompt this description.

He sincerely hopes that he is standing in the old paths and dealing in Truths which have been made known from the beginning,and which will be responded to by the instincts of every christian heart.

What he aspires to, is to be a means of reminding his many better brethren of an armory that all know of, but which in the confusion arising from the sudden and ferocious assault upon the State was overlooked, not forgotten; and he will be most happy if others betters qualified than himself, shall make more efficient and glorious use of these all-conquering weapons.

He has prepared the work he now offers to the public at odd intervals in the midst of other engagements that have severely tasked mind and body; and he is not ashamed to confess, with honest simplicity, that he believes he could, with more time and leasure, have presented his subjects more analytically and compactly, and with fewer errors of style.

It is due, however, to add, that in the author's opinion, it would be sinful to aim at too much brevity, or to avoid all repetition ; for whoever will undertake to instruct a community on moral questions must conquer that false pride which aims only to please the critical, must often indulge in repetitions, and must be ready to present the same important idea in many different forms.

Much of the redundancy of the following work, was, therefore, designed : the Author's great aim was and is to do good, and all he asks of the public is to receive his contribution to the deliverance of his country in the spirit with which it is offered.

He feels perfectly sure that he points a gallant, devoted and bleeding nation to the only road to independence and peace ; a road not of his discovery, but which God himself has cast up, broad and obvious, and along which he has every where put way-marks so plain that he may run who reads. He has endeavored to heed this command : "Thus saith the Lord, stand ye in the ways, and see and ask for the old paths, wherein is the good way, and walk therein, and ye shall find rest for your souls." Jer. 6, 16.

He does indeed, offer his work to the public with emotions of intense anxiety which cannot be expressed ; but none of these yearning thoughts concern his own fate as an author, while all are directed with trembling interest to the manner in which his dear countrymen shall receive the counsels of Him who says by His Word and His Providences, " Give ye ear, and heed my voice ; hearken and hear my speech." Is. 28, 23.

C. II. W.

SCRIPTURAL VIEWS

OF

NATIONAL TRIALS.

CHAPTER I.

A view of the American Crisis from a Worldly stand-point.

The United States and the Confederate States of America are now waging with each other one of the most bloody and terrible wars known in the history of the human race.

The former power is the assailing party; and its avowed purpose is the subjugation or extermination of the latter.

The Confederate States are contending for separate national existence and independence; and this power is carrying on the war, on its part, in a manner consistent with its professed object. It stands on the defensive—it seeks only to protect its own; and if left to itself it would desire no advantage of its enemy. It believes that the existence of other distinct nations on the continent is not inconsistent with its own rights and interests; and it is willing to accord to others what it claims for itself, the privilege of living under a government and laws of their choice.

The United States regards the establishment of other independent powers on the soil of North America, as an infringement of its rights and disastrous to its interests; and in aiming at the utter destruction of the Confederate States it professes to believe that it is struggling for its own existence.

It would have all its subjects to believe that whatever men can value in time is at stake in the issue; and it would place under the ban of civilization and christianity the people on whom it is making war, as a race whose extermination would be a deliverance to the world.

In consistency with these professions it has gathered up all its vast energies, and hurled them, with furious hate and zeal, at the vitals of its enemy ; and it has summoned to its aid every fierce and cruel and licentious passion of the human heart.

It regards no evil under the sun as so great as the existence and freedom of the people of the Confederate States ; and hence whatever may tend to bring calamity and destruction on these is supposed to add to the sum of human happiness.

It has, therefore, called for a sword upon the warrior, and upon his wife and children—for battle in the open field, battle by the assassin's dagger, battle by the midnight torch, and battle by poison, famine and pestilence.

Such is the present position of the contending parties : the purpose on each side is simple, the issue is clearly defined and well understood.

Those engaged in this strife trace it to political causes ; and like all actors in a drama, their view is limited to the scenes through which they are passing and their immediate causes and results.

The defendants suppose they saw the beginning of the crisis in the rapid progress of a fanatical spirit in what is now called the United States, inimical to their peace and interests ; the aggressors charge the convulsion to an institution of society peculiar to one section of a country that has been rent in sunder never to be re-united.

In short one class of politicians find the solution of this awful convulsion in African Slavery, and another in opposition to it ; and here again the issue between the parties is made up, is sharply defined, definite, single and simple.

The views of the parties as to the means of deciding this tremendous contest are equally plain ; and while the purposes of the respective belligerents remain unchanged there can be no compromise, and no end to the strife until one side or the other fails in power to prosecute its aims against the resources of the other, or against the influence of foreign nations.

The view from this worldly stand-point is full of darkness. No satisfactory or sufficient cause for such a gigantic struggle can be discovered—for no one in full possession of his reason, and acquainted with the history of the world, can even imagine the possibility of any remuneration to the assailants for the loss of liberty and of human life, and for the tremendous expenditure of means which their efforts involve. All sensible persons know that success will place the subjects of the aggressive power in the same position with the assailed, for military conquest on such a scale inevitably implies the conversion of the conquering nation into a colossal and jealous military despotism, the great mass of whose people must belong, in person and property, to the chief of the State, to enable him to hold his empire together. But the world knows that the permanent subjugation of a civilized and determined people, covering a territory as large, diversified and fertile as that of the Confederate States, is utterly impossible; and that if the armies of the invaders even had possession of the entire country there would be continued and formidable insurrections in the regions over-run, and probably rebellions on the part of the enslaved and oppressed masses in all parts of an empire necessarily despotic in the extreme.

The moment the Confederate States ceases to exist in name, the spirit of hatred and rivalry which induced the people of the aggressive power to endure so many privations would be extinguished; and these having then the disposition to consider, rationally, their situation, would become restless and turbulent, and ready to join hands with those who promised destruction to the central tyranny whose existence and integrity would be inconsistent with individual rights in any part of the empire.

And thus, from the politician's point of observation no termination to the most terrible and exhausting struggle of modern times, can be discerned: the whole scene, from this position, is a dreary picture of causeless and endless desolation.

2

CHAPTER II.

View, from a political stand-point, of the position and conduct of the worldly element of Society, in the commencement of the Contest.

The person who writes the history of the Confederate States of America, during the first stages of the present Revolution, will find that the honor of the nation does not require any ingenious marshalling or embellishment of facts. Viewed without reference to their religious bearings, the actions of the people were really illustrious ; and the records of the past furnish no parallel, in political contests, to the energy, enthusiasm and endurance which have characterized the inhabitants of the country.

Every class of the population seemed, instinctively and simultaneously, to comprehend the position of things—and every rank of Society, each sex, and all ages have performed their part with a devotion and heroism that would dignify purposes even less generous and noble.

As the first and chief desire was for the elements of worldly strength, God seemed to answer favorably all the prayers on this subject.

We asked for a zealous and politically-united people—and He inspired the whole nation with one heart and one soul in regard to its issue with the public enemy.

The prejudices of rank, the antipathies of old party combinations seemed to be instantly obliterated from the public mind : and those who were for the former Union, and those who were against it were divided now only by an emulous desire to outdo each other in efforts and sacrifices for the New Confederacy.

We were fearful of domestic discord, and especially of servile insurrections ; yet the bosom of Society has never been ruffled by any internal forces, while not a single effort at armed resistance to lawful authority has been detected among the slaves, except in those places occupied by the forces of the enemy.

The widow has cheerfully given her mite to the general cause, and the very poorest have contributed their earthly all in freely offering the strong arms of the husbands and brothers on which they leaned ; and never in the history of slavery on the continent did the ruling race feel so little apprehensions from the African element of society as it has done since it has witnessed the result of attempts by a hostile and formidable power, with immense armies on the soil, to seduce or force the negroes into rebellion against their masters.

We were not without anxiety that the machinery of a complex political system formed by a confederation of Sovereign States, would at first be wanting in the energy. and unity of purpose and action essential to the safety of the country at such a time; but the General and State Governments, in their organized capacities, have been in nearly perfect accord with each other, and the whole machinery of authority has worked as smoothly as it is possible to operato any organism dealing with and controlled by creatures with human passions and infirmities.

We prayed for courage and military ardor among our troops; and we have had an army, gathered without difficulty from every rank. and walk of life, animated with a zeal, heroism and contempt of danger and suffering, which ranks it with the best the world has ever seen.

We were afraid that the free citizens of a Democracy would not readily submit to the discipline necessary to the safety and success of armies; but while no mere worldly cause ever attracted to its standard hosts of such a character as have been mustered into the Confederate service, men of learning, men of wealth, men of ease, men accustomed to the exercise of every human right, men who left loving and beloved families in want at home, mechanics, farmers, planters, merchants, members of the learned professions, teachers and students, no soldiery have ever exhibited more uncomplaining patience, more persevering endurance, more intrepid constancy amid every difficulty, danger and suffering that can befall the human body, and wear out the energy of the human soul.

In short, the whole community gave itself in heart, body and estate to the new order of things; and in behalf of this Government of its choice it has met the storm of a fierce and most cruel war with a unity of purpose, feeling and sympathy, an energy, zeal and devotion, never before known, under such trials, in any temporal cause.

Rulers and subjects, citizens and soldiers, men and women, labored and sacrificed with one heart and one purpose; and the loss of property, the deprivation of former comforts, the separation of families, the exile from home, the exactions and oppressions of pitiless tyrants and brutal soldiery in temporary possession of the soil, the sundering of the most sacred ties of nature, the wasting scourges of the camp and the slaughter of numerous and terrible battles only served to draw the people of the Confederate States into a closer political union with each other, to deepen and strengthen their at-

tachment to the cause for which they have suffered so much, and to
it in a clearer light before their minds the worldly views of the
issue between them and their enemies.

The whole nation now comprehends its position and prospects as
far as these can be understood from a political point of observation,
and according to the principles of human reasoning; the power that
wars upon it has declared its purpose; and its actions plainly indicate that this is not an empty threat.

The destiny of both the contending parties seems to be staked on
the issues of war, of pitiless and savage war: of a war to be waged
as long as one power is able to attack and the other to defend.

Looking then at the state of things in the light of carnal philosophy, there is but one hope of deliverance to the Confederate States
—and that is, that their power of physical resistance will be sustained until their antagonist is exhausted, or turned from his purpose by the fear of foreign intervention.

The public action of the whole country is consistent with this correct view of its position; and Government and people on bending
all their energies in the direction which, to human sagacity, alone
promises success.

The former has not failed to adopt measures to enlighten foreign
Governments as to the true character of the contest, and their interests, in its early termination in favor of the Confederate States;
and all classes of the population have made up their minds to submit cheerfully to whatever is thought to be necessary to strengthen
the military defenses of the country.

They can yield nothing to their adversary without making utter
ship-wreck of all that is dear to freemen—they are ready to surrender every thing to the requirements of their own cause.

They are, in their political sentiments, the most united people on
the face of the whole earth—they are, in principle, the most loyal
to their own authorities.

They are thoroughly imbued with an unconquerable spirit of resistance : they are straining every nerve for the development of war-
like resources, they are prepared to brave and endure every affliction
which human malice can invent, and they are ready to sacrifice every
thing but the cause which has united and armed them.

Human wisdom, human strength, and human patriotism are here
displayed to the utmost extent consistent with human infirmity ;
and yet, is there not a universal impression that something still is
wanting in the acting of this grand and solemn drama? Has every
character been represented on the stage? The statesman, the hero,

the patriot have nobly sustained their parts and will receive their just meed of praise from a gazing and interested world; but has not the greatness of the tragedy been marred in the performance by leaving out the most important character of all? Has the christian philosopher taken his right position on this illustrious stage?

Has he been the real hero of the piece, filling his own proper place to which every other is subordinate, thus preserving the unity and completeness of the drama, developing its just ideas before the audience, and displaying the true relation of every scene and by-play to the one central and controlling plot of which every other is but a part and incident?

Has mere political agreement succeeded in uniting society in all its ramified interests, and made it a perfect, consistent moral machine living and moving to one end?

Has loyalty, by itself, here manifested in its most noble worldly aspects, been sufficient to draw from the soil of the popular heart those manly, generous, self-denying and virtuous actions and sentiments in all the relations, dealings and responsibilities of the individual necessary to give enduring life and stamina to a nation?

Have we not all felt a partial eclipse of that sun which alone can clothe the moral world with beauty and strength? has not the whole machinery of state, perfect in its order and arrangements, suffered for the want of healthful energy and proper direction in those spiritual, religious springs which constitute the vital forces of all communities?

There is a universal impression that this terrible tragedy has a deeper meaning than the mere political issues at stake; and that human wisdom and human power can do no more to bring to an early close a contest which, to those who look at it in the light of worldly philosophy alone, is one of the most painful and inexplicable mysteries of time.

No one dare to say that the Confederates have not succeeded for the want of the carnal appliances of States; people, rulers and soldiers have done and endured more than the most sanguine had reason to expect, and yet they seem as far off as ever from an object which all believed would be accomplished with much less sacrifice, enthusiasm and courage.

Men of the world have a right to feel that they have done their part, and performed it well; but the clouds still thicken on the devoted land, and the tempest howls in fiercer fury through all its borders.

"What more can we do?" asks the statesman, the soldier, the cit-

izen. "What is the solution of this awful mystery?" is the question in every heart. "*There be* many that say, who will show us
any good?" *Ps.*iv. 6 ; and the object of the succeeding pages is to furnish to a gallant and bleeding nation a true and satisfactory answer
to this all-important question. It is drawn from a source that cannot lie ; and it directs the suffering and beloved countrymen of the
writer to the origin and remedy of all their afflictions. It is not a
quack nostrum of the author's own discovery : it is the very balm of
God for those whom He has torn and to whom He Himself speaks.
"To-day if ye will hear His voice harden not your hearts."

CHAPTER III.

The Bible View of Revolutions.—The absolute and universal Sovereignty of God, and its results.

We are taught in the Holy Scriptures, the only infallible Standard of Truth, that there is one God, Almighty, of whom, and through whom and to whom are all things.

We are taught, also, that He created all things, and for His pleasure they are, and were created : " For by him were all things created, that are in heaven, and that are in earth, visible and invisible, whether they be thrones or dominions, principalities or powers : all things were created by Him and for Him."

This God is a God far off and near at hand ; and while He fills heaven and earth, creating and holding the worlds in order, there is not a sparrow that falls to the ground without His permission.

Every event that occurs, from the launching of a planet to the movements of an insect, is under His immediate and special control : and all things are directed by Him to His own glory.

All things, therefore, material and immaterial, animate and inanimate, visible and invisible, must have a moral purpose and significance ; and hence nothing was made for itself, and all created beings, all matter, and all events, powers and dominions are connected with one universal system of Providence, and are made to display the Divine perfections.

Among the attributes of the Deity are perfect goodness, and perfect and immutable justice ; and it has pleased Him to make a sublime display of these in the means He has devised to save members of a rebellious and fallen race from the consequences of their sins.

Our world has been the theatre of those most amazing events, the incarnation, crucifixion and resurrection of Jesus Christ, the eternal Son of God ; and by this means the honor of God's broken Law has been vindicated, and He can be just, and the justifier of every sinner that believes.

From the time of Adam's transgression and fall this Saviour has been announced and preached as the Light and Life of the world : and a Church has been established of the believers in Him, whose mission it is to preach the glorious gospel of the blessed God to every creature

Different means have been adopted, at different times, to warn the world that it lies in wickedness; and we are to believe, and we can know by a proper study of the history of those times, that the gospel agencies before the flood, and under the Jewish dispensation, were the most effectual for preserving a knowledge of God's Holy Law, and for making it a means of saving the human race from utter destruction.

As the whole universe, then, has a moral meaning connected with a display of the Divine attributes, all the events of time on earth are to be solved with reference to that holy and unchangeable Law which was revealed as the Life of the world, to its violation, and to the means of grace adopted for the deliverance of those who have incurred its penalties.

The entire history of the world turns on these points—in these, and these alone, we have an explanation of the mystery of time.

The state of the earth is made to conform to the condition of man upon it, and to the system of grace for his redemption; and the labor necessary to procure food and clothing, the hostility of the elements, the rigor of the seasons, disease and bodily infirmities are not only necessary punishments for sin, but disciplinary influences rendered essential by the depraved nature of man to restrain him from that unbridled licentiousness to which he is prone, and which would hasten the extinction of the race.

In the same light we are to construe all national changes: they are ever the immediate result of obedience to or violation of the Law of God in the institutions and heart of the nation, and they are, also, intimately connected with the progress of the Church.

However obscure, or weak or remote a people may be, their existence and history are not independent or exceptional events, having no connection with the one grand, consistent course of Divine Providence; and while the end of every change in the condition of nations—whether savage or civilized, christian or pagan, will be made to minister to the progress of the means of grace, it will, also, be invariably and strictly in conformity with the immutable principles of Divine Justice.

This is the uniform doctrine of Scripture, all of which is given by inspiration of God; and this is, also, the teaching of the facts recorded in it. All history, as it appears on these inspired pages, is a history of the Church, and also, a series of moral and just retributions; and national sins and national afflictions are well understood to be always and inseparably connected as cause and effect.

Whatever the character of the incidents related—whether they occurred in the ordinary course of things, or whether by miraculous displays of the Divine power, they are so stated under the inspiration of God, that we never for a moment mistake their meaning.

From the high and unclouded summit of revealed Truth, the world and all that it contains, its material things, its actions and its revolutions are beheld as one moral system, under the immediate control of the Infinite Mind, and directed to His righteous ends : nor is there a particle of matter, a living creature, a passion, idea or entity of any kind that exists for itself or by itself, or that is not in its origin and results, an integral part of a harmonious and consistent plan which will be made to minister to the glory of the Divine Power.

God, in the Holy Scriptures, is universally represented as the Sole Architect and Proprietor ; and all the labor and passion of creatures, whether they be moral or natural, animate or inanimate, are made to minister to His righteous ends. By this same light the meanest insect that creeps in the dust of the earth, is seen to be His creation, living and moving and having its being for His moral purposes—Hell and its reprobate hosts can only minister to His glory, and all the elements of society, human and angelic, and the whole moving machinery of worlds and systems of worlds are the servants of His will and the ministers of His pleasure.

When, therefore, we read in the Bible of the rise, progress and fall of nations, we are never in danger of misunderstanding causes, relations or results : the Truth which beams from the infallible Word, makes all these so clear that he may run who reads.

We do not often see, nor do we care to know, the intricate machinery of state, the intrigues of individuals, of party strifes and the clash of rival and sectional interests of the various countries, whose history stalks before us on the page of inspiration ; and so occupied are our minds with the true solution of events, and of their one grand moral lesson, that we forget those mediate agencies and results which rank highest in profane or uninspired narratives.

We are here introduced behind the scenes, and behold the Author of the Drama of Life, and the casting of the plot and arrangement of the actors—and we are not deceived or carried away by the performances and exhibitions of the stage.

We do not behold occurrences as the result of the triumph or defeat of factions, or of measures of administrative policy ; nor will we be led into the error of basing the power of a nation on its natural resources, or its weakness on the number or strength of its rivals.

God hath spoken—we have heard this—"that power belongeth unto God." *Psalm* lxii, 11.

We are made to know what constitutes the strength of kingdoms, and what it is that disgraces and destroys nations; and we are allowed to see when these elements of greatness and decay exist in the vitals of a State, and our whole attention is absorbed with their normal and inevitable development.

As we survey the progress of men and communities, we understand the part which each performs, and its relation to the general plan: and all events are seen to revolve about one central and controlling idea, and that is, that the whole series is a system of retributions, a moral lesson, manifesting the innate depravity of man, the evil and malignity of sin, and the righteousness and goodness of God, who is still causing the wrath of man to praise Him, and still advancing the general good of the world.

We behold, in the sacred text, the struggles of nations, not as mere contests for national supremacy, belonging wholly to the domain of political history, and under the exclusive control of temporal agencies: but we see in all the guidance of the Divine Hand, and we know that all are mutually dependent parts of one harmonious system of Moral Economy.

In the inspired narrative, many nations and millions of people pass before the reader, in vast processions, briefly and impressively displaying their virtues and vices, their varied fortunes and their final end; but all this grand and solemn panorama, with its thousands of shifting scenes, and its myriads of actors, is clearly understood to be one connected drama, ever directed by the unerring and the all-controlling, the never-suspended, and the special Providence of God to His own glory, and to the extension of His kingdom of righteousness and peace on earth.

In short, the sacred volume discloses by its *facts*, as well as by its *doctrines*, that God is a Moral Being, that His whole creation has a moral purpose, and that all the events of time are made subservient to this end—that every revolution and all the progress and history of kingdoms are special providences, to be understood only by their relations to an immutable moral Law, displaying the righteousness of the Supreme Ruler, and working together for the advancement of His ever living Church.

Does any one ask for the proof of these positions? Let him search the Scriptures—they are *all* cited as a text in point.

Nor is there any want of orthodox teachings on these subjects in the religious Literature of the Confederate States; and the author's object in stating these fundamental truths of Scripture here—truth taught in a thousand familiar formulas, and known to the whole mind of the Church—is to bring the reader to this as the proper starting point for a just examination of the circumstances of the times

There is no difficulty in gaining the assent of any one versed in the Scriptures of eternal Truth to these positions as correct statements of elementary principles of the Divine Economy—but while we are all ready to receive and acknowledge certain great propositions of the Divine Government as abstract truths, it is hard for us to give them a practical and living application to those events in which we are personally interested, and which take stronghold of the sympathies and feelings of our carnal nature.

The teachings of the historical part of the revealed Word must be studied in the Scriptures themselves; nor is it at all necessary to quote here the numerous Texts which declare the being, attributes and prerogatives of the Supreme Ruler. But for the purpose before the author, it may be well to cite certain Texts which are specially and peculiarly applicable to the circumstances of the times; and he makes these quotations, not to add to the stock of religious knowledge, common to all the Church; but to bring before the mind of th e christian public, in their true relations and connections, the facts of the times and those eternal Truths by which they are to be solved.

PROOFS AND ILLUSTRATIONS OF FOREGOING DOCTRINES.

The first chapter of the Prophecy of Ezekiel illustrates the above doctrines by visions more expressive than human language—and such vivid representations are not uncommon in the Holy Scriptures. When the inspiration of the prophet began he was a captive in Chaldea; and the universal Providence and sovereignty of God were set before him in the grand and imposing manner related below :

"Now it came to pass in the thirtieth year, in the fourth month in the fifth day of the month, as I was among the captives by the river of Chebar, that the heavens were opened, and I saw visions o God.

In the fifth day of the month, which was the fifth year of king Jehoiachin's captivity,

The word of the Lord came expressly unto Ezekiel the priest, the son of Buzi, in the land of the Chaldeans by the river Chebar; and the hand of the Lord was there upon him.

And I looked, and, behold, a whirlwind came out of the north, a great cloud, and a fire infolding itself, and a brightness was about it, and out of the midst thereof as the colour of amber, out of the midst of the fire.

Also out of the midst thereof *came* the likeness of four living creatures. And this *was* their appearance; they had the likeness of a man.

And every one had four faces, and every one had four wings.

And their feet *were* straight feet; and the sole of their feet *was* like the sole of a calf's foot : and they sparkled like the colour of burnished brass.

And *they had* the hands of a man under their wings on their four sides; and they four had their faces and their wings.

Their wings *were* joined one to another; they turned not when they went; they went every one straight forward.

As for the likeness of their faces, they four had the face of a man, and the face of a lion, on the right side : and they four had the face of an ox on the left side; they four also had the face of an eagle.

Thus *were* their faces : and their wings *were* stretched upward; two *wings* of every one *were* joined one to another, and two covered their bodies.

And they went every one straight forward : whither the spirit was to go, they went; *and* they turned not when they went.

As for the likeness of the living creatures, their appearance *was* like burning coals of fire, *and* like the appearance of lamps : it went up and down among the living creatures; and the fire was bright, and out of the fire went forth lightning.

And the living creatures ran and returned as the appearance of a flash of lightning.

Now as I beheld the living creatures, behold one wheel upon the earth by the living creatures, with his four faces.

The appearance of the wheels and their work *was* like unto the colour of a beryl : and they four had one likeness : and their appearance and their work *was* as it were a wheel in the middle of a wheel.

When they went they went upon their four sides : *and* they turned not when they went.

As for their rings, they were so high that they were dreadful; and their rings *were* full of eyes round about them four.

And when the living creatures went, the wheels went by them : and when the living creatures were lifted up from the earth, the wheels were lifted up.

Whithersoever the spirit was to go, they went, thither *was their* spirit to go; and the wheels were lifted up over against them; for the spirit of the living creature *was* in the wheels.

When those went, *these* went; and when those stood, *these* stood : and when those were lifted up from the earth, the wheels were lifted up over against them : for the spirit of the living creature *was* in the wheels.

And the likeness of the firmament upon the heads of the living creature *was* as the colour of the terrible crystal, stretched forth over their heads above.

And under the firmament *were* their wings straight, the one toward the other : every one had two, which covered on this side, and every one had two, which covered on that side, their bodies.

And when they went, I heard the noise of their wings, like the noise of great waters, as the voice of the Almighty, the voice of speech, as the noise of a host : when they stood, they let down their wings.

And there was a voice from the firmament that *was* over their heads, when they stood, *and* had let down their wings.

And above the firmament that *was* over their heads *was* the likeness of a throne, as the appearance of a sapphire stone : and upon the likeness of the throne *was* the likeness as the appearance of a man above upon it.

And I saw as the colour of amber, as the appearance of fire round about within it : from the appearance of his loins even upward, and from the appearance of his loins even downward, I saw as it were the appearance of fire, and it had brightness round about.

As the appearance of the bow that is in the cloud in the day of rain, so *was* the appearance of the brightness round about. This *was* the appearance of the likeness of the glory of the Lord. And when I saw it, I fell upon my face, and I heard a voice of one that spake."—*Ezekiel, Chapter* 1st.

The prophet first saw a whirlwind—an apt illustration of the violent revolutions and convulsions in the moral and physical forces of nature. There was a great cloud with the whirlwind, and clouds and darkness, to mortal vision, accompany the storms and commotions of the world ; but there was also a fire infolding itself, and a great brightness, indicating the wise and holy purposes of every dispensation however violent and terrible it may seem.

Out of the midst of the brightness came the likeness of four living creatures ; and in the appearance of these we have a wonderful description of the pure and exalted intelligences that act as the messengers of Heaven and execute its will.

In every storm and whirlwind—in every commotion and revolution whether among animate or inanimate things, they are present.

By these creatures, and upon the earth, was a wheel, with a wheel within; and their rings were so high that they were dreadful.

The classical heathen represented the course of Fortune by a wheel; and it is indeed the most fit emblem of the mutations of time, indicating both progress forward and the continual changes and overturning of things by which it is effected.

A wheel within a wheel has become a proverbial expression to denote the intricacy and complexity of systems moved by various and apparently contradictory springs, to one end or purpose; and doubtless the common illustration is derived from the vision of Ezekiel.

The mysterious combination of wheels which the prophet saw was a complex unity; and all the infinite and apparently contradictory variety of events constitute one harmonious system in the counsels of God. One wheel was on the earth, and thus all the rolling over of things here is part of the one uniform system of Divine Providence; and the immense and dreadful circumference of the rings shows the all-embracing extent of this one, uniform and pervading control.

The rings of the wheels were full of eyes: and thus we are most impressively taught that the perpetual whirl and rotation which elevates one to-day and depresses him to-morrow, is not a blind fatality, but a uniform and intelligent method, guided by infinite and unfailing wisdom.

In this complicated but perfect plan there is no accident, no chance events, no waste of force, no real conflict of machinery; but the wheels, the rotations of time, ever accompany the living creatures, are ever found to be the result of the one living power, the one ever-present intelligence beyond whose immediate guidance nothing can occur.

The direction of these wheels was always straight forward: to whatever point of the compass they went, it was never a backward motion, and thus, however tortuous, conflicting and retrograde may seem to mortals the eddying currents of time's eventualities, they are but the complications of the one grand and consistent scheme of Providence, that goes continually forward to the accomplishment of the ends of Infinite Wisdom.

Above and by the wheels, the rotations of time, were the living beings, or creatures, the intelligent and pure messengers who execute the Divine Will: and over these was a glorious firmament, the bright atmosphere of holiness that emanates from the presence of the Supreme Majesty, and which, always gleaming as a halo over the heads of his ministers, authenticates their Divine mission, and displays the ever-present righteousness and justice of God in all their movements.

Above this was the likeness of a throne, as the appearance of a sapphire stone; and upon the likeness of the throne was the likeness as the appearance of a man above upon it.

"And I saw," says the prophet, "as the color of amber, as the appearance of fire round about within it, from the appearance of his loins even upwards, and from the appearance of his loins even downwards, I saw as it were the appearance of fire, and it had brightness round about.

As the appearance of the bow that is in the cloud in the day of rain, so was the appearance of the brightness round about. This was the appearance of the likeness of the glory of the Lord."

It is evident that the Being here referred to is Christ, the Second, equal Person of the blessed Trinity, the everlasting and almighty Son of God; "the likeness as the appearance of a man," and the bow, symbolical of a dispensation of grace prove it, while the Invisible Father has never been represented by any similitude or image to mortal eyes.

Thus God, in the person of Christ, presides immediately over the whole course of things; and wherever the wheel of fortune or destiny rolls, there is His throne, there His authority, power and presence, for there is no destiny but the will of God, and through Christ He works out His bright designs.

By these amazing appearances, this combination of images we have an inspired representation of the causes and workings of all created things: there is presented before us a model of the mechanism of the whole moving frame of nature, with its complication of machinery, and simplicity of design, its unity of purpose, certainty of action and ever forward movement amid apparent collisions and accidental explosions, with the single, unerring and almighty power that controls and directs it to its destined work. Nothing happens outside of this single system: to its regular and normal action are to be referred all contingencies in the moral and physical universe, the earth-quake and tornado, storm and pestilence, the rise and fall of empires, the division of States, the phenomena of nature, the creation of worlds and the feeding of insects.

All existence, material or immaterial, is directly under the Throne of omnipotence: wherever there is a display of force, animate or inanimate, there is the control of the omnipresent and almighty God.

And how literally and beautifully does the wonderful vision of Ezekiel speak to our minds the descriptions of other inspired writers of the ways of Providence! how are the various characteristics of these dispensations, scattered through the volume of revealed Truth, are combined into one perfect and glowing picture!

It is said by the prophet Nahum. (1st, 3rd).

"The Lord hath his way in the whirlwind, and in the storm, and the clouds are the dust of his feet."

And though "Clouds and darkness are round about him"—yet, "righteousness and judgement are the habitation of His throne."— Ps. xcvii, 2.

"A fire goeth before Him, and burneth up His enemies round about."—Ps. xcvii 3.

Yet "Mercy and Truth are met together—righteousness and peace have kissed each other" (Ps. lxxxv, 10.) through Jesus Christ the ever living source of grace to a fallen world.

He is set as King upon the Throne; and however dark and terrible may seem the casualties of time, over all the troubled scene, on the bosom of every stormy cloud, the bow of promise is seen, indicating all these as agencies in the benign and merciful dispensations of the Redeemer's Kingdom.

In Deuteronomy, iv, 39, we have this authoritative and comprehensive declaration of the rule of the Supreme Governor—"Know, therefore, this day, and consider it in thine heart, that the Lord, He is God in Heaven above and upon the earth beneath."

Here God claims to rule not only in spiritual, or what is commonly considered as moral affairs, but in those which are usually regarded as political and temporal; not only over rational and responsible creatures, but in all the material brute agencies of the universe.

Speaking through the lips of Isaiah, the same glorious Being says, "I form the light and create darkness: I make peace and create evil: I the Lord do all these things" (xlv, 7.)

The Apostle John declares that "God is light, and in Him is no darkness at all"—and when, therefore, Jehovah professes to be the author of darkness, it is not of darkness or confusion in His own counsels, or to His own all-seeing Eye.

The reference is to those mysterious dispensations which confound the wisdom of the creature—to those Providences which are not to be understood on principles of human philosophy and which unsettle and confound the calculations of human sagacity.

"The day of the Lord," says Amos, "is a day of darkness" (v, 18): that is to say God often comes to work out His plans in a way contrary to all human expectations, by processes that render the wisdom of the wise but foolishness, and under circumstances that veil all creature sight in darkness and doubt.

Yet however dark, and mysterious and unexpected the event—
however it may, in *our* estimation, bring an eclipse over the whole
world of science, and arrest even all moral progress, the obscuration
is God's own special work, and the apparent darkness will minister
to the glory of Him who dwells in unapproachable light.

In *Amos Chap.* iii, *v's.* 4, 5, 6, we have this language.

"Will a lion roar in the forest when he hath no prey? will a
young lion cry out of his den if he has taken nothing? Can a bird
fall in a snare upon the earth, when no gin is for him? shall one
take up a snare from the earth, and have taken nothing at all? Shall
the trumpet be blown and the people not be afraid? shall there be
evil in a city and the Lord hath not done it?"

The meaning of these passages is obvious: by such familiar illustrations God would impress on our minds that all judgements are
his, that his Providence is special as well as general, that He does
everything on fixed plans, and is ever successful in all His underta-
kings.

In the above verses, and in the quotation from Isaiah, He represents Himself as the author of evil; the meaning of which is that calamities are sent by Him, and while sin is the work of the Devil,
even this has its allotted bounds and shall be used to add to the
glory of the Universal Sovereign.

As lions do not roar for nothing, so God does not permit revolutions to happen without a moral purpose: and storms, convulsions and earth-quakes, like the roaring of the lion for his prey, are
the voice of the Almighty, pursuing His certain plans.

It is said in Job, (v, 6,) "affliction cometh not forth of the dust,
neither doth trouble spring out of the ground:" whatever the circumstances of the times, whatever the agencies by which commun-
ties or nations are scourged, the special Providences of God are there.
and the malice of fiends, the inventions and actions of men
and the forces of brute matter will be made to work His will.

In the following passages we have a similar statement of the special dealings of God for moral ends, in all the phenomena of nature

"And offer a sacrifice of thanksgiving with leaven, and proclaim
and publish the free offerings: for this liketh you, O ye children of
Israel, saith the Lord God.

And I also have given you cleanness of teeth in all your cities,
and want of bread in all your places: yet ye have not returned unto
me, saith the Lord.

And also I have withholden the rain from you, when *there were*
yet three months to the harvest: and I caused it to rain upon one

4

city, and caused it not to rain upon another city : one piece was rained upon, and the piece whereupon it rained not withered.

So two or three cities wandered unto one city, to drink water: but they were not satisfied : yet have ye not returned unto me. saith the Lord.

I have smitten you with blasting and mildew · when your gardens and your vineyards and your fig trees and olive trees increased, the palmerworm devoured them : yet have ye not returned unto me. saith the Lord.

I have sent among you the pestilence after the manner of Egypt your young men have I slain with the sword, and have taken away your horses ; and I have made the stink of your camp to come up unto your nostrils : yet have ye not returned unto me, saith the Lord

I have overthrown some of you, as God overthrew Sodom and Gomorrah, and ye were as a firebrand plucked out of the burning : yet have ye not returned unto me, saith the Lord."—Amos, iv, 5–11.

Thus all calamities, in whatever shape they come, are the result of sin, and are either judgements for it or admonitions to repent ; and the extent of the evil and the agency employed are no evidence of its being more or less the result of Divine intervention.

The evil may be confined to an individual, a city or province, or it may involve nations and the world—it may be slight or terrible, and it may be accomplished by means of fire, water, pestilence, earth-quake or tornado, by creeping insects, by ferocious beasts, or by men or devils, and still it is the special dealing of God for sin, it is His voice, uttered for a purpose and which the wise will heed as they will the lion's roar.

The most impressive illustrations of the doctrines of this chapter are those in which Jehovah claims the crawling things of the dust as the unerring and effectual ministers of His will—and in the Prophet Joel (Chapter ii) the Majesty of Heaven and earth calls an army of locusts His army, and plainly declares them invincible by carnal power, not to be resisted even by all the wisdom of men, except by moral means, and by appeasing the wrath of their Creator.

But no uninspired statement of principles or facts can so forcibly present the views contended for as the following text from the Oracles of Truth : " But God prepared a worm when the morning rose the next day, and it smote the gourd that it withered."—Jonah, iv, 7.

A single member of the vilest and weakest family of living things, whose life is but an hour, and whose world a few inches of space, is the direct creation of Almighty Power—and the instinct that guides it to the prolongation of its brief existence by preying on the nearest vegetable production, is an important link in. the chain of special Providences by which the world is taught, chastened, afflicted and blessed.

Of a similar import are the words of our Saviour, in *Mathew*, x, 29—" Are not two sparrows sold for a farthing? and one of them shall not fall to the ground without your father.

But the very hairs of your head are all numbered."

Can human language be more explicit?

But let us for a moment turn to a few passages of more general import—and here we will first quote a verse found in the beginning of this chapter, begging the reader to mark how all-comprehensive in statement and how full and perfect in detail is the language used :

" For by Him were all things created, that are in heaven, and that are in earth, visible and invisible, whether they be thrones or dominions, or principalities or powers : all things were created by him and for Him "—*Col.* i, 16.

" The Lord hath made all things for Himself : yea even the wicked for the day of evil," Proverbs, xvi, 4—and to this agrees the language of Revelation (*Chap.* iv, 11,) " Thou art worthy O Lord, to receive glory, and honor and power, for Thou hast created all things, and for Thy pleasure they are and were created."

" Whatsoever the Lord pleased, *that* did he in heaven, and in earth, in the seas and all dark places," (*Ps.* cxxxv, 6); and to every work of His hands He says, as He declared to Pharaoh, " and in very deed for this cause have I raised thee up, for to show in thee my power." *Ex.* ix, 16.

He is a God at hand, and a God afar off; He fills heaven and earth, and there is no secret place where any can hide from His dominion. *Jeremiah*, xxiii, 23, 24.

He is " the Most High......that liveth forever, whose dominion is an everlasting dominion, and His kingdom is from generation to generation. And all the inhabitants of the earth are reputed as nothing : and he doeth according to His will in the army of heaven, and *among* the inhabitants of the earth ; and none can stay His hand, or say unto Him, what doest thou ?"—*Daniel*, iv, 34, 35.

In *Revelation*, iii, 14, Christ declares Himself to be " the beginning of the creation of God "—that is, He is the cause, origin and author of all ; and thus He is declared to be not only the son of God, and God, but the ultimate solution or reason for all the works of creation.

In the same book of Revelation, *Chapter*, v, 13, the inspired writer says, " And every creature which is in Heaven, and on the earth,
and under the earth, and such as are in the sea, and all that are in
them heard I, saying, Blessing and honor, and glory, and power, be
unto Him that sitteth upon the throne, and unto the Lamb for ever
and over."

Thus all things that are made, testify, in some form, to the glory
of Him who reigns over all ; and the voice of their praise directed
to the Lamb, connects the whole creation with a moral system, and
exalts the Saviour as the Maker, Proprietor and end of all.

He has the keys of hell and of death, (*Rev* i, 18,) : all the works
of creation and Providence, all the events of time and eternity have
an inseparable connection with His moral Government, "for of Him,
and through Him and to Him are all things: to whom be glory for
ever and ever. Amen."—*Rom*. xi, 36.

CHAPTER IV.

Bible Views of National Revolutions, continued.—God's holy attributes, and man's depravity, and the consequences.

It is a fundamental principle of the Christian system that God is perfectly holy, just and wise; and that as His power is absolute, without limit, or impediment from any source or cause; so its exercise is always righteous, without error, accident, confusion or injury.

But in one of the worlds created by the Supreme Architect, and under His immediate, absolute and perpetual control, there are violence, trouble and suffering—why is this?

If nothing had been revealed to the rational inhabitants of this world but the attributes of its Sovereign, a proper belief in these would require a solution of their troubles on the part of those concerned, in their own dispositions and actions.

But the Divine Disposer has not left any room for doubt; and He has given to man a full account of the origin and cause of death and of every human wo.

The first man, created in a state of holiness and happiness, rebelled against his Maker, fell from his sinless condition, and involved himself and his posterity in a state of impurity and wretchedness; and all the confusion and afflictions of time are the result of sin, and of consequent disobedience to the Divine commands.

Death was denounced to the federal head of the human race as the consequence of disobedience; but it has pleased the beneficent and almighty Ruler of the universe to suspend the full execution of the judgment pronounced on Adam and his descendants, that they might become the subjects of a system of grace, devised with a wisdom, goodness and mercy that will fill all creatures with wonder for ever

The bodies of men became immediately subject to death; and all were to be exposed to labors and trials which were partly punishments, as they were the results of the acts of those concerned, but which were, also, a wholesome discipline, a wise and benevolent economy, designed to hold in check the passions of a depraved race, to remind it continually of its fallen and dangerous condition, and to lead it to the glorious and infallible remedy for every distemper of time.

A perfect Saviour was provided for the inhabitants of a world ruined by its own perversity; and it was and is the design of an offended God that repentance and remission of sins through the atonement of this Divine Redeemer, should be preached to all men, for many thousands of years.

A rebel world is, therefore, kept from destruction by Him against whom it has deeply revolted, expressly on account of the intercession of Christ, the Son of God, and that all who will, may through Him, escape the penalty of their acts, and be prepared to enjoy eternal holiness and felicity in Heaven; and hence while the earth remains it will be characterized by events different from those which occur in any other part of the universe.

Upon it the powers of good and evil come in contact: sin against a holy, immutable and absolute God is on it, mingling in all its affairs, and while it is restrained from the full development of its tendency to utter ruin, it is not punished with that strict justice which is its reward and which is in store for it.

In the perfect plans of God it will meet with adequate retributions: but where it is sincerely repented of it has been atoned for in the infinite sufferings of Christ, and where it is not, its adequate and eternal reward is only suspended for a season that its subject may have opportunity of accepting the salvation provided, and of escaping from the certain wrath to come.

By this plain and divinely revealed theory of the mystery of time, all its painful phenomena are to be accounted for.

The earth has to be closely cultivated to cause it to yield its fruits for the subsistence of human life: the elements of Nature seem hostile to the race of man, and his brief existence is purchased by continual toil and anxiety.

He comes into the tho world with suffering, and in every condition, he is subject to disease, disappointment and sorrow; and very soon he passes for ever from this stage of being by a process from which the instincts of natural life shrink in ghastly terror.

This life of burden and travail is more than deserved by man for the innate depravity of his nature, and by his sinful actions; and it is, also, a disciplinary system absolutely necessary to prevent the evil tendency of a fallen race from ripening, like the sins of Sodom, into incurable rottenness, while it is a merciful and perpetual admonition of the wrath of God, and a living, practical and solemn remembrance of the pains and penalties of that second death which is the certain doom of all the unrepenting sons of Adam.

Such is the wise and just plan of God's dealings with man, in this world, as an individual and an immortal being; and the same system is applied to him in his national capacity, with such modifications as the circumstances of his position plainly require. ,

Nations, as such, are purely temporal beings, and must, therefore, receive, in time, the full reward of their deeds; and though as public or political organisms they have no souls, they are composed of moral or responsible beings, and must be judged and dealt with according to the dispositions and actions of the persons who compose them.

They are composed of men, and man is a rational and accountable agent, everywhere, and always under the immediate Government of God; and hence they will all be judged by the Divine Law, their sins being measured by the extent of their opportunities, and the wilfulness and stubbornness of their offences.

But while the Divine economy proceeds on this fixed and universal rule towards men in their social and political capacities, it has, also, been so adjusted, by infinite wisdom, as to make it perpetually subservient to the interests of the Redeemer's Kingdom; and though every national change or affliction will be caused by the disposition and conduct of the nations concerned, it will, likewise, be made to promote the cause of the Church on earth.

Convulsions are decreed as an element in the advancement of the Kingdom of Christ, because the character of nations and not the plans of God, render them inevitable; and while they are thus the agents of the Divine Will in promoting the progress of the system of grace, they are, also, the awards of the righteous Judge for the sins of those concerned.

Here, then, is the certain solution of all the toils, mutations and sorrows of time : here is the divinely-given account of the origin and uses of every evil which befalls a people.

All national as well as all individual suffering, is the certain result of a violation of the Law of God—and the offence of the afflicted parties may be in his and their dispositions, or in both actions and dispositions.

The affliction is a penalty, incurred by the sufferer ; but as the nations exist and suffer in a world governed by a system of grace, and as they are made instruments in this system, the chastisements which their own conduct has merited, may be, also, a means of reforming them, and of leading them to greatness and happiness by making them efficient promoters of righteousness and truth on earth

This is the whole and satisfactory history of the origin and uses of every national trial or revolution that ever has happened, or that ever will occur, in any part of the world; but with these propositions are connected a number of others of such importance to all communities, and especially to those situated like the people of the Confederate States, that they are reserved for separate chapters.

In the mean time, let all endeavor to receive and apply, in their length, breadth and depth, the great scriptural teachings already stated : that the Sovereign Maker and Guide of the universe is almighty and infinitely holy, and that, therefore, sin and suffering are everywhere and always regular and inevitable cause and effect.

It would be a most deplorable and awful state of things if it were possible for any creature to suffer without an adequate cause in himself ; and if such an accident should occur, no rational being could ever again feel safe.

If such things could happen, God would either be unjust, or less than omnipotent ; and either supposition is contrary to the whole teaching of Scripture, and revolting to the instincts of the Christian heart.

The honor of the Divine Nature is interested in preserving every moral creature from undeserved injury ; and if one momentary pang could be causelessly inflicted, it would fill the universe with uncertainty and horror. Every being with moral sentiment would at the same time sustain a shock : for no one could feel secure, and no one would ever forget this illustration of the imperfection or injustice of the Divine Economy.

The case of the Christian, called on to suffer persecutions on account of his godly life in Christ Jesus, is no exception : the Christian, as such, is a spiritual being, and in his heaven-born nature can not be injured by men or devils.

His light afflictions, which are but for a moment, work out for him a far more exceeding and eternal weight of glory ; and all that the malice of the world and of hell can effect, will only enable him to display more conspicuously the divine origin of his faith, will serve to weaken the hopes and affections that were doing him an injury, and will strengthen the cause which he has espoused.

The believer is required to fill up the measure of Christ's afflictions : but when his sufferings are not merciful chastenings to work out in him the peaceable fruits of righteousness, they will glorify God by furnishing an illustration of the hatefulness of sin, of the mercy and forbearance of the Supreme Ruler, of the superior and saving character of the new life of the Christian, and be thus an effectual warning and a powerful appeal to a world lying in wickedness.

Thus the steadfast sufferings of the Christian, for his Divine Master, are his most precious works: he is, by such means, made an illustrious co-worker with God, and enabled to add to his crown, i life many stars of rejoicing.

The Church also is a spiritual body; and though it is established for a work of time, it is subjected to a discipline, whose origin and ends take hold of eternity.

Its outward organization and its elements of worldly power may be impaired; but it will not be in the power of created things to touch the purity or energy of its divine life. This is God's husbandry: and the machinations of His enemies will only serve in the end to distinguish its excellency over all the inventions of creatures, to burn from it the tinsel of baser metals, to manifest before the universe the righteousness, goodness and justice of its Head, and the malice, baseness and cruelty of His opponents, and to enhance the glories of those triumphs which await it in time and in eternity, and in which will participate, in heaven, all who have served it by doing or suffering on earth.

But . . . ms, as such, can have no remuneration in time or eternity for afflictions they have not deserved; and though a future generation might profit by the sufferings of the present, how will this compensate those who have died in darkness and sorrow?

Let no one deceive himself; any other theory for individual or national trial is dishonoring to God, and full of difficulty and hopeless gloom.

The extent, nature or instrumentality of the affliction does not affect the truth of the propositions above enunciated; and though the party suffering may incur his trials and disasters in the prosecution of an enterprise just in itself, they are not the less the reward of his own conduct, and in such cases are sent on account of existing dispositions or of past offences or both.

And as already intimated, it is not because the Kingdom of Christ, from the plans of God, needs revolutions and violent mutations among the powers of the world, that they occur; and it is both absurd and impious to claim that if our nation is not suffering as the Church, it is at least undergoing trials as a high privilege to aid in the progress of the Redeemer's Cause.

God will certainly "overturn, overturn, overturn......until He come whose right it is," (*Ezekiel, xxi*, 27); but while the grand result of *all* changes in the earth is thus made known, a sufficient cause for the troubles of every people will always be found in their own hearts and conduct with respect to the Divine Law by which all nations are to stand or fall.

This is not the proper place to prove what we must infer from the whole Divine Economy, that all have had some opportunity of knowing the requirements of this law; it is sufficient to say that this inference of the Word of Truth is easily susceptible of proof from the facts of history, and can not be doubted by those enlightened by the Word and Spirit of God.

PROOFS AND ILLUSTRATIONS.

The Prayer of Daniel.

The first citations to sustain the positions of this chapter, teach by both facts and doctrines; they express the inspired views and show the actions of great and holy men under national trials, and are intended for the instruction of persons similarly situated in every age and place

The character of Daniel is well known to the Bible student. He was a patriot in the highest sense of the word; and he manifested his love for his people and country under the circumstances best calculated to try them.

Personal interests and honor are so identified with those of country, that it is mostly impossible to know the source and sustaining motives for public spirit; and no doubt many men have done and suffered much for their nation from selfish instincts without being aware of the real influences by which they were controlled.

But there can be no misapprehension with regard to the nature and origin of Daniel's feelings for his countrymen.

He would have lost, instead of gaining, as far as worldly power and consideration are concerned, by the restoration of his people to their own country and himself with them; and while the exile and dispersion of his race had been a means of advancing him to the most illustrious position of worldly grandeur, it was any thing else but a credit to him to be considered as a lover and favorer of the dispersed and despised family of Jacob.

The children of Israel, as a race, were hated and persecuted; and in Daniel's time they were in exile and bondage, weak and wretched, their country a desolation, and their name a reproach.

But Daniel had been advanced to the highest honors and dignities of the greatest and most magnificent empire on earth; and while he had every thing to hope from the confidence and favor of this power, an association and intimacy with his people was alike dangerous to his honor and to his life.

His personal merit and the favor of God were securing for him the most illustrious name and position on earth—and his family and national affinities could win for him nothing but shame and 'hatred.

On the one side were the highest prizes which can tempt worldly ambition to forget and despise kindred and nation; on the other were the most disgraceful and terrible penalties which men can inflict offered as the apparently certain reward for adhesion to the cause of his people.

None of these things could move the steadfast heart of the illustrious Hebrew from its attachment to the home and the cause of his fathers; and as no man in modern times can expect to be his superior in piety, faith and godly zeal, so none can hope to become more distinguished for a display of unselfish and exalted attachment to country and people.

History and Analysis of Daniel's Prayer.

When the Hebrew prophet uttered the prayer quoted below, and which has been recorded for the instruction of after times, he had fresh in memory his captivity among a people who hated, oppressed and despised his race without a cause.

He knew by inspiration that all the blessings in store for the world were to come through the medium of his own race; and he was fully aware, from observation, that much as this nation had offended God, by their rebellions and idolatries, they were, as a whole, infinitely superior to those by whom they were hated and afflicted.

Among them were to be found the only worshippers of the true and living God; and if no other examples were to be found the prophet could see in himself, and in his fellow-captives, Shadrach, Meshach, and Abednego, the most illustrious evidences of the superior tendencies of the Jewish faith and polity. The faithful among the descendants of Jacob were the only stars which shone upon the dark night of paganism and abomination in which the world was immersed; and those who made war on the Jews and sought to destroy their race and worship were actuated as much by hostility to the religion of the God of Heaven as by dislike to the children of Israel. In fact, the instruments by which the chosen race were scourge, were generally licentious, cruel and abominable; and such was the corruption of manners in the empire where Daniel had recently been a captive, such the general, incurable and indescribable depravity of the nation that the name of Babylon has been adopted, by the authority of God Himself, to represent all that is most base, wicked, obdurate and detestable in His human enemies.

The gods of the heathen were all the rivals and foes of Jehovah—and those who executed the justice of Heaven on the Jews exulted in the idea that they were opposing its Holy Majesty.

All these things were perfectly familiar to Daniel; and he was an eye-witness both of the abominations of the enemies of his people, and of the cruel wrongs which they heaped upon them.

But it is to be observed that these things are not recited in the narrative part of the prophet's petition; he does relate a history, but he selects only the two great facts which it concerns the afflicted to know

He mentions, repeatedly, the sins of his people, and their consequence, national troubles; and there is no allusion whatever to the character, motives or conduct of the instruments of these troubles.

Confessions, in Daniel's Prayer.

The prophet confesses in the most emphatic manner :

1. The sins of his people as the cause of all their afflictions.
2. That *all* had sinned, not excepting himself. The kings, princes and fathers are enumerated among the guilty, and *all* Israel are confessed to have transgressed.
3. That God is righteous in all his works, among which is cited the fact of His watching upon the evil to bring it upon His own chosen people.
4. That the plan of God's judgments had been revealed—and that there was not only no mystery in the fact that the Jews were scourged at the hands of Jehovah's enemies, but that the reasons for these things had been plainly given before they occurred.

Petitions, and the ground on which they are based.

As Daniel does not refer to or characterize the motives of the enemies of his race and of his God, so he leaves their judgment wholly to Him to whom vengeance belongs. He does not presume to direct the Justice of Deity, and his whole appeal is for mercy to those who suffer the righteous consequences of their own actions.

He bases these petitions for deliverance not on the merit of those concerned, not on sympathy or pity for their harsh and long sufferings—for to have done this was to have offered an insult to the God whose aid was implored.

If there had been undeserved punishment, then the Almighty was to blame : if the mere amount of afflictions had made the chastened parties objects worthy of Divine favor, then a change of conduct and disposition was not important, and punishment or rebukes to this end were unnecessary chastenings, and therefore, cruelties from the Divine Hand.

Daniel asks for the deliverance of his race " for the Lord's sake :" he prays for it in the name of God's mercy, and for the sake of His own glory.

In short, the great points in the inspired prayer of this glorious patriot, this illustrious prophet, this holy man to whom the assurance was given direct from Heaven that he was greatly beloved, were that sin, wilful sin against God's holy and reasonable law, and affliction, were inseparable cause and effect—and that deliverance from merited calamity was only to be expected when it was consistent with the covenanted mercy, the righteousness and goodness of God. This road would necessarily lead through the repentance and reformation of the people concerned ; and it was only on such conditions that inspired men of old who spake as they were moved by the Holy Ghost, asked for the removal of the afflicting hand of Jehovah.

Let the reader now carefully study the prayer recorded for his guidance ; and let him as he reads keep in mind the circumstances and surroundings of its Author. He was one of a race scattered and peeled ; and had been born in a land which was then desolate from the successive and awful ravages of the enemies of its nation's God.

It and its people were an astonishment among the nations ; its inhabitants, after enduring every calamity, had been carried away captive by a " bitter and hasty people," its temple burned with fire, its palaces despoiled, its women ravished, its children dashed in pieces in the streets, its kings and nobles degraded and cruelly maimed, its elders and princes dragged away in chains and reduced to slavery.

The prophet and his race had been dwelling among those who had desolated their land and desecrated their holy things; and for long years he had seen his people and their faith a taunt and reproach to the fierce, remorseless and depraved heathen into whose hand God had sold them. Yea, he had seen the most sacred vessels, dedicated to the holy service of Almighty God, profaned by an idolatrous and debauched king and his profligate courtiers and shameless courtezans in their filthy orgies while they blasphemed that Power whose people they had conquered, insulted and oppressed by Its permission.

He knew from the careful study of the Divine Word that the day of restoration for the race whom his heart followed in all their trials and wanderings was about to dawn ; and with his soul filled with ar-

lent desire for this result he approaches the mercy seat. He kneels
down in sight of the pollutions of the god-hating despisers of his
people—and in this far land, with the groanings of the captive He-
brews and the scoffs of their licentious tormentors sounding in his
ears, he turns his face to Jerusalem, and his thoughts to that home
of his heart, and pours forth his prayer for deliverance.

He remembers and places in their proper position towards each
other only causes and results, sin and punishment—and thus his
words ascend to the Throne of Grace, and receive an immediate and
most gracious response.

THE PRAYER.

"In the first year of Darius the son of Ahasuerus, of the seed of
the Medes, which was made king over the realm of the Chaldeans :

In the first year of his reign, I Daniel understood by books the
number of the years, whereof the word of the Lord came to Jeremiah the prophet, that he would accomplish seventy years in the
desolations of Jerusalem.

And I set my face unto the Lord God, to seek by prayer and supplications, with fasting, and sackcloth, and ashes :

And I prayed unto the Lord my God, and made my confession,
and said, O Lord, the great and dreadful God, keeping the covenant
and mercy to them that love him, and to them that keep his commandments ;

We have sinned, and have committed iniquity, and have done
wickedly, and have rebelled, even by departing from thy precepts
and from thy judgements :

Neither have we hearkened unto thy servants the prophets, which
spake in thy name to our kings, our princes, and our fathers, and
to all the people of the land.

O Lord, righteousness belongeth unto thee, but unto us confusion
of faces, as at this day ; to the men of Judah, and to the inhabitants
of Jerusalem, and unto all Israel, that are near, and that are far off,
through all the countries whither thou hast driven them, because of
their trespass that they have trespassed against thee.

O Lord, to us belongeth confusion of face, to our kings, to our
princes, and to our fathers, because we have sinned against thee.

To the Lord our God belong mercies and forgivenesses, though we
have rebelled against him ;

Neither have we obeyed the voice of the Lord our God, to walk
in his laws, which he set before us by his servants the prophets.

Yea, all Israel have transgressed thy law, even by departing, that
they might not obey thy voice ; therefore the curse is poured upon

us, and the oath that is written in the law of Moses the servant of God, because we have sinned against him.

And he hath confirmed his words, which he spake against us, and against our judges that judged us, by bringing upon us a great evil : for under the whole heaven hath not been done as hath been done upon Jerusalem.

As it is written in the law of Moses, all this evil is come upon us : yet made we not our prayer before the Lord our God, that we might turn from our iniquities, and understand thy truth.

Therefore hath the Lord watched upon the evil, and brought it upon us : for the Lord our God is righteous in all his works which he doeth : for we obeyed not his voice.

And now, O Lord our God, that hast brought thy people forth out of the land of Egypt with a mighty hand, and hast gotten thee renown, as at this day ; we have sinned, we have done wickedly.

. O Lord, according to all thy righteousness. I beseech thee, let thine anger and thy fury be turned away from thy city Jerusalem. thy holy mountain : because for our sins, and for the iniquities of our fathers, Jerusalem and thy people are become a reproach to all that are about us.

Now therefore. O our God. hear the prayers of thy servant, and his supplications, and cause thy face to shine upon thy sanctuary that is desolate. for the Lord's sake

O my God, incline thine ear, and hear ; open thine eys, and behold our desolations, and the city which is called by thy name : for we do not present our supplications before thee for our righteousnesses, but for thy great mercies.

O Lord, hear ; O Lord, forgive ; O Lord, hearken and do ; defer not, for thine own sake, O my God : for thy city and thy people are called by thy name.

And while I was speaking, and praying, and confessing my sin. and the sin of my people Israel, and presenting my supplication before the Lord my God for the holy mountain of my God ;

Yea, while I was speaking in prayer, even the man Gabriel, whom I had seen in the vision at the beginning, being caused to fly swiftly. touched me about the time of the evening oblation.

And he informed me, and talked with me, and said, O Daniel. I am now come forth to give thee skill and understanding.

At the beginning of thy supplications the commandment came forth, and I am come to shew thee ; for thou art greatly beloved therefore understand the matter, and consider the vision "—*Daniel*. ix, 1-23.

PRAYER OF NEHEMIAH.

Can any one doubt the glowing patriotism of Nehemiah? He was a Jew, in high favor in a foreign court, being cup-bearer to Artaxerxes, King of Persia ; and he flourished at the time of the restoration of the Jews from the Babylonish captivity, and the rebuilding of Jerusalem. Soon after this enterprise was begun it met with heavy discouragements; but Nehemiah, full of zeal for God and for his nation, asked permission to join the feeble band who, amid great distresses and persecutions, were laboring to restore the holy city.

Having gained the consent of his Sovereign he entered on his work of love ; and for a number of years he devoted his time, his energies and his princely income to it, laboring with untiring zeal in the face of danger and under the most trying difficulties.

When this illustrious and godly man heard of the disasters of those who entered before him on the sacred and Divinely enjoined task of rebuilding Jerusalem preparatory to the restoration of its holy worship, he utters the prayer which is given below.

Its recitals and petitions are similar to those of Daniel's—and like the petition of the latter prophet it was inspired as a part of the Sacred Oracles, intended for the instruction and guidance of after ages.

The reader will consider, the history and analysis of Daniel's prayer above given, as applicable, in the main, to that of Nehemiah —and his special attention is invited to this emphatic utterance of a great, good and inspired man,—" both I and my father's house have sinned."

" The words of Nehemiah the son of Hachaliah. And it came to pass in the month Chisleu, in the twentieth year, as I was in Shushan the palace,

That Hanani, one of my brethren, came, he and certain men of Judah ; and I asked them concerning the Jews that had escaped, which were left of the captivity, and concerning Jerusalem.

And they said unto me, The remnant that are left of the captivity there in the province are in great affliction and reproach: the wall of Jerusalem also is broken down, and the gates thereof are burned with fire.

And it came to pass when I heard these words, that I sat down and wept, and mourned certain days, and fasted, and prayed before the God of heaven.

And said, I beseech thee, O Lord God of heaven, the great and terrible God, that keepeth covenant and mercy for them that love him and observe his commandments :

Let thine ear now be attentive, and thine eyes open, that thou mayest hear the prayer of thy servant, which I pray before thee now, day and night, for the children of Israel, thy servants, and confess 'the sins of the children of Israel, which we have sinned against thee : both I and my father's house have sinned.

We have dealt very corruptly against thee, and have not kept the commandments, nor the statutes, nor the judgements, which thou commandedst thy servant Moses.

Remember, 1 beseech thee, the word that thou commandedst thy servant Moses, saying, *If* ye transgress, 1 will scatter you among the nations :

But *if* ye turn unto me, and keep my commandments, and do them ; though there were of you cast out unto the uttermost part of the heaven, *yet* will I gather them from thence, and will bring them unto the place that I have chosen to set my name there.

Now these *are* thy servants and thy people, whom thou hast redeemed by thy great power, and by thy strong hand.

O Lord, I beseech thee, let now thine ear be attentive to the prayer of thy servant, and to the prayer of thy servants, who desire to fear thy name : and prosper, I pray thee, thy servant this day, and grant him mercy in the sight of this man. For I was the king's cupbearer."—*1st Chapter Nehemiah.*

PRAYER OF EZRA.

Ezra was one of those who labored with holy zeal for the restoration at Jerusalem of the religious polity of the chosen people ; and he entered on his task some years in advance of Nehemiah. He was a returned exile, a leader of his people, full of wisdom and the Holy Ghost, and gave himself to the cause of his country and of the true Church with which it was associated with untiring patience and zeal, and an unfaltering faith.

He was honored by God as an instrument in the great work of revising that part of the scriptures written before his time, and of publishing a correct copy.

While he was laboring for his nation and his God with a piety and fidelity which none can surpass, he hears of a trespass of his people, and then, under the direction of the Holy Spirit, pours forth the prayer below.

Its recitals and confessions are characterized by the same spirit 'with those already quoted ; and while the immediate occasion of the prayer was an offence committed about the time it was offered, it narrates briefly, but distinctly and emphatically, the system of God's dealings with His people, and the causes of all their calamities.

6

"Now ... these things were done ... since ... that ...
The p... Israel and the pri... of the Levites, ... eg.
a... by the ... the people of the lands, ... of g ...
their ... of the ... the Hittites, the Peri-
z... the ... the ... the Moabites, the Egyptians,
and the Amorites.

... here ... h ... for themselves ...
the ... ... they mingled themselves with the
pe... of ... so that ... the ... princes ... hath been
ch... in this trespass.

And when I heard this thing, I rent my garment and my mantle,
and ... of the hair of my ... and of my ... and sat down
astonished.

Then were ... assembled unto me every one that trembled at the
word of the God of Israel, because of the transgression of those
that had been carried away; and I sat astonished until the evening
sacrifice.

And at the evening sacrifice I arose up from my heaviness; and
having rent my garment and my mantle, I fell upon my knees, and
spread out my hands unto the Lord my God.

And said, O my God, I am ashamed and blush to lift up my face
to thee, my God: for our iniquities are increased over our head, and
our trespass is grown up unto the heavens.

Since the days of our fathers have we been in a great trespass unto
his day; and for our iniquities have we, our kings, and our priests,
been delivered into the hand of the kings of the lands, to the sword,
to captivity, and to a spoil, and to confusion of face, as it is this
day.

And now for a little space grace hath been shewed from the Lord
our God, to leave us a remnant to escape, and to give us a nail in his
holy place, that our God may lighten our eyes, and give us a little
reviving in our bondage.

For we were bondmen; yet our God hath not forsaken us in our
bondage, but hath extended mercy unto us in the sight of the kings
of Persia, to give us a reviving, to set up the house of our God, and
to repair the desolations thereof, and to give us a wall in Judah and
in Jerusalem.

And now, O our God, what shall we say after this? for we have
forsaken thy commandments,

Which thou hast commanded by thy servants the prophets, saying,
The land, unto which ye go to possess it, is an unclean land with the

... of the people of the lands, with their abominations, which have filled it from one end to another with their uncleanness.

Now therefore give not your daughters unto their sons, neither take their daughters unto your sons, nor seek their peace or their wealth forever: that ye may be strong, and eat the good of the land, and leave it for an inheritance to your children forever.

And ... upon us ... for ... our God hast punished ... our ... Are, and hast given us such deliverance ... ; Should we ... break thy commandments, and join ... with ... wouldst not thou be angry ... till thou hadst consumed us, so that there should be no remnant nor escaping?

O Lord God of Israel, thou art righteous; for we remain yet escaped, as it is this day: behold, we are before thee in our trespasses: for we cannot stand before thee because of this."—Ezra ix.

... THE GOVERNMENT OF DAVID

...

The incident referred to, and which is thus inculcated of Truth by facts quoted in this chapter, is thus related

" Then there was a famine in the days of David three years, year after year; and David enquired of the Lord. And the Lord answered, It is for Saul, and for his bloody house, because he slew the Gibeonites.

And the king called the Gibeonites, and said unto them; (now the Gibeonites *were* not of the children of Israel, but of the remnant of the Amorites; and the children of Israel had sworn unto them; and Saul sought to slay them in his zeal to the children of Israel and Judah;)

Wherefore David said unto the Gibeonites, What shall I do for you? and wherewith shall I make the atonement, that ye may bless the inheritance of the Lord?"—*II Samuel,* xxi, 1–3.

It is no answer to the force of these examples that the Jews were a peculiar people, under a peculiar dispensation. It is true that the descendants of Abraham and the proselytes joined to them, constituted the visible Church on earth; and to them were committed the Oracles of God, and the true worship of this Holy Being in the sacrifices and ceremonies which typified Christ and His atonement. But all that can be said is that the Israelites, enjoying special advantages, were laid under greater obligations than other nations; but the principle of the Divine Government as applied to all was and is precisely the same, and that is, that every people must be judged by the Moral Law, the extent of their offences being measured by their opportunities. That all have some means of knowing this law we are not permitted to doubt, the Oracles of Truth declaring that " the wrath of God is revealed from Heaven, against all ungodliness and unrighteousness of men, who hold the truth in unrighteousness.

Because that which may be known of God is manifest in them; for God showed it unto them.

For the invisible things of Him from the creation of the world are clearly seen, being understood by the things that are made, *even* His eternal power and Godhead; so that they are without excuse:

Because that, when they know God, they glorified Him not as God, neither were thankful; but became vain in their imagination, and their foolish heart was darkened

Professing themselves to be wise, they became fools;

And changed the glory of the uncorruptible God, into an image made like to corruptible man, and to birds and four-footed beasts, and creeping things......And even as they did not like to retain God in *their* knowledge, God gave them over to a reprobate mind, to do those things which are not convenient;

Being filled with all unrighteousness, fornication, wickedness, covetousness, maliciousness; full of envy, murder, debate, deceit, malignity; whisperers, backbiters, haters of God, despiteful, proud, boasters, inventors of evil things, disobedient to parents,

Without understanding, covenant breakers, without natural affection, implacable, unmerciful:

Who, knowing the judgment of God, that they who commit such things are worthy of death, not only do the same, but have pleasure in them that do them." *Romans i,* 23 and 28–32.

Here is the inspired statement of the opportunities which all have had to know God, and of the manner in which the idolatrous nations have used them; and in the next chapter of the same book we are clearly informed of the method in which the Righteous Ruler will proceed in His judgments, to render to every man according to his deeds.

" For there is no respect of persons with God

For as many as have sinned without the law shall also perish without the law; and as many as have sinned in the law, shall be judged by the law.

For when the Gentiles, which have not the law, do by nature the things contained in the law, these having not the law, are a law unto themselves:

Which shew the work of the law written in their hearts, their consciences, also, bearing witness, and their thoughts, meanwhile accusing, or else excusing one another.' *Rom. ii,* 11–15.

The law here referred to is the Decalogue; and they who have it not in writing, manifest a sense of its commandments, once written on the hearts of men, *first,* by those moral acts which evince a moral sense, and *secondly,* by the operations of their conscience.

" The absence of all moral acts in the lower animals, shews that they have no law, or sense of moral obligation. But , no matter how diversified may be their circumstances, all evince that they are under a moral law "

" The Gentiles are not excusable, although not amenable to the written laws of the Jews, since they have a law written upon their hearts, by which they shall be judged, and according to which they shall be punished." " When they practice any of the virtues, or perform moral acts, these acts are the evidence of a moral sense: they show that the Gentiles have a rule of right and wrong, and a feeling of obligation, or in other words, that they are a law unto themselves."

And "men are to be judged by the light they have ever-lly enjoyed."

The ground of Judgment is their work, the reward is Judgment is clean, unmiserably."

. . . .

. . . . God.
. . . .

. . . . "As surely as I am . . all the
. . . . "IN,
. . . . Jam
. . . . or, justice and truth,
. . . .

T . . . .
. . . . that
. . . . for
. . . . Cor.

. . . .
. . . . of G . . . .
. . . . Joh . . . .
. . . . Verily T . . . . that
. . . .

. . . .
. . . .
. . . .
. . . .
. . . .

. . . .
. . . .
. . . .
. . . .
. . . of the F . . . .
. . . . die."

. . . . is not equal. . . H . . . . O
. . . . are not your way . . up . . hill.

W . . . . pass from his righteousness, and
. . . . for his iniquity that he
hath done shall he die.

Again, when . . turned away surely away from his wickedness
that . . . . and doeth that which is lawful and right,
he shall save his soul alive.

. . . . ; and turneth away from his . . . . the
. . . . he shall surely live, he shall not die.

Yet saith the house of Israel, The way of the Lord is not equal

House of Israel, are not my ways equal? are not your ways unequal?

Therefore I will judge you, O house of Israel, every one according to his ways, saith the Lord God. Repent, and turn yourselves from all your transgressions; so iniquity shall not be your ruin.

Cast away from you all your transgressions, whereby ye have transgressed; and make you a new heart and a new spirit: for why will ye die, O house of Israel?

For I have no pleasure in the death of him that dieth, saith the Lord God; wherefore turn yourselves, and live ye."—*Ez.* 18. 25–32.

"Yet the children of thy people say, The way of the Lord is not equal: but as for them, their way is not equal.

When the righteous turneth from his righteousness, and committeth iniquity, he shall even die thereby.

But if the wicked turn from his wickedness, and do that which is lawful and right, he shall live thereby.

Yet ye say, The way of the Lord is not equal. O ye house of Israel, I will judge you every one after his ways."—*Ez.* 33. 17–20.

"But we are sure that the judgment of God is according to truth."—"For there is no respect of persons with God." (See *Rom.* 11). 1 *Pet.* 1. 17. *Acts* 10. 34–35. *Ecc.* 12. 14.

"All thy commandments are truth."—*Ps.* 119. 151—"all thy commandments are righteous." Do 172. *Ps.* 111. 2–3. *Rom.* 7 12. *Ps.* 19. 7, 8, 9.

"Shall not the judge of all the earth do right?"—(*Gen.* 18. 25). *Job* 8. 3, and 34. 10, 11, 12. *Deut.* 32. 4. 2 *Chron.* 19. 7. *Ps.* 89. 14, and 98. 2. *Jer.* 18. 7, 8, 9, 10. *Prov.* 5. 21, 22. 2 *Chron.* 16. 9. *Ps.* 21. 8, 9. *Micah* 5. 9. *Luke* 19. 27. *Ps.* 2. 10, 11. *Nahum* 1. 2, 3: 7, 8, 9, 10. *Hab.* 3. 12. *Is.* 28. 17–22, and 24. 1–21. *Jer.* 25. 31, 32, 3. *Is.* 60. 12, and 26. 21. *Ps.* 30. 3. *Is.* 66. 15, 16.

Such are the judgments in the judging world of Him who "is righteous in all His ways, and holy in all His works."—*Ps.* 145. 17.

"He doth not afflict willingly nor grieve the children of men...... Out of the mouth of the Most High proceedeth not evil and good."—*Lam.* 3. 33–38. He Himself asks, "Have I any pleasure at all that the wicked should die," (*Ezek.* 18. 23). and not that he should return from his ways and live?"

Then, "**wherefore doth a living man complain, a man for the punishment of his sins?**" *Lam.* 3. 39, for "God is King over all the earth," *Ps.* 47. 7, and "the works of His hands are verity and judgment."—*Ps.* 111. 7. *Hosea* 14. 9.

CHAPTER V.

BIBLE VIEWS OF NATIONAL TRIALS, CONTINUED.

Whatever may be the nature of a nation's cause, and whatever the character of the instrumentality by which it is afflicted, when it suffers, it is chastened for sin.

It was intimated in the previous chapter, that the cause in which a nation may be engaged at the time it is afflicted does not affect the character of its trials; and that however just may be the enterprise in which it suffers, the calamities or reverses which it encounters are the judgments of a righteous God for sin.

There is in the Holy Scriptures an illustration of this proposition precisely in point, and it covers all the ground so completely that it would hardly seem necessary to quote any other passage.

It was made a religious obligation on the Jews to exterminate the corrupt inhabitants of Canaan; the command to this effect was often and emphatically repeated, and when God enjoined this duty, none could doubt that He would confer the power to perform it.

Soon after Joshua, a good and inspired man, entered on this sacred task, an expedition which he sent against the town of Ai was disastrously repulsed—and what were the conclusions and conduct of the chosen leader of Israel? Did he consider occasional defeats as necessarily incident to a work in which the Almighty was aiding?

Did he conceal the repulses of his arms from the people, and encourage them to go forward without fear as God was certainly with them, according to His own oft-repeated promise to be? Did he try to persuade his officers and soldiers that the check with which they had met was a success in disguise, and that the All-wise Disposer was operating through such disasters for their final triumph?

Joshua was too well instructed in the ways of God, and too fearful of offending his Divine Master, to countenance anything so dishonoring to the Supreme and Holy Majesty of Heaven and earth; and he adopted the only course which would show a just appreciation of the attributes of Jehovah, and which could therefore lead to his own success.

He instantly recognized defeat as an indication of the displeasure of God—and he knew and confessed that the disaster to his arms was sent from Heaven.

With such confessions in his heart and on his lips, and while he and his elders are solemnly honoring God by publicly confessing that their defeat was His work, he is informed of the cause of his difficulty, and directed what to do to prevent future and worse calamities.

The time of the inhabitants of Canaan had come—the measure of their iniquities was full, and God had chosen the Jews as the instruments of His vengeance upon a people, whose pollutions could no longer be borne. But in the defeat at Ai, the Divine Arbiter was against the arms of His people, though He was with their cause; for they had sinned against them, and He designed to chasten them that their trespass might be exposed, and repented of, and the nation prevented from plunging into deeper iniquities. One in the camp of Israel had contaminated himself with the accursed thing: and the people being blessed with a wise and godly leader, their reverse at Ai was made a means of arresting the progress of abominations which would have caused God to desert them, and give them up to destruction.

Thus the interpretation of a reverse in a way consistent with the power, justice and goodness of the Almighty, and humiliating to himself and his people, led Joshua to success; and no commander can receive a check in a cause more sacred or one in which he can have such authoritative assurance that God is with it.

The leader of Israel was not so foolish and so impious as to fear that a confession of the displeasure of Heaven would strengthen his enemies, and injure his own cause; he was well aware that if Jehovah was for him, he could not be defeated, and he was inspired to know that the honor of this perfect Being required every reverse to be considered as directly sent by Him, and for the offences of those concerned.

By such a course he not only did not weaken his cause, but he avoided all further defeats; and this example remains a solemn, emphatic and perpetual admonition to the nations.

The history referred to is recorded in the 7th chapter of the Book of Joshua, and is as follows:

"But the children of Israel committed a trespass in the accursed thing: for Achan, the son of Carmi. the son of Zabdi, the son of Zerah, of the tribe of Judah, took of the accursed thing: and the anger of the Lord was kindled against the children of Israel.

And Joshua sent men from Jericho to Ai, which is beside Bethaven, on the east side of Beth-el, and spake unto them, saying, Go up and view the country. And the men went up and viewed Ai.

7

And they returned to Joshua, and said unto him, Let not all the people go up; but let about two or three thousand men go up and smite Ai: and make not all the people to labour thither: for they are but few

So there went up thither of the people about three thousand men: and they fled before the men of Ai.

And the men of Ai smote of them about thirty and six: for they chased them *from* before the gate *even* unto Shebarim, and smote them in the going down: wherefore the hearts of the people melted, and became as water.

And Joshua rent his clothes, and fell to the earth upon his face before the ark of the Lord until the eventide, he and the elders of Israel, and put dust upon their heads.

And Joshua said, Alas, O Lord God, wherefore hast thou at all brought this people over Jordan, to deliver us into the hand of the Amorites, to destroy us? would to God we had been content, and dwelt on the other side Jordan!

O Lord, what shall I say, when Israel turneth their backs before their enemies!

For the Canaanites and all the inhabitants of the land shall hear *of it*, and shall environ us round, and cut off our name from the earth: and what wilt thou do unto thy great name?

And the Lord said unto Joshua, Get thee up; wherefore liest thou thus upon thy face?

Israel hath sinned, and they have also transgressed my covenant which I commanded them: for they have even taken of the accursed thing, and have also taken, and dissembled also, and they have put *it* even among their own stuff.

Therefore the children of Israel could not stand before their enemies, *but* turned *their* backs before their enemies, because they were accursed: neither will I be with you any more, except ye destroy the accursed from among you.

Up, sanctify the people, and say, Sanctify yourselves against tomorrow: for thus saith the Lord God of Israel, *There is* an accursed thing in the midst of thee, O Israel: thou canst not stand before thine enemies, until ye take away the accursed thing from among you.

In the morning therefore ye shall be brought according to your tribes: and it shall be, *that* the tribe which the Lord taketh shall come according to the families *thereof;* and the family which the Lord shall take shall come by households; and the household which the Lord shall take shall come man by man.

And it shall be, *that* he that is taken with the accursed thing shall be burnt with fire, he and all that he hath : because he hath transgressed the covenant of the Lord, and because he hath wrought folly in Israel.

So Joshua rose up early in the morning, and brought Israel by their tribes ; and the tribe of Judah was taken :

And he brought the family of Judah ; and he took the family of the Zarhites : and he brought the family of the Zarhites man by man ; and Zabdi was taken :

And he brought his household man by man ; and Achan, the son of Carmi, the son of Zabdi, the son of Zerah, of the tribe of Judah, was taken.

And Joshua said unto Achan, My son, give, I pray thee, glory to the Lord God of Israel, and make confession to Him ; and tell me now what thou hast done ; hide *it* not from me.

And Achan answered Joshua, and said, Indeed I have sinned against the Lord God of Israel, and thus have I done :

When I saw among the spoils a goodly Babylonish garment, and two hundred shekels of silver, and a wedge of gold of fifty shekels weight, then I coveted them, and took them ; and, behold, they are hid in the earth in the midst of my tent, and the silver under it.

So Joshua sent messengers, and they ran unto the tent ; and, behold, *it was* hid in his tent, and the silver under it.

And they took them out of the midst of the tent, and brought them unto Joshua, and unto all the children of Israel, and laid them out before the Lord.

And Joshua, and all Israel with him, took Achan, the son of Zerah, and the silver, and the garment, and the wedge of gold, and his sons, and his daughters, and his oxen, and his asses, and his sheep, and his tent, and all that he had : and they brought them unto the valley of Achor.

And Joshua said, Why hast thou troubled us? the Lord shall trouble thee this day. And all Israel stoned him with stones, and burned them with fire, after they had stoned them with stones.

And they raised over him a great heap of stones unto this day. So the Lord turned from the fierceness of his anger. Wherefore the name of that place was called, The valley of Achor, unto this day."

From this it plainly appears that God may be with the cause of a people and temporarily against their *arms ;* and it is, as is, evident from this passage, and in fact, from the whole Sacred Word that however just a nation may be in its controversy with another, all its afflictions are the result of its own offences, and an admonition to repentance.

This truth is illustrated by so many examples in sacred history, and is so essential to the honor of the Divine Nature as it is revealed to us, that it seems almost absurd to argue it to a Christian community; yet such is the imperfection and perversity of human nature, that it is incapable of applying to itself the plainest doctrines, and such as it has often taught in theory, when they come in contact with carnal pride and passion.

Men, in all ages, have supposed that when God comes to judge them, He will do it by that pomp and display with which the carnal heart inseparably connects the dignity and grandeur of earthly royalty; and they think that if the Deity were to do as the Pharisees required of Jesus Christ, to shew them a sign from Heaven, that is, to suspend the laws of Nature and overpower their senses, they could believe He had come.

Besides, when man is smitten by the instrumentality of his fellow, his passions are more likely to blind his judgment than when he is afflicted by brute agencies that have no will, and cannot think, judge and hate.

Over these latter, as they are not self-acting, and have no senti-ments good or bad, the Almighty is supposed to exercise a more immediate control; and when a whole nation or a considerable part of it is scourged by drouth, by floods, earthquake or pestilence, there is a solemn impression of the agency and displeasure of the Divine Ruler.

But if plagues, even by irrational matter, be very partial in their influence, human pride stands in the way of a just interpretation; and a small community from whom the rains of Heaven are with-held will not acknowledge that it is chastened of God, because it sees other neighborhoods which it regards as no better or even worse than itself, enriched with the precious treasures of the clouds. And yet, to the truly wise, such partiality of nature is more impressive and instructive than a general course which might be attributed to general laws; and this is precisely the kind of cases put by the prophet Amos, (*Chap.* iv. See pages 25 and 26 of this work) to shew conclusively the admonishing hand of an angry God.

But when man is punished by the instrumentality of his fellow-man—by one who has passions and a body like his own, one whom he sees drawing what he conceives to be false conclusions and acting on wrong and unjust motives, and whom he can meet and strike with his own weapons, he is blinded by his passions to the true springs of things, and contracting his vision to the issue between him and his fellow, he cannot realize that the eye of the Invisible sweeps over a wider range, or that His all-embracing Providence has made this controversy but an incident in another and more important drama.

If his human antagonist be unjust and cruel, and the contest be one of life and death, its immediate origin in the passions of his adversary, and its issue as depending on his will and strength, wholly monopolize his thoughts; and his philosophy running in this extremely narrow channel of carnal wisdom is apt to limit the interest of the Almighty to these phenomena, when in fact the whole controversy and all its passions and contingencies, are themselves but parts of a greater work of God, and all ministering to its results.

But if God always takes sides with us when unjustly assailed by rational creatures, then He has endowed with life and the power of action beings whom He cannot prevent from inflicting wrong; and though He may be defending us against these enemies, yet He created them, and thus is responsible for the injustice which they commit. Can any Bible reader entertain such an idea of God for a moment? Can any one raised and educated in a christian land believe in and respect a Deity who will not himself afflict without cause, but who bestows being and life on others who can and will involve the innocent in undeserved suffering?

The truth is, that God often makes nations the instruments for chastising each other—and he does it not for the merit of the agency used but out of His sovereign will, and for reasons which can generally be easily comprehended.

That this most important matter may be well understood, let a common case be cited.

There is war, bitter and fierce, between two neighboring powers; and in this contest one party, actuated by malicious envy or the lust of domination, is seeking, unprovoked, the subjugation or destruction of the other, while the assailed or defendant is simply endeavoring to maintain his national independence. The ancient Jews were often placed in this latter situation; and the nations who invaded them with fire and sword were their inferiors in moral character, and generally actuated by hatred for the God of Israel.

Now, the chosen race were repeatedly involved in sore calamities by such invasions; and disinterested spectators, viewing these providences in the calm light of history, can easily discover their wise and obvious reasons.

Disasters thus brought on a people educated to believe in the immediate superintendence of an Almighty and Holy God, are best calculated to induce them to examine their existing dispositions and their former conduct. If there is no sin in the cause in which they suffer calamities, then why are they afflicted? Why does God permit an impious and savage foe to heap mischiefs on them, while they are standing in defence of their homes? The answer is so obvious, that the distant reader is astonished to find how blind and infatuated the descendants of Abraham often were; and it seems to us that nothing but incurable madness could have prevented a nation, instructed by the living Oracles, from profiting by such impressive admonitions of their unfavorable position with the Divine Power.

It should be added, that it is of the essence of the punishment that it is inflicted, while the sufferer is defending himself without offence in this matter; and if nations were to endure calamities only while engaged in unrighteous wars, how could they be reformed?

If a people have reason to believe that its disasters are caused by the sinful manner in which it engaged in or carries on a war, it will not look further for causes of the Divine displeasure; and in such cases, chastening providences would not lead to the discovery and healing of sores that previously existed.

But let a still more impressive illustration, and one which has happened, be taken: let it be supposed that a nation is involved in a deadly and most afflictive war which it did not seek, and which assails its very right to existence, for which no rational mind can discover any motive of interest or ambition in the attacking party. A great, free and prosperous power, interested in peace, converts itself into a colossal and imperial despotism for the purpose of destroying a neighbor, whose industry is important to it, and whose government founded on the free principles which formerly characterized its own, would have been an important ally in a world unfriendly to liberty; and it enters on its bloody work with the full purpose of succeeding or of being itself ruined.

The inauguration of this dreadful strife throws a gloom over the better hopes of all the world; and every step in its progress is marked by sacrifices which cause the heart of philanthropy to bleed.

The assailants, in the prosecution of their work, free themselves of their own bonds, their humanity, and their wealth and comfort, as a gladiator would disrobe himself of his garments; and threatening vengeance on all who interpose to arrest their insane fury, they grapple their victims with a hold that nothing can break but the utter destruction of one side or of both.

The assailed ask only to be let alone; they stand within their own frontiers, and in defence of home they fall by the thousand, while the burning torrent of invasion rolls its smoking course in all directions over the devoted land, consuming peaceful villages, converting provinces that smiled with plenty into desolate wastes, and daily increasing the multitude of the homeless and houseless.

Who hurled these maniac legions with reckless and insatiate fury upon a nation desiring peace, and not provoking war?

Such a phenomenon, beheld from a distance, has a moral which cannot be mistaken : and the people who have searched in vain for a reason for their calamities in their conduct to their human enemies, must have incurred the displeasure of Heaven, in some other way.

God is omnipotent and a God of Justice : why then does he permit a nation to suffer such cruel wrongs while defending a cause so righteous?

Why are the authors of those calamities precipitated upon such dire havoc of their own interests in their attempts to ruin those who are merely defending themselves?

As already stated, such a case has occurred ; and when the passions which this dreadful crisis in the world's history has aroused, have passed away, the leadings of Providence will appear so palpable that the chief wonder in regard to the strange era will be the fact that any among the people interested, with Moses and the prophets before them, could fail to improve the lessons taught.

There is another reason why the Deity should choose to inflict the chastening which it designs on an offending people through the agency of another human power actuated by wicked motives ; and that is, that the character of the latter may discover itself to the world as it appears in the sight of Heaven, and thus justify in the eyes of all men the retributions in store for it For example, the Babylonians had reached a depth of depravity of which the christian public could have had no conception but for its connection with the afflictions of the visible Church ; and had we known of this great empire only from the descriptions of profane history, we would have supposed that its total destruction was a loss to the world.

God saw and marked the spiritual loathsomeness of this mistress of the nations ; and he allowed the wickedness of the nation to develop itself in the chastenings which He designed for His own peculiar people, that thereby a double purpose might be accomplished. In this way the Jews were justly afflicted for their offences—and at the same time the instruments of this Providence were allowed to display their nature in those acts which would cause the whole earth to rejoice at their extermination.

All the existing great powers of the world were employed as agencies in chastising the children of Israel for their sins; and while the latter were admonished of the displeasure of Heaven in a way to make them easily understand, if they would, their diseased moral condition, the former proved their true character and justified their coming desolations.

God did not cause the iniquities of those who, with cruel and impious motives, made war upon His people; but He saw their corrupt hearts ripening for destruction, and He turned their passions into channels to work out His own righteous purposes both with respect to themselves, and those whom He chastened by them.

And such events are constantly occurring in history; the Sovereign of the universe beholds depravity ripening for death in the heart of a nation, and He sees sins in another people which He designs to rebuke, and He allows the iniquity of the former to display itself in malicious and, as far as it is concerned, causeless wrongs upon the latter. And thus the power to be chastened is impressively admonished of the displeasure of Heaven, and the assailing party has publicly proved its character before it receives at the Lord's hand the righteous award which awaits it.

It remains only to add a caution of infinite moment to those concerned, and broadly based on the scriptural views above presented.

When a nation, standing in defence of its undoubted rights, is unjustly assailed by a rival power, it has no reason to conclude from this fact alone that God is with it in the ordinary sense of the word; but the position of the people with respect to the Divine Power is to be judged of by what occurs to them in the progress of the struggle.

If they are afflicted, they may be perfectly sure of the displeasure of Heaven for their existing dispositions, or for previous and unrepented offences; and whether God will be with their cause or not depends wholly on the manner in which they receive His admonitions.

It is a favorable sign that good is designed when a community is scourged in the beginning of its national career, and when engaged in a cause not sinful; for rebukes at such times are best calculated to produce proper self-examinations, and reformations the most easily effected at such times, are generally more thorough, and are always more lasting.

But the purposes of the Deity will not be defeated: calamities come from Him, and are sent for sin, and the lifted rod will not be laid aside till the offending party is healed or destroyed.

PROOFS AND ILLUSTRATIONS.

The Jewish nation was scourged, at different times, by most of the powers of the world cotemporary with them.

That *all* nations were inferior, in general moral character, to the Israelites, bad as these often were, we have abundant reasons to believe. The modern student is sometimes misled on this subject by the thorough exposure of the moral pollutions of the Jews in their history, the infallible Word of God, and by the want of a true christian light in the Literature of the heathen to reflect their spiritual condition. Had the state of society in the great idolatrous nations of antiquity been depicted by an inspired prophet, living among them, and thoroughly acquainted with their habits—or had their inner life and character been described by any one, whose standard of morals was taken from the Divine Law, the representation would have filled the modern Christian world with disgust and loathing. But we have a right to conclude that the descendants of Jacob were, in general character, the first race on earth :

FIRST. Because they were God's chosen people, they were His visible Church on earth, were trained by Him, had His Word among them, and were constantly instructed by inspired men.

SECONDLY. The jealousy with which the laws of their Divine King guarded them against social intercourse with *all* other races, unless the latter would adopt their religion and become incorporated with them, is a plain and impressive evidence of the greater depravity of every other people.

THIRDLY. Everything left by the civilized pagans of antiquity which illustrates their religious, moral and social habits, speaks a uniform language of a depth of pollution inconceivable to the present Christian world.

FOURTHLY. The Holy Scriptures, by their facts and doctrines, teach the same lesson ; and there is abundant evidence in profane history of the treachery, ferocity, cruelty, sensuality and profligacy of the nations who warred upon the Jews.

Yet to these "terrible of the nations," God often sold His people for their sins ; and this was done, while these very rods of the Divine Vengeance lifted up themselves against Him who wielded them.

All the pagan world hated the Jews, because it was in heart bitterly hostile to the God of Israel ; but the righteousness of the great King allowed those who followed banners that openly defied His sovereignty, to encamp about the holy City, and to offer in sight of

His Temple, sacrifices to some rivals that would usurp His throne and majesty

He permitted the base worshippers of wood and stone to vex His people and to desolate their land, blaspheming His Holy Name, while they unconsciously executed His Sovereign Will; and while these vile heathen were thus made instruments for the chastening of a better but rebellious and sinning people, their ravages were more pitiless and terrible than anything known in the horrors of modern, civilized warfare, and their motives were impious and detestable.

But when these idolaters were perpetrating their barbarities on the Jews, they were writing in permanent records, for the judgment of posterity, the monstrosities of their moral life; and thus they were themselves preparing a vindication of that justice which has since rained such awful desolations upon them. Philistia, Ammon, Edom and Moab—Assyria, Babylon, Syria and Egypt, and other powers were used as agencies in the chastisement of the chosen race; and upon all of these God has long since executed righteous judgment, their own actions in connection with His Church and the writings of the prophets solemnly impressing upon the mind of the whole world the source, cause and meaning of the awful desolations with which their names will be forever associated.

The whole history of the Jews, as recorded in the Old Testament, is referred to as a quotation in point; and nearly all the prophecies illustrate what has been asserted of both fact and doctrine. The student of the inspired Word will find that every calamity which befell the Jews, through any agency, was sent from Heaven for their sins; and that notwithstanding the fact that they were always hated, at heart, by all the other powers of the world, they were never injured when walking blameless in the precepts and ordinances enjoined upon them. Moses spoke truly when he told them that obedience to God's commands was "their life," and that they never could be harmed, unless "their Rock had sold them" for their offences; and all their history and all the warnings of their prophets, constitute a special message from Jehovah, the same unchangeable God forever, to every people who have His Word.

It would be out of the question to incorporate in this work all those portions of the sacred Scriptures which are herein referred to; and it would seem almost unjust to the force of the lessons which they richly convey, to extract only such parts as are consistent with the limits of this work. The reader cannot go amiss for authority to almost any part of the Old Testament.

A number of passages quoted in the last chapter are applicable to some of the points in this; and the reader is asked to consult the Book of Judges; Ezekiel xxv. 20, 31, 32; Jer. xlvii. 48, 49, 50, 51; Isaiah xxxii. 34, 47 : 10, 13, 14, 15, 21.

It is not necessary to add more; but attention is called to the important teaching of the following brief quotations :

"They chose new gods; there was war in the gates."—(*Jud.* v. 8.)

"O Assyrian, the rod of mine anger, and the staff in their hand is mine indignation."—(*Is.* x. 5.)

"Calling a ravenous bird from the east, the man that executeth my counsel, from a far country."—(*Is.* xlvi. 11.) "Thou hast set up the right hand of his adversaries."—(*Ps.* lxxxix. 42.)

"Deliver my soul from the wicked, which is thy sword : from men which are thy hand, O Lord, from men of the world which have their portion in this life, and whose belly thou fillest with thy hid treasure."—(*Ps.* xvii 13, 14.) (It will be seen here that the Psalmist recognizes the wicked as the sword of God—and states that they are fed or sustained by Him, until they have done His will.)

This sword is sheathed when a man or nation is without offence before God—for "when a man's ways please the Lord, he maketh even his enemies to be at peace with him."—(*Prov.* xvi 7.)

CHAPTER VI.

Bible Views of National trials, continued.—A striking illustration of the truth of the propositions of the previous chapter

The Holy Scriptures teach that there is a devil and other fallen angels, wicked and reprobate spirits who rebelled against God, fell from their first estate, and are held in penal chains for everlasting fire.

The chief of these spirits is a liar from the beginning, and the father of lies : he is the impersonation and sum of sin, and therefore embraces in his nature all that is vile, false, cruel, destructive, and detestable.

He is in perpetual antagonism to God, and the opponent of the obedience and happiness of his creatures ; and as sin has been introduced into this world by Adam's fall, and dwells in the hearts of all unconverted men, Satan is permitted, for wise and holy purposes, to plant here the enginery of his infernal arts.

He is allowed to be a tempter, not to make men sinners, but to develop what is in man, and expose to a fallen race its dangerous condition and its need of a change.

The power, for mischief, which the Prince of darkness is permitted to exercise over mortals, is proportioned to their native depravity ; and when men are said to be seduced by him, they are simply under the influence of passions before latent in them, and which the Devil has drawn out into action.

This Arch Mischief Maker hates all the race of mortals as a consequence of his hostility to God : he and his legions have never, in any possible way, been harmed by any of the children of Adam, and yet he pursues them with undying malice.

Now what has the Church ever taught in regard to this state of things ?

Has it held that when man sins under the influence of the tempter, he is to be excused—and that God will not condemn him, but take his part ?

Has it taught that it is inhuman to denounce sin and not to exulpate the sinner, because he is the victim of the causeless spite of the enemy of God and man ?

If this were the doctrine of the Scriptures and of the Church, then it might be considered unpatriotic to believe that a nation, afflicted by enemies whom it had not injured, was blameless before God; but no such idea has ever, for a moment, been entertained by the orthodox believers in the Holy Oracles.

Though Satan is man's enemy from the inherent malice of his own reprobate nature, the victim of his arts is considered as justly suffering the penalty of his sins ; and not even the most holy angels, much less erring mortals, are permitted to bring railing accusations against an adversary whom the righteous Judge permits for a season to be a tempter.

For to assert that his power is iniquitous, is to condemn Him who permitted him to exercise it ; and all that is allowed to that creature is to despise this fiend for his sinfulness and opposition to God, to resist and fly from him as the enemy of all that is good and pure, and to repel his arts by the means which God has taught are most effectual to that end.

Men are allowed to contend with him ; but they must do it not with his own devices, but with the armor which the Almighty Sovereign is ready to lend to all who would escape from error.

A nation cannot have more malicious enemies than the dusky legions of hell : and the worst people that ever existed are infinitely better than the Devil and his angels.

And if it is not unchristian and inhuman to hold that the mortals who are afflicted by their sins, that is by Satan's devices, are justly dealt with, how can it be unpatriotic to say that a community wantonly assailed by malicious men is righteously chastened by the Almighty ?

Has God more control over devils than over men ?

Has he less pity for those whom the Arch Fiend leads into disasters than for such as are afflicted through other instrumentalities?

These reflections bring us naturally to another and most important consideration ; and that is, that the maxim about fighting the devil with fire, is the very coinage of hell

As already stated, creatures are allowed to contend with the great Adversary of God and of all good beings, are expressly commanded so to do ; but they must fight in a way consistent with the nature of the issue, and of the prize at stake. Satan's object is to make them like himself : this accomplished, he has effected all the mischief that even his mind can conceive. To be like him is to be an utter, awful and eternal ruin : and therefore the great stake in all contests with him is the character which the party he wars on is to assume.

Now to adopt his weapons is to assume his nature—and this done, his victim is conquered.

And so, when individuals and states are assailed, in the wise and merciful Providence of God, by wicked and malicious powers of the earth, they must not only trust in the Almighty, but they must fight for themselves; but, if they expect the favor of Heaven, they must contend on the principles sanctioned by it.

Beyond all doubt, a community is often assailed by mortal enemies precisely on the plan which permits the assaults of Satan; and that is, to test the character of the assailed, and permit it to see if it is really deserving of the aid of a holy God, although it is without blame as to its human antagonist.

If its national enemy is vile, treacherous and cruel, this national foe is contending on those principles which are detestable in the sight of Heaven, and which are the best evidences of merited judgments; and if the assaulted party resort to similar means it yields the most important issue at stake, and gives itself up as conquered.

If a good people are assaulted by a bad, the distinction between them is lost as soon as the former adopt the habits of the latter; and it is a mockery to suppose that men can contend for virtue and freedom by the means which belong to vile and slavish natures.

What is the worst condition to which a wicked and pitiless tyrant can reduce a people?

A virtuous freeman can die in triumph for his cause—he can wear chains in a dungeon, and lift up his serene and unconquered soul in proud defiance of his enemy; but when he becomes the victim of cruel and servile passions, he is conquered and ruined!

The moment he undertakes to fight his adversary with his own base principles, he has given up the contest as one between freedom and slavery, and whichever way the issue of arms may terminate, virtue and liberty have fallen, and the wicked policy which put the assailant in motion, has completely triumphed.

This is an extremely fruitful subject, and its importance demands that it should be presented in another light.

A striking feature in the conduct of all wickedly aggressive nations is the disposition on the part of the ministers of religion to deal out God's vengeance on all they deem His foes.

There is no better sign of the workings of Satan; and from the constant habit of this wicked one he is styled, by way of eminence, the Accuser.

It is undoubtedly a part of the Christian's duty to rebuke a world lying in wickedness; but there is an infinite difference between reproofs administered to evil doers, and charges preferred against them, especially railing charges, at the throne of Omnipotence.

The good man will not fail, when acting according to his christian instincts, to denounce sin; but not even the Archangel Gabriel dares to denounce the offender before God.

When the clergymen or priests of the assailing party thus impiously assume to direct the vengeance of Jehovah, their conduct should not excite the fears of the other side, much less an emulous spirit; and an attempt at a defence in kind against such denunciations betrays a want of true religious character, and a fearful trifling with the attributes of Jehovah.

If our enemies curse and rail, their blasphemy will not justify ours; and the principle involved is not changed by the fact that we may think we have the greater reason to imprecate the vengeance of Heaven.

Doubtless, all who indulge in this kind of preaching justify themselves on the ground that they are calling for justice on the enemies of God; and such mad-men, in opposing nations, are separated not by principle, but only by their own opinions as to which have the better claim to the privilege of wielding the thunderbolts of Omnipotence.

Each acts as if God's jealous prerogatives were to be delegated to men: yea, each claims the right for mortal hands to seize the lightnings of Almighty Vengeance, and to blast whomsoever he may deem the enemies of the Most High.

God has not left the throne where He has sat in awful majesty from eternity; nor has He laid aside His royal prerogatives to be appropriated as abandoned jewels by the first daring finder.

When impious mortals assume to administer or direct His justice, their blasphemy can hurt only themselves and the nation which encourages them; and the people who are the objects of their hatred are safe from their malice just in proportion to their horror of such proceedings.

Doubtless, there is no nation but has among its spiritual guides some foolish men, ready to defend themselves and their people by such weapons as may be used against them; but such preachers, instead of adding to the strength of their country, are a weakness and a curse; and in a community wickedly assailed and struggling with manly fortitude for the cause of justice, they are of all classes, the most contemptible and pernicious.

Such men are to be dreaded as a moral leprosy; they would introduce into the heart of the nation the plague from which it has tried to escape by arraying itself in arms.

They encourage the public enemy by their sins, the principles of their religious guides—and they stand between an afflicted people and the unfailing channels of God's covenanted mercies.

They are terrible only to the cause they defend; and the dangers of the state may be surely estimated by their influence and popularity.

They bring into the camp of the brave defenders of the right an accursed thing; and as long as they are tolerated, there can be no certain hope of success.

PROOFS AND ILLUSTRATIONS.

Let the reader consult the 1st chapter of Job as an illustration of what it is permitted to Satan to do—and of the manner in which good man receives his assaults. It was Satan who was the instrument of Job's calamities—yet this godly man exclaimed, "The Lord gave, and the Lord hath taken away; blessed be the name of the Lord." "In all this," says the inspired historian, "Job sinned not, nor charged God foolishly"—(i. 22.) He did afterwards complain of God's dealings—and in doing so he sinned, and was rebuked by God himself as the reader will find in chapters xxxviii and xxxix. In chapter xl. v 1-5, we have these instructive words

"Moreover the Lord answered Job, and said,

Shall he that contendeth with the Almighty instruct him? he that reproveth God, let him answer it.

Then Job answered the Lord, and said,

Behold, I am vile; what shall I answer thee? I will lay mine hand upon my mouth.

Once have I spoken; but I will not answer: yea, twice; but I will proceed no further

"I also will not henceforth drive out any from before them of the nations which Joshua left when he died:

That through them I may prove Israel, whether they will keep the way of the Lord to walk therein, as their fathers did keep it, or not." -(Judges ii. 21-22.)

"And they were to prove Israel by them, to know whether they would hearken unto the commandments of the Lord, which he commanded their fathers by the hand of Moses."—(Judges iii. 4.)

"Howbeit, in the business of the ambassadors of the princes of Babylon, who sent unto him to inquire of the wonder that was done in the land, God left him, to try him, that he might know all that was in his heart."—(2 Chron. xxxii. 31.)

"And he shewed me Joshua the high priest standing before the angel of the Lord, and Satan standing at his right hand to resist him..

And the Lord said unto Satan, The Lord rebuke thee, O Satan, even the Lord that hath chosen Jerusalem rebuke thee : is not this a brand plucked out of the fire?

Now Joshua was clothed with filthy garments, and stood before the angel."—(*Zech.* iii. 1-3.)

" Be sober, be vigilant ; because your adversary the devil, as a roaring lion, walketh about, seeking whom he may devour :

Whom resist steadfast in the faith, knowing that the same affli - tions are accomplished in your brethren that are in the world."— (1 *Peter* v. 8-9.)

" Whereas angels, which are greater in power and might, bring not railing accusation against them before the Lord."—(2 *Pet.* ii. 11.)

" Yet Michael the archangel, when contending with the devil he disputed about the body of Moses, durst not bring against him a railing accusation. but said, The Lord rebuke thee"—(*Jude* 9.)

" To me *belongeth* vengeance, and recompense."—(*Deut.* xxxii. 35.)

" Judge not, that ye be not judged.

For with what judgment ye judge, ye shall be judged : and with what measure ye mete, it shall be measured to you again."—(*Mat.* vii 1-2.)

" Therefore thou art inexcusable, O man, whosoever thou art that judgest ; for wherein thou judgest another, thou condemnest thy-self ; for thou that judgest doest the same things.

But we are sure that the judgment of God is according to truth against them which commit such things.

And thinkest thou this, O man, that judgest them which do such things, and doest the same, that thou shalt escape the judgment of God ?"—(*Rom.* ii. 1-3.)

" Speak not evil one of another, brethren. He that speaketh evil of *his* brother, and judgeth his brother, speaketh evil of the law, and judgeth the law : but if thou judge the law, thou art not a doer of the law, but a judge.

There is one lawgiver, who is able to save and to destroy : who art thou that judgest another ?"—(*James* iv. 11-12.)

" But God is the judge : he putteth down one, and setteth up an-other."—(*Ps.* lxxv. 7.)

" Let no man say when he is tempted, I am tempted of God : for, God cannot be tempted with evil, neither tempteth he any man :

But every man is tempted, when he is drawn away of his own lust, and enticed.—(*James* i. 13-14.)

9

CHAPTER VII.

Mysterious Dispensations of Providence

Human nature is fallen and depraved, and in this condition is ready to assign its trials to any cause rather than the true one.

It is on this account that men often characterize the dealings of God towards them as mysterious and inscrutable : and in so doing the blame for afflictions is ingeniously shifted from the suffering creature to the plans of the great Creator.

People do not suppose they are impugning the wisdom, power or goodness of God, when they refer to His afflictive dealings as conducted on principles not to be understood ; but they do plainly say by such language that the cause for these distresses is not to be discovered by the mortals concerned, and is not a necessary result of their actions or disposition.

Still, they are willing to admit that the Divine Disposer has good reasons for His course in the premises—but if He has, they are not to be understood by finite minds, and therefore cannot be explained on any principles of human philosophy.

This explanation of the ways of Providence towards man is extremely offensive to the Supreme Ruler—and indeed it is well calculated to impair the confidence of His creatures in Him as a perfect Being.

To say the least, it represents Him as allowing His subjects to suffer without knowing the cause ; and thus attributes to His Government such radical and fatal imperfection as to render the results of good and evil action wholly uncertain.

In fact this course of reasoning removes all obligations to obey God at all ; for if His dealings with His creatures are to be conducted on rules not revealed and not to be understood, why should His written Law be regarded ? If the Almighty Sovereign has two systems of action towards His subjects, the one made known and the other reserved in His own infinite Mind, are not His creatures in a most deplorable condition and without inducement to do good, or to abstain from evil ? is there any distinction between good and evil ?

What is the purpose of a written Law if it alone is not to judge all the actions and dispositions of those to whom it is given ?

This whole idea of mystery is a subterfuge, a sinful invention of

human pride which would degrade the Creator rather than confess
a fault in self; and it is in direct conflict with the plain teachings
of that Word which has been revealed from Heaven as the certain,
eternal and immutable rule of life and death.

God has been "manifest in the flesh," in the person of His co-
equal Son; and it is to this Being, so known to us, by His own appearance among us, and by His full and complete Word that "all
judgment is committed." There is not a mysterious, invisible, unknown power behind the Son, reversing His decisions—but "the
Father judgeth no man, but hath committed all judgment unto the
Son, that all men should honor the Son, even as they honor the
Father. He that honoreth not the Son, honoreth not the Father
that sent Him."—(*John* v. 22-23.)

To refer afflictions, therefore, to a mysterious will of the Father,
over and beyond the system of Christ's Kingdom and Rule, is a dis-
honouring of the Father, even though we insert a saving clause to the
effect that this inscrutable Will is righteous.

And this Son emphatically says, "And if any man hear my words,
and believe not, I judge him not: for I came not to judge the world,
but to save the world. He that rejecteth me, and receiveth not my
words, hath one that judgeth: the word that I have spoken the same
shall judge him in the last day. For I have not spoken of myself;
but the Father that sent me, He gave me a commandment, what I should
say and what I should speak. And I know His commandment is
life everlasting: whatsoever I speak, therefore, even as the Father
said unto me, so I speak."—(*John* xii. 47-50.)

What can be more explicit? God has no other rule of action towards His creatures than that revealed in connection with and by
His Son Jesus Christ; and Christ Himself will not judge by arbi-
trary will, but according to the commandment of the Father, and
which commandment He has made known by Himself and His prophets, as the Word that is to judge all men, test all actions and dispositions, and award all retributions. In this sure Word all that
is necessary for man to know, all that concerns *his* welfare in time
and eternity, is fully and plainly stated. This eternal truth is exalted in judgment: this is the rod of iron that smites all nations,
the rule that accounts for all the mutations and afflictions of time.
There is no mystery in any of these things: the reasons and principles of all God's dealings with us are plainly stated, and "belong
to us and to our children."

FURTHER PROOFS AND ILLUSTRATIONS.

It is to be noted that in the prayer of Daniel, quoted on pages

18 and 39, he repeatedly states the fact that he and his people had departed from *the* laws of God—that they had not obeyed *His voice* —and that the afflictions of the Jews were *a confirmation of the Word of God revealed to them*. He repudiates all idea of mystery, and emphatically recognizes the cruel sufferings of his race at the hands of abominable and God-hating idolaters, as the true fulfilment of the righteous Law made known by Jehovah, and violated by his people. Nehemiah is careful to teach the same doctrine in the prayer recorded for our instruction: and it occurs in the inspired petitions of other holy men.

"The secret things belong unto the Lord our God: but those things which are revealed *belong* unto us, and to our children for ever, that *we* may do all the words of this Law."—(*Deut*. xxix. 29.)

"For he established a testimony in Jacob, and appointed a law in Israel, which he commanded our fathers, that they should make them known to their children:

That the generation to come might know *them*, *even* the children *which* should be born; *who* should arise and declare *them* to their children:

That they might set their hope in God, and not forget the works of God, but keep His commandments."—(*Ps*. lxxviii. 5-7.)

"To the law and to the testimony: if they speak not according to this word, *it is* because *there is* no light in them."—(*Is*. viii. 20.)

"Surely the Lord God will do nothing, but he revealeth his secret unto his servants the prophets."—(*Amos* iii. 7.)

"The secret of the Lord *is* with them that fear him; and he will shew them his covenant."—(*Ps*. xxv. 14.)

All mystery in the ways of God is only with those who do not heed the voice of His Word: to such as fear Him He reveals all His methods of dealing, and they know how to escape His judgments

CHAPTER VIII.

Bible Views of National trials, continued.—The manner in which National trials are made to promote the cause of Christ on earth.

It is important that the reader should not misunderstand the doctrines of the preceding chapter.

God is not accountable to His creatures for any of His ways; and no one can stay His hand and say what doest thou? But as a just and good Sovereign He has revealed all that it is necessary for His subjects to know; and He has set before men life and death, and plainly indicated the road to each. He has fixed the boundaries between right and wrong; and He has made known the plan and reasons for His judgments towards every creature in all his relations.

Every Christian is assured that *all* the dispensations in which he is interested are for his good; and he ought, also, from the doctrines of the Divine Charter of his faith, to believe that every national trial will display the glory of God, and advance the cause of His Kingdom on earth

No one who exercises a true faith in the teachings of the Revealed Word can doubt what has been already stated concerning the origin and the general result of all national changes and afflictions, nor does such faith need the corroborating influence of facts to sustain it. The best evidence to it is the Word of God which cannot lie; but the Almighty Disposer is ever confirming His truth before the eyes of His creatures, and at this age in the history of the world, the advocate of the Scriptures is enabled to answer the skeptical and to sustain the faith of the weak by pointing to the methods by which public trials promote the ends referred to. It is unnecessary to enumerate all of these—but it is well to refer to some in order to turn in the right direction the thoughts of those who are passing through dark dispensations, and to bring before them considerations which not only afford light and encouragement, but, also, indicate the path of christian duty.

FIRST. The destruction of a nation may be of great service to the cause of the Church; but in such cases the measure of iniquity will be full and the day of grace passed

Such a doom does not come without previous warning; and it falls only on those who have hardened themselves against the admonitions of God, who have corrupted all their ways before Him, and who are seen by the Divine Mind to be beyond reformation and only a source of evil to the world. Nations, like individuals, do have their days of grace; and when the time of their probation is over, and they are found joined to their idols, they will suffer the final and righteous judgments of Heaven on all the unrepenting workers of iniquity

This doom never overtakes any people without ample warning; and its perfect justice will be always manifested by the obdurate natures of those concerned

The people, therefore, who fear this fate are not those who are in most danger of suffering it; and its approach is usually preceded by that awful delusion denounced against those who persistently pervert the truth, of being contented with their ways, justified in their own eyes, and given up to believe a lie. It is unnecessary to undertake to show how the destruction of such a nation may advance the cause of the gospel; the facts of every case will be so plain that none can mistake their import.

SECONDLY. Public calamities may serve to reform a nation; and when we are permitted to see this result, we need no further explanation of their uses:

Here again the manifestations of the popular heart will furnish to the Christian patriot unerring signs of coming events; and if he witnesses a disposition to tremble at the Word of God, and to look at home for the cause of trouble, an openness to the truth, and a desire to discover the sins of self, he may be assured that the trials of his country are intended to improve its moral condition, and that this good result is hastening on.

THIRDLY. If a nation is neither destroyed nor reformed by its trials, the righteousness of God is vindicated by solemn admonitions to repent; and when reproofs have been often administered, and there has been no improvement on the part of those chastised, the friend of truth beholds impressive displays of Divine goodness and forbearance, and the world is prepared to justify that final stroke of wrath which will surely come.

FOURTHLY. A community which God has destined to an important work in the cause of the Gospel may, in the commencement of its political or organic life, be educated by trials for its coming task.

God, in the rightful exercise of His sovereignty, may and does often choose individuals and nations for peculiar positions of influence and responsibility; but, as He repeatedly assured the Jews, this is not for the righteousness of the instrumentalities selected, and these must, therefore, be trained for their work.

If a nation is seen to be teachable, it will be placed in such circumstances as will be likely to discover to itself its existing disposition—and its trials will be continued until it is turned from its errors and is brought to a higher standard of faith and morals than that which generally prevails. These views are clearly illustrated in the history of the Jews.

It is obvious now that when the descendants of Abraham were delivered from the bondage of Egypt, they were of a low-moral type compared with that of the people who entered Canaan under the lead of Joshua: but even Moses himself was not aware of the baseness of that generation which God liberated from the power of Pharaoh until its character was proved in the trials of the desert.

We know from history, as well as from the assurance of God Himself, that the mere descent from Abraham did not constitute the Jews a superior race; nor were they rendered worthy of their illustrious career by the knowledge of the high destiny for which they were designed.

The repeated assurance from a Divine source, that they were chosen for a great and glorious work did not fit them for it, nor elevate them to a nobler character; nor did all the amazing displays of Jehovah's power in their behalf, and of His affection for them, serve to purge out the old leaven of their natures, nor to string themselves with more manly sinews.

These important facts were to be discovered by the schooling of the wilderness; and it was not until after they had been long instructed by God through His Word and His Providences, that the Israelites, as a race, seemed at all superior to the idolatrous and corrupt nations who were cotemporary with them.

But God having chosen them to a great destiny, educated them for it; and the first part of their training was designed to impress upon them their native depravity, their innate aversion to a holy life, their inability in themselves to choose or to follow out an illustrious career, and notwithstanding their ceremonial purity and their nearness, in name, to God, their fixed attachment to vices that would reduce them, if left to themselves, to the level of the heathen world.

The Sovereign of the universe may select other communities for places of peculiar honor; and though no other nation, as such, will ever occupy the place of the Jews in the sense of being the chosen race, and of constituting the visible Church, yet in all ages some of the powers of the world are prepared to occupy positions which are made to contribute in a special manner to the advancement of the Redeemer's Kingdom.

When a nation has been born under such christian influences as
will enable it rightly to interpret the Providences of God, and com-
mences its career with great and continued troubles, there is reason
to hope that it is designed for a high and useful destiny; but let
no one be deceived by this remark

*It is not for their inherent virtue that communities are thus chosen
of God for an illustrious service, and sent out to the wilderness of
trouble to be trained; but their trials are caused by the fact that they
are wholly unfit for their coming fate and are so refractory that they
will not be taught until the rod has been unsparingly used.*

When, therefore, the afflictions of a people, under 'the circumstances above indicated, serve only to enhance the virtue of the
concerned, in their own estimation—and when the conviction of
benevolent designs on the part of Providence is a source of pre-
sumptuous pride and an argument against repentance and reformation, the trials of the nation are not preparing it for greatness, but
are premonitions of coming destruction.

If calamities serve to purify, elevate and ennoble a new people, they
presage a glorious future; if they do not, there is not only no reason for hope, but there is abundant cause to fear a base career and
an ignoble end.

Thus God, in the just exercise of His prerogatives, may smite a
people for its sins in the very opening of its career, to prove its disposition, to discover its nature to itself, and its need of reformation,
and the result of these trials on national character will be a strong
indication of their purpose on national destiny.

PROOFS AND ILLUSTRATIONS.

Some of the propositions of this chapter are mere statements of
facts which need no other confirmation than a knowledge of the
course of past events—and the following quotations sustain the
others.

" Thus saith the Lord God unto Jerusalem, Thy birth and thy
nativity is of the land of Canaan; thy father was an Amorite, and
thy mother a Hittite.

And as for thy nativity, in the day thou wast born thy navel was
not cut, neither wast thou washed in water to supple thee; thou
wast not salted at all, nor swaddled at all.

None eye pitied thee, to do any of these unto thee, to have com-
passion upon them; but thou wast cast out in the open field, to the
loathing of thy person, in the day that thou wast born.

And when I passed by thee, and saw thee polluted in thine own blood, I said unto thee *when thou wast* in thy blood, Live; yea, I said unto thee *when thou wast* in thy blood, Live.

Now when I passed by thee, and looked upon thee, behold, thy time *was* the time of love; and I spread my skirt over thee, and covered thy nakedness: yea, I swore unto thee, and entered into a covenant with thee, saith the Lord God, and thou becamest mine.

Then washed I thee with water; yea, I thoroughly washed away thy blood from thee, and I anointed thee with oil.

I clothed thee also with broidered work, and shod thee with bad gers' skin, and I girded thee about with fine linen, and I covered thee with silk.

I decked thee also with ornaments, and I put bracelets on thy hands, and a chain on thy neck.

And I put a jewel on thy forehead, and ear-rings in thine ears, and a beautiful crown upon thy head.

Thus wast thou decked with gold and silver; and thy raiment *was* of fine linen, and silk, and broidered work; thou didst eat fine flour, and honey, and oil; and thou wast exceeding beautiful, and thou didst prosper into a kingdom.

And thy renown went forth among the heathen for thy beauty; for it *was* perfect through my comeliness, which I had put upon thee, saith the Lord God."—*Ezekiel* xvi. 3—14.

Under the figurative language used above, God would impress with infinite force, upon the minds of the Jews their obligations to Him for all that distinguished them from other nations. He chose them not for their righteousness—but He clothed them with moral beauty, because He had selected them for His people.

And as they were without excellence when He set His love upon them, so were they without power or influence; it was not because their virtue, wisdom or strength made them important to God that they were chosen, but He who set them apart for His service Himself fitted them for their work.

"The Lord did not set His love upon you, nor chose you, because ye were more in number than any people; (for ye *were* the fewest of all people.")—(*Deut.* vii. 7.)

The people thus chosen were to be educated by the Word of God and by trials.

"And thou shalt remember all the way which the Lord thy God led thee these forty years in the wilderness, to humble thee, *and* to prove thee, to know what *was* in thine heart, whether thou wouldst keep His commandments, or no."—(*Deut.* viii. 2.)

CHAPTER IX.

The subject of Chapter VIII, continued.—The most doubtful case stated and discussed.

There is one class of national tri,*, which would appear to be a painful mystery to many professed christians who believe they see more of evil than of good in the immediate results of such afflicting dispensations, and who can derive comfort only from a vague hope that God will accomplish His beneficent ends by means inscrutable to mortal vision.

That the unhappy doubts in which this subject is involved may, if possible, be removed, let an extreme case be taken for discussion.

A people whose springs of national life have felt the healing power of Divine Truth, is involved in a defensive war.

The whole nation, as a body, is under the influence of an orthodox and evangelical Church : the christian element of Society is strong in numbers, in learning, wealth and position. Society is blessed with the thousand civilizing agencies which spring from the deep hold of religious principle on the popular mind, all classes enjoy the means of a sound education, the gospel is regularly preached to the whole nation by a learned and godly ministry, wise and just laws are faithfully executed, a diligent attention to the honest and useful arts of peace causes the face of nature to smile with beauty, and creates an abundance which disarms robbery of the plea of necessity, and the wealth and zeal of the Church are founding and supporting seminaries filled with pupils in training for the Lord's service.

In the midst of this state of things Society is shaken to its foundations with the rude shock of war—of a war on the issue of which the very existence of the nation is staked, and whose successful prosecution will long and severely task all the energies of the country.

War, in Christian nations at least, appears, under all circumstances, to be demoralizing : it takes away the restraints of law and of public opinion, relaxes the influence of education, removes large bodies of men from the softening power of female society and of family associations, and from the wholesome discipline of daily labor for the means of subsistence, sharpens the public appetite for unhealthy excitements, fosters idleness and dissipation, accustoms all classes to scenes of ferocity and carnage, impoverishes honest men, paralyzes useful enterprise, and opens a wide and inviting field for fraud, dishonesty, avarice, revenge, hatred and sensuality.

Every reformatory agency of society seems to be embarrassed and to suffer—the operations of the Church to be contracted and weakened, and the humanizing voice of law and letters to be hushed.

All the manifestations of iniquity are fearfully increased : idleness and drunkenness become more general and are the fruitful parents of other vices, and profanity, oppression, robbery and murder abound.

Such are the results of war under any circumstances, if it is long continued ; but in the case supposed, the contest is for national existence, and the assailants in the strife, strong in numbers and resources, and filled with the ferocious energy of mad fanaticism, strike at the vitals of the country by every weapon which cunning can invent, and which malice can wield.

They summon to their aid all the bitter passions of the human heart ; and thus they provoke to hatred and cruelty on the other side, and the struggle becomes a prolonged tragedy of unrelieved horrors.

Every step of its progress adds a still darker page to the history of human depravity and suffering ; and such is the apparently rapid degeneracy of the times that each year of the strife seems to bring the parties interested a century nearer to a savage condition.

What religious advantage can the spectator behold in such a struggle ?

How can the christian inhabitants of the nation so cruelly assailed discover more of good than of evil in a state of things which has deranged the whole machinery of Society, paralyzed nearly every moral agency, and forced a people devoted to peace, to abandon its beneficent arts, and to give themselves universally to the destruction of war ?

If the nation is immediately led to repentance or reformation, the uses of the afflicting Providences are obvious to all ; but when such results do not seem to follow, how can the christian philosopher console himself for the calamities of the times except by simple reliance on the goodness and power of God, and a belief that Infinite Wisdom will, in some way unknown to mortals, accomplish its beneficent ends from seeming evil ?

The Christian, under such circumstances, is *not* always shut up to rayless darkness ; and he will find in the following considerations ample reasons for justifying the state of things imagined, and which sometimes occurs, as a necessity to the progress of the Gospel.

FIRST. The word demoralization as applied to those phenomena of Society which result from war is often used in an improper sense, and one in conflict with fundamental doctrines of the revealed Word

The *amount* of crime is increased by war—but the *source* of evil; the unconverted human heart, is not rendered. *more capable of sin.*

The sum of all sins is to be alienated from God, and in a state of rebellion to Him ; and this is the condition of every man by nature, and each one in this state is capable of any iniquity which man has ever perpetrated. ' " The heart *is* deceitful above all *things* and desperately wicked : who can know it ?" (*Jer.* xvii, 9.) " And God saw that the wickedness of man *was* great in the earth, and *that* every imagination of the thoughts of his heart *was* only evil continually." (*Gen.* vi, 5.) " Behold, I was shapen in iniquity; and in sin did my mother conceive me." (*Ps.* li, 5.) " God looked down from heaven upon the children of men, to see if there were *any* that did understand, that did seek God.

Every one of them is gone back : they are altogether become . filthy ; *there is* none that doeth good, no, not one." (*Ps.* liii, 2, 3.) " He that trusteth in his own heart is a fool." (*Prov.* xxviii, 26.) " This *is* an evil among all *things* that are done under the sun, that *there is* one event unto all : yea, also the heart of the sons of men is full of evil, and madness *is* in their heart while they live, and after that they go to the dead."—*Ec.* ix, 3.

" For out of the heart proceed evil thoughts, murders, adulteries, fornications, thefts, false witness, blasphemies."—*Math.* xv, 19.

" Now the works of the flesh are manifest, which are *these*, Adultery, fornication, uncleanness, lasciviousness,

Idolatry, witch craft, hatred, variance, emulation, wrath, strife, sedition heresies,

Envyings, murders, drunkenness, revellings, and such like." (*Gal.* v, 19-21.) " For we ourselves also were sometimes foolish, disobedient, deceived, serving divers lusts and pleasures, living in malice and envy, hateful, *and* hating one another." (*Titus* iii, 3.) Such is the character of the natural or unconverted man, as drawn by the pen of inspiration : and if the reader desires further light on this subject let him ponder the following terrible passage : " What then? Are we better *than they?* No, in no wise ; for we have before proved both Jews and Gentiles, that they are all under sin ;

As it is written, There is none righteous, no, not one : .

There is none that understandeth, there is none that seeketh after God.

They are all gone out of the way, they are together become unprofitable; there is none that doeth good, no, not one.

Their throat is an open sepulchre; with their tongues they have used deceit; the poison of asps is under their lips:

Whose mouth is full of cursing and bitterness :

Their feet *are* swift to shed blood:

Destruction and misery *are* in their ways:

And the way of peace they have not known :

There is no fear of God before their eyes." (*Rom.* iii, 9—18.) This awful description of unconverted men, Jews and Gentiles, savage and civilized, educated and ignorant, is sustained by numerous other texts in the Holy Scriptures; but enough has been quoted to prove the assertion that every son of Adam, in his natural state, can be guilty of the worst crimes ever committed by a member of his race.

The unchanged heart is a fountain of all iniquity : and a thorough appreciation of this fundamental truth is the first step in every judicious and useful effort to promote the welfare of the human race, and an essential pre-requisite to a just appreciation of the necessity of a Divine and crucified Saviour.

Now, in a nation that has long enjoyed the blessings which flow from the gospel, there springs up a state of things unfavorable to the full and practical recognition of the doctrine in question ; for all but those who are instructed by the Holy Spirit are tempted by their carnal pride to attribute the advanced state of civilization, and the general prosperity, to human agencies, and to the more noble natures of the new races of men. A subtle but fatal form of infidelity even creeps into the bosom of the visible church ; and all literature begins to breathe the same spirit, so flattering to human vanity, so opposite to the teachings of revealed truth, and so dishonoring to the economy of grace. If the growth of the nation in learning and prosperity is more rapid than its progress in vital godliness a deceitful and dangerous condition of things supervenes ; and if this course of affairs should not be interrupted by some Providential intervention, the truly christian element of society would soon be buried in a mass of pernicious errors filling the influential positions in the Church, and leading the people to ultimate ruin.

Such, for instance, has been the history of the region once embraced within the limits of the United States ; and the unexampled prosperity of the country, due alone to the vital godliness of those who laid the foundation of its greatness, aided in the development of doctrines the opposite of those on a just appreciation of which the lasting peace of the nation depended.

Religion is not an inheritance from man to man, but a Divine gift to its possessor; and while the externals of piety were transmitted, the native depravity of those who enjoyed blessings purchased by the faith of their ancestors, found in this very prosperity an argument to flatter their own pride at the expense of the Truth of that God whom they professed to honor. The new state of the world was attributed to the advancement of the arts of peace, results were put for causes, and it was proudly maintained that man, on this Hemisphere, had triumphed over the infirmities which had marked his career in all other places, and in all past ages; and the Church not only did not rebuke this impious language which found utterance in periodicals, in books, in political and anniversary harangues, and in the actions and teachings of reformers and professed philanthropists, but it admitted into its own strong-holds men who held, under specious disguises, principles that would lead to its betrayal.

The natural human heart was the same it had ever been; but its depraved instincts were held in check by law, by education, and by a state of public opinion formed when vital christianity had a stronger hold on the heart of the nation.

But every thing was a sham : the laws were made on the supposition that Divine Truth had a more powerful influence on the public mind than it was really exerting; men of the world crowded into the Church under the same impression, and were careful to present a decent and consistent exterior, and teachers of abominable and destructive heresies took infinite pains to wrap their deadly poisons in learned technicalities scented with the odor of approved Theology

But law, and education, custom, interest and public opinion had only built a covering over the mouth of the volcano, and imprisoned the elements of destruction in the bowels of the mountain; and when the people fondly imagine that the flames are extinguished and are building their hopes on the very jaws of death, God sends an earth-quake which opens a mouth for the devouring element, and soon the air is darkened with smoke and cinders, and the country devastated with a deluge of burning lava. The nature of man is found to be the same it ever was; and when convulsions open the way, there is poured forth from his heart such streams of destructive iniquity that all cavils are silenced, all the ingenious theories of infidel reformers about human perfectibility, are exploded and disgraced, and the great foundation doctrine of man's depravity is plainly revealed to all who have eyes to see. The remedy, for the time, seems harsh, but the disease to be removed is infinitely more injurious; and though society suffers by the unlocking of the fathormless abyss of human depravity and the letting loose of all-the untamed beasts of prey that inhabit there, the amount of genuine christianity is not diminished, and the energies of the Church, roused to unwonted activity, are directed with a better sense of the great work before it, and of the only means by which it is to be accomplished.

In such convulsions, the wickedness always inherent in the heart of man, is developed into action; and while it is thus made a source of great suffering within the scope of its power, its melancholy and dangerous condition is impressively revealed, and the havoc which it makes of the best interests of society, exposes the quackery of those who had pronounced it whole, and prompts to an earnest desire for the medicine which alone can heal it.

Thus, we can discern an important and glorious use for those terrible forms of national affliction stated above; and the demoralization of these awful lessons is only apparent, being but an outward development of existing depravity, permitted by God for the sweeping away of the refuge of lies, opening the eyes of the nations to the only hope of a fallen world, and impressing on the Church the paramount importance of its only mission, to preach Jesus Christ and Him crucified as the power and wisdom of God.

And cannot the American Christian, dark and as is the ordeal through which he is passing, see light in these suggestions? How eloquent is the language of the revolution which shakes the continent and solemnizes a gazing world! It is God's argument, overthrowing with irretrievable destruction, the sophistries of a people who had used His blessings for the perversion of His truth! By this terrific explosion Jehovah declares that American Institutions are not a new gospel; and the moral of the tragedy is not that republicanism is a failure, or learning injurious, or popular privileges pernicious, but that MAN IS DEPRAVED, and in his best estate, without the transforming power of a living christianity, is worse than a beast of prey.

> "Amidst the woods the leopard knows his kind,
> The tiger preys not on the tiger brood;
> Man only is the common foe of man."

This is a lesson of the American crisis, written in letters of fire, for the admonition of the nations; and mark with what appropriate means does Infinite Wisdom cause a false and impious philosophy to undermine its own foundations and disgracefully expose its own absurdity!

In one part of the country rent in twain, there was a great and increasing degeneracy in the theory of moral doctrines; and the true, scriptural idea of Christ's atonement was explained away, as inconsistent with the divinity of human nature.

Bad actions and an evil state of society were admitted; but these were attributed to forms of government and to laws There was a growing impression that all the vices of the world were curable by human agencies; and that much of the trouble of the past was caused by ignorance, and by unjust government. The philosophy of the region referred to, did not account for the origin of ignorance and of evil government; it presumed that these had happened in some way not derogatory to the general nobility of man, and it contended that at all events the people in one part of America, and especially in New England, were now fully apprized of all that was necessary to reform the world. And now this people, who depended on political theories to do the work of Christ, are, through the agency of their government, seeking to heap the most direful calamities on the head of millions of their former fellow-citizens.

They who contended that the great secret of human progress consisted in the right of the people to choose their own rulers and to make their own laws, are invading with fire and sword half a continent for daring to select its own form of government without their consent; and the community who held that personal bondage, even when a semi-savage was the slave and a civilized christian the master, was an outrage on the dignity of human nature, are waging a bitter and terrible war with the avowed purpose of destroying or enslaving a whole christian nation. Those who could not bear to look on a gallows erected for the execution of murderers, cannot satiate their thirst for blood, with the crimson torrents that flow over battle fields piled with the gashed victims of ruthless war—the believers in human perfectibility would deprive a large portion of the human race of every right of man; and they who contended that American Institutions were a new Gospel, perform with frantic joy, a bloody war-dance over their grave, and wildly exult in the exchange of liberty, with peace and fraternity, for a despotism that gratifies their lust for conquest and spoliation.

The people who taught that rebellion against God was not such a depravity in the creature as to render him incapable of good in himself, are endeavoring to prove that opposition to their authority has rendered a whole nation of men, women and children unworthy of life; and they who regarded the doctrine of hell as an invention of bigotry, consider no punishment too terrible or too long for those who refuse their domination.

In short, those who would secure the peace of the world by reason and philosophy, are waging against the united appeals of all christendom, the most cruel, exhausting and irrational war of modern times; and they who believed in man's innate power to sustain himself and to reach his own best good, have been permitted to present the awful spectacle of a deliberate national suicide in the midst of unexampled prosperity!

And let us turn for a moment to the demonstrations of this doctrine of depravity on that end of the continent where the Church had still maintained a doctrinal purity.

Here orthodoxy of profession had taken the place of vital godliness: and as the Church standards and philosophy still spoke a pure language, the display of infirmity has characterized the actions of individuals rather than that of public or political organisms.

And can any one look upon the scenes presented in the bosom of Society, in a gallant nation, heroically struggling for existence and independence, and doubt that man is a hopelessly fallen being, and always and everywhere, terrible to himself, without the sanctifying power of a new life from above?

Does not the state of things present an overwhelming demonstration of the truth and necessity of the Gospel?

What is here to corrupt men but their own hearts?

They have not been led astray by theological errors; they have not been debased by their public cause, for it is noble and generous, and demands for its success a virtuous and heroic people.

They have not been debased by bad laws or by corrupt political teachings; and they are placed in a position in which it is perfectly obvious that their liberties, their property, their security, their peace among themselves, all their immediate and remote temporal interests depend on their union in feeling and sympathy, their brotherly kindness and regard for each other.

They are, almost literally, one family : they are cut off from the sympathy, aid and intercourse of all the world, they are shut up to themselves, and under God, to their own exertions, a formidable and ferocious enemy pressing on all their frontiers, and their destiny as a nation trembling in the balance.

And what is the spectacle which their inner life presents? Threatened with famine and cut off from all the granaries of the world, they have to be restrained by the strong arm of the law from converting the staff of life, every pound of which is precious, into a dead-

11

ly poison; surrounded by the infuriate legions of a power that aims to destroy their liberties and confiscate their property, they aid the public enemy and enhance the common dangers and trials, by preying on each other.

But why undertake to draw a picture of what every one sees and feels? What pen can do justice to that insatiate greed of gain which seems to have petrified the hearts of a large portion of the community, and has filled society with swarms of devouring extortioners. speculators and thieves?

What language can represent to foreign ears the dark and cheerless condition of a society that has felt the blighting power of selfishness developed to insanity, and where men, cut off from the sympathies of the world, are never consoled for public trials by domestic charities?

It is not necessary to dwell on this state of things: suffice it to say, that when man had wrapped himself in assumed perfections and claimed as his native glory the lustre which the Gospel had shed on his race, God disrobes the veiled idol of the nineteenth century and sets it before the world in all its inherent vileness.

Man, as a moral being, is seen in all America to be but a mass of leprous corruption—and it is found that there is no power in creature skill to give life, health and beauty to this body of death.

This lesson of the times is of infinite value: with the general wreck of human improvements, there has also fallen a delusion that was surely leading to the undermining of those foundations on which the better hopes of the world must stand.

The Church will be called back from many vain speculations and much unprofitable labor, to a more vivid, profound and practical apprehension of the truth as it is in Jesus Christ—the true Christian will have a more active realizing sense of his task in a world lying in wickedness, and stripping himself of all the dialectics of philosophical Theology, and oppositions of science falsely so called will go to his task with the Spirit of Paul at Corinth, knowing only Christ and Him crucified.

The world must now see that human skill has signally failed to heal the source of all human woes; and the true messengers of that Gospel which ignores circumcision and uncircumcision as nothing, and proclaims individual regeneration through the grace of God in a crucified and Divine Redeemer, as the only hope of men and of nations, will find that this terrific storm has blown down many barriers that stood in their way. The vital christianity of the age has not been diminished or impaired; and though the number of true

disciples may be small, they will hear and rally to the voice that
speaks in trumpet tones from these commotions,

"Men of God, go take your stations;
Darkness reigns o'er all the earth;
Loud proclaim among the nations,
Joyful news of heavenly birth:
   Bear the tidings,
Tidings of the Saviour's worth.

"What tho' earth, by hell excited,
Should oppose the Saviour's reign!
Plead His cause to souls benighted;
Fear ye not the face of man;
   Vain the tumult,
Earth and hell will rage in vain."

As the subject is not yet finished, the quotations from Scripture
are reserved for another chapter.

CHAPTER X.

The subject of Chapters VIII & IX continued.

One method by which the cause of the gospel may be advanced by such revolutions as that which now rages in America has just been considered : and two others will now be suggested for the consolation and encouragement of the christian who lives in these troublous times.

The order commenced in the previous chapter will be preserved in this—and we now come to a *Second* use of wars in christian states. The nominal church is apt to become corrupt after a long career of peace with the world and of influence over it. This is by no means owing to the character of christianity, but results wholly from the depravity of men.

When the gospel acquires such power in the heart of a nation as to influence public and private action, unconverted men crowd into the Church from worldly motives ; and as religion is not inheritable, the descendants of a christian generation may be outwardly under the same influence, and yet far different in inward life and character.

And thus in the course of a few generations an apparently ortho dox Church may be encumbered with a vast amount of dead material ; and not only so, but as the seemingly christian element extends its influence over the wealth, enterprise and learning of the country, the weak and the false portion of the Church will begin to judge of its prosperity by the extent of its carnal appliances.

In time all will begin to rely too much on worldly means; and there will follow a most deceptive and diseased condition of things, and one which the devout christian will deplore, while he will fear it is beyond the reach of human remedy.

The real gold of the Church will be hid in a vast amalgam of baser metals, gilded over ; and nothing but a chemical test from God Himself, or a furnace heated by Him, will separate the parts, and free the precious ore from its vile admixtures.

At such times the visible Israel seems to consider that its only business is to decorate and fortify Jerusalem by carnal art ; and there is a vast expenditure on its walls, bastions and towers, on its streets and synagogues. The chief energies of the Church are devoted to the founding of seminaries, the construction and ornamentation of houses of worship, and the writing of learned and polished essays for critical audiences; and while the vast majority of the human race are sitting in darkness and the shadow of death, a Church, great in numbers, wealth and education, considers that it is performing its mission to a dying world by assembling every Sabbath in its costly and luxurious temples, listening soberly to well written discourses, and contributing the hundredth part of its worldly income to the support of a few poor and faithful men who are laboring earnestly amid the wide destitutions of the domestic and foreign field.

In the mean time religion is made as easy as possible to the mixed multitude who have honored God with their nominal adhesion to His cause ; and the lines of the Church and of the world so fade into each other that there is a large frontier ground which seems to be common to both.

The keen eyes of infidelity easily detect in the society of professed believers nearly every vice of the outside world, only clad in more sober hues ; and it becomes a really doubtful question whether the argument drawn from the conduct of its membership weakens or strengthens the cause of the Church.

Has not many a devout follower of the meek and lowly Jesus, in America, seen and mourned over the reality of this picture?

Have not such, in contemplating the difficulties in the way of their beloved Zion, often exclaimed "Return, O Lord, how long? Let thy work appear unto thy servants, and thy glory unto their children.

And let the beauty of the Lord our God be upon us."

In the midst of this state of things, there is a shaking of heaven and earth, of Church and State : the day of the Lord comes, and the messenger of the covenant sits in His temple as a refiner and purifier of silver.

But this day of the Lord is a day of darkness and gloominess : it is a time of quaking, the face of the covering cast over all people is destroyed, and the towers fall.

Many that shone as bright stars in the christian firmament, shoot from their spheres and go out in darkness—not a few of the grand pillars of the Church fall into ruins, and the earth is strewn with the wreck of Zion's outward bulwarks.

But though God sifts the Church with a seive, not a single grain of wheat is lost ; and the storm which seems to have blown down the Church, does but disentangle its vital element from the vast encumbering structures with which the world had hemmed it in.

The convulsions of the nation seem to be demoralizing because they shake every man who is wrongly placed into his right position; and while multitudes who wore the livery of Heaven are now arrayed with the enemies of God, every true soldier of the cross is left, and the army of the faithful, feeling more completely its dependence on its Almighty leader, gathers more closely around His standard, and throwing away every encumbrance, and clothing itself in the whole armor of God, goes forth to battle and to conquer.

The foundations of a purer Church are always laid in troublous times—and though the new house will be inferior in earthly grandeur, its glory will exceed that of the former, and in it will the Lord give peace to His saints, and from it will flow living waters for the healing of the nation.

And are not such results more than compensation, to the christian mind, for all the apparent wreck and ruin caused by war?

THIRDLY. While such convulsions break from their hold the vast parasitic growth that had interwoven its entanglements with all the energies of the Church, and leave the really christian element unfettered by the world, renovated in spirit, and animated with a more just conception of its mission, they also shake down many barriers of prejudice and false philosophy that stand in its way, and open up a wider and more fruitful field for its labors.

This proposition will be best illustrated by a reference to facts open to the observation of all the readers of this work; and let the christian patriot of the Confederate States behold in its true light the condition of things about him.

Is this an unfavorable time for the presentation, or for the reception of gospel truth?

What difficulties has this revolution interposed in the way of the true work of the Church?

The work of erecting sacred edifices has been arrested—the Seminaries languish, and men are not in a condition to go quietly through old routines, nor to sit calmly and amuse themselves by grappling with the learned dialectics which, in times of peace, furnished them with a weekly intellectual repast.

The old and easy channels of communication between the Church and the very small portion of the world which it reached, have been interrupted; the few shady high-ways over which the ancient machinery of stated Committees and permanent Boards penetrated, on a smooth track, short distances into the least dangerous part of the enemy's country, have been destroyed.

A large portion of the well-dressed and well-behaved audiences of many fashionable Churches have disappeared: Choirs have been broken up, and organs and bells cannot be obtained.

. A number of flashy preachers have felt a call to more ambitious occupations; and many godly ministers, many faithful office bearers have been driven from their charges, and many hopeful flocks have been scattered, and are now homeless and houseless.

A large number of congregations have been dispersed, and a great many christians have been taken from their usual avocations, and have gone into the service of the country; but is all this a loss to the service of Christ?

Let the account be balanced, let gains and losses be set against each other.

Not a few who had a name to live, have joined the world; and by this movement the camp of the faithful is purged of traitors, and dead weights are removed from the energies of the Church.

The *mechanics* of the Church have been greatly damaged: but the spirit of Christ was not in these; and too much reliance on them in the past was a serious obstacle in the way of the more efficient means of God's appointment.

Old routines and established formulas of conducting public religious affairs have been almost abolished; but these were not only not the prescribed channels of Divine grace, but they were often a great hindrance to the direct, earnest and simple preaching of · the gospel to a world lying in wickedness.

The multiplication and ornamentation of Church edifices was not enlarging the congregations of perishing sinners, hungering for the Word of Life; and in many places good men were giving their whole attention to piles of brick and mortar, while every street corner furnished more opportunities of reaching the destitute than were to be found in the gorgeous tenements on which had been bestowed so much of the time, thoughts and means of liberal-minded christians.

Flourishing congregations have been scattered all over the country, driven into exile among all sorts of people; and by this means the good are mixed with the evil, the salt of christianity, which was too much accumulated in store houses, is diffused where it is needed, and every grain with a true savor, is made to accomplish five times what it did before.

A great multitude of professing christians have gone into the various departments of the public service; but if they were good men the spirit of Christ did not forsake them when they left their homes.

Let us select an humble christian as an example of many—and let us contrast his spiritual life and work in peace and war.

He was a consistent member of a flourishing Church, enjoying the services of a learned and eloquent minister; and while he was punctual in his attendance at the house of worship, and gave what he could spare to its treasury, this was about all he could contribute to the service of the Lord.

His example did not seem of much importance amid so many blazing lights that paled his glimmering taper; and in a community accustomed to a certain unctuosity of manner in those who led in public exercises, he could not pray or speak before others to edification.

He was not practised in the mechanics of the Church, and could not swaddle and present his ideas with those approved technicalities which had become more important than the thoughts which they decorated.

This man goes into the ranks of the Confederate army, and messes and sleeps with rude men, from far different sections, men who have enjoyed none of his privileges, and who have never before been in such intimate contact with a follower of Christ.

He is not afraid to talk and read to these daily companions; his little taper shines with a steady light in a dark place, and to those who share his blanket, and stand by his side in the storm of battle, or drink from his canteen as life ebbs from their fainting hearts, he presents, in simple words, the glorious gospel of the blessed God with a power and to a purpose seldom reached by those who study in their closets the wants of a dying world.

And how many thousands of instances of this sort may have occurred since the war commenced! How many humble followers of the Saviour, whose lips were sealed at home by the conventionalities of a cramping, artificial system, have been enabled to speak a word in season to those whom the Church, with all its wealth and learning, had never reached at home, and who owed their contact with Christian men and their interest in their prayers and sympathies to a revolution which had borne down all barriers of separation and commingled saints and sinners on its eddying currents?

It is true that this concussion has, to a wonderful extent, shaken together the population of a large country, loosing, as it were, every man from his station, and mingling the whole multitude into a rolling mass of humanity, the component parts of which, like drops of water in a boiling whirlpool, are ever changing places: but will the cause of the Church, in a land of which the professed christian element constituted a large proportion, gain or lose by this mixing process?

Would it not seem that God had broken, by this revolution, the stereotype into which the Church had cast itself, and had dispersed its membership to the four winds, thus forcing it to a more literal observance of the solemn and perpetually binding injunction to go "into all the world and preach the gospel to every creature."

God's fire is in Zion; but as His people had carefully walled it in with brick and stone, He has demolished their furnaces, and scattered the live coals far and wide over the dry leaves of the forest.

Those that do not kindle into new flames were never truly ignited—but every vital spark will still burn, and the warmth and light and purifying power of the celestial element will be diffused through all the dark habitations of the land

Again: a night of darkness and storm has come upon the nation; and never before in the history of the country, did the true Christian enjoy such opportunities of demonstrating, beyond all cavil, the Divine origin of the faith which he professes.

Many zealous followers of Christ have, doubtless, often wished that they had the power once bestowed on prophets and apostles of stopping the mouths of gainsayers and of convincing the doubtful by work by miracles; and God has now conferred on them the glorious privilege of doing what, to the eyes of the world, will be as amazing as an interruption of the regular course of nature. They have but to walk consistently with their profession, in order to make miraculous displays before the unbelieving: to be honest while all others are falling before the power of Mammon, when there is neither law nor public opinion to restrain cupidity from fraudulent acts and unjust exactions—to exhibit hearts blooming with tender charities in an atmosphere cold and blighting as the polar blast—to do justly, to love mercy and to walk humbly with their God, at a time when judgment is turned away backward, and justice standeth afar off, when truth is fallen, and he that departeth from evil maketh himself a prey.

At such a time a really good man is "as a hiding place from the wind, and a covert from the tempest; as rivers of water in a dry place, as the shadow of a great rock in a weary land."

It is a time of darkness and tempest; and how sweetly shines upon the bosom of this night of horrors, the serene light of christian example!

The saints have but to trim their lamps and set them on their windows; and every passing way-farer, out in this dreadful storm which has blown out every other light, will feel and confess the obligations of the world for the only illumination which cannot be extinguished.

12

And while individual christians can, in these various ways, accomplish more than at ordinary times, the Church as a body, is placed nearer to the heart of the public than in times of peace.

The tremendous shock with which the world trembles has given unwonted activity to the popular mind: and the spectators of a tragedy where scenes of still deepening horror crowd each other, are peculiarly susceptible of religious impressions.

The entire public of the Confederate States has felt that God is moving in this storm; and whatever is offered as a revelation from the invisible world, attracts the most devouring attention.

The Wicked One has witnessed this hungering for spiritual food, and he is trying to satiate it with ashes: he beholds how the furrows of the field are gaping for seed, and he is busily sowing them with pernicious errors.

He is turning those who would hear from the other world, "unto them that have familiar spirits, and unto wizards that peep, and that mutter;" and scarcely a day passes that the arch-fiend is not feeding the eager multitude with visions of blind boys, and dreams of queer old women, and prophecies of dying quacks.

Many are saying "lo here is Christ, lo He is here;" and breathless attention is elicited to such vile fabrications as stories of wonderful sights in the Heavens, and strange voices in the earth, and mysterious inscriptions on the products of nature.

Foolish or wicked fanatics carnalize the Spiritualisms of Scripture: sensation mongers tell of swords and chariots in the clouds, and of legends written by invisible hands on the sand, and thousands listen with breathless interest to miserable impostures which at other times would only excite contempt.

All are eagerly enquiring "What is the will of Heaven?" and all are ready to hear, with an attention never awakened before, the message of the Divine Power.

In the meantime, the chosen head of the nation and the leaders of the army, with wise and devout patriotism, encourage the enquiring and bleeding population over whose interests they watch, to look upward for light and help; and the lungs of all the ministers of the Confederacy could not fill the ears that would listen, nor could all its presses supply reading matter to the eyes that would examine the answer from God.

The Church can stand upon its high places and command the solemn attention of a whole nation while it proclaims the Divine Will: and will it not with the truth in its hands go out among the eager and enquiring multitude and cry,

" O generation, see ye the word of the Lord."—(*Jer.* ii. 31.) If it does not, the fault will be its own : if a glorious harvest is not reaped from these convulsions, it will be because the professed followers of Christ were not willing in the day of His power.

PROOFS AND ILLUSTRATIONS.

This chapter and the two which precede it relate more to facts than doctrines. They contain suggestions as to the manner in which national trials promote the cause of the Church, it having been previously proven that such is, in part, their design; and from the nature of things these suggestions do not need illustrations from the Divine Word.

These suggestions are based on the general principles of the Divine Economy already discussed, and demonstrated by copious extracts from the Holy Scriptures; but the very methods above indicated as means by which wars and civil commotions and revolutions may be made to subserve the interests of the Redeemor's Kingdom, are repeatedly adverted to in the Sacred Oracles.

It is unnecessary to quote all the passages in point; but the reader is referred to *Is.* xxiv. xxv. xxvi. xxvii. Do. ii. Do. xxxii. 14 to 20. *Zech.* xiv. 6–5. *Luke* xxi. 25–28. *Jer.* xxx. xxxi. *Hosea* ii. and many kindred passages.

" Because, even because they have seduced my people, saying, Peace : and *there was* no peace ; and one built up a wall, and, lo, others daubed it with untempered *mortar* :

Say unto them which daub *it* with untempered *mortar*, that it shall fall : there shall be an overflowing shower ; and ye, O great hailstones, shall fall ; and a stormy wind shall rend *it*.

Lo, when the wall is fallen, shall it not be said unto you, Where is the daubing wherewith ye have daubed *it* ?

Therefore thus saith the Lord God ; I will even rend *it* with a stormy wind in my fury ; and there shall be an overflowing shower in mine anger, and great hailstones in *my* fury to consume *it*.

So will I break down the wall that ye have daubed with untempered *mortar*, and bring it down to the ground, so that the foundation thereof shall be discovered, and it shall fall, and ye shall be consumed in the midst thereof : and ye shall know that I *am* the Lord.

Thus will I accomplish my wrath upon the wall, and upon them that have daubed it with untempered *mortar*, and will say unto you, The wall *is no more*, neither they that daubed it."—(*Ezekiel* xiii. 10–15.)

" Behold, the Lord hath a mighty and strong one, *which as* a tem—

pest of hail *and* a destroying storm, as a flood of mighty waters over-flowing, shall cast down to the earth with the hand.

The crown of pride, the drunkards of Ephraim, shall be trodden under feet :

And the glorious beauty, which *is* on the head of the fat valley, shall be a fading flower, *and as* the hasty fruit before the summer : which *when* he that looketh upon it seeth, while it is yet in his hand he eateth it up.

In that day shall the Lord of hosts be for a crown of glory, and for a diadem of beauty, unto the residue of his people,

And for a spirit of judgment to him that sitteth in judgment, and for strength to them that turn the battle to the gate."—(*Is.* xxviii. 2-6.)

" Judgment also will I lay to the line, and righteousness to the plummet : and the hail shall sweep away the refuge of lies, and the waters shall overflow the hiding place."—(*Is* xxviii. 17.)

" Israel is an empty vine, he bringeth forth fruit to himself : according to the multitude of his fruit he hath increased the altars , according to the goodness of his land they have made goodly images." —(*Hosea* x. 1.)

" And Ephraim said, Yet I am become rich, I have found me out substance : in all my labours they shall find none iniquity in me that *were* sin.

And I *that am* the Lord thy God from the land of Egypt will yet make thee to dwell in tabernacles, as in the days of the solemn feast." —(*Hosea* xii. 8–9.)

" And I will bring you into the wilderness of the people, and there will I plead with you face to face.

Like as I pleaded with your fathers in the wilderness of the land of Egypt, so will I plead with you, saith the Lord God.

And I will cause you to pass under the rod, and I will bring you into the bond of the covenant."—(*Ezek.* xx. 35–37.)

" When the enemy shall come in like a flood, the Spirit of the Lord shall lift up a standard against him."—(*Is.* lix. 19.)

CHAPTER XI.

Bible Views of National Trials—continued. The comparative sins of Nations not always to be judged of by their comp rrative afflictions, at any given time.

The compensations and retributions of Providence to temporal beings are not to be judged of by isolated facts in their history. While sin is the cause of all affliction, the greatest apparent sufferer at any given time, is not thereby proved to be the greatest offender; and when we would estimate the character of a community or political organization by its calamities we ought to know the whole series of afflictive dispensations of which it has been the subject, and all the results of these Providential dealings, immediate and remote.

It is a plain inference of principles already stated that we have no right to decide on the comparitive iniquities of a people from the trials they are enduring at any particular period : this judgement must be reserved to those far future times which shall see the fruits produced by these trials, and, also, the dealings of God with the nation in question, and with all its cotemporaries, to the end.

It is for the ignorant, the proud, the self-righteous, the bigoted and obdurate, to assume to themselves superior virtues on account of their exemption, at the time, from the calamities that have overtaken others; but the instructed christian will understand that the feet of all unrepenting offenders will slide in due time.

When the Divine Master chastens a guilty party, it should be any thing else than a source of self-complacency to His other subjects who have broken His Law ; and the meting out of the reward of his deeds to one offending creature is an assurance to all the guilty of the certain retribution in store for them.

And on the other hand, it is wholly unbecoming in those who are justly brought into judgement to refuse to know they are offenders because there seems not to be a general inquisition; it is an impeachment of the righteousness and wisdom of God to suppose that because all who have violated His commands are not arraigned at the same time, the corrections of His hand are not the result of His displeasure.

To the Supreme Arbiter must be left the judgement of each, and the manner ; vengeance is His, and He is not to be directed in His dealings by the views of His subjects.

It is both foolish and dangerous in us to refuse to believe it is

God who is dealing with us, because our cotemporaries are not put
on trial with us; it is sufficient for us to be assured that when troubles come upon us they are Divinely sent, and our great concern is
not to enquire why others are not chastized or what will befall them,
but to learn the uses of our own trials, and seek deliverance from
them, in God's own appointed way

It must, also, be borne in mind that God's view of His creatures
is absolute not comparative; and that before Him the guilt of each
is a fixed and certain quantity, ascertained according to the position,
acts, and advantages of each with reference to one infallible standard.

When the Almighty arraigns His erring creatures at the Bar of
His Justice, this is not to interplead with each other; they do not
stand before Him as accusers of others, but to answer, each one, for
his own offence.

There is one Law-Giver and one Judge who does not seek or need
the counsel of any of His creatures; and when He calls for repentance it is an insult, a horrible aggravation of guilt to point His
wrath to the sins of others

PROOFS AND ILLUSTRATIONS

For proofs of the important points stated in this chapter the reader
is referred to the texts of Scripture already quoted, and to the many
other passages of like import to which they lead him.

The doctrines are fully sustained by previous discussions and references, and only a few more quotations from the inspired Word
will be added here.

"There were present at that season some that told Him of the
Galileans, whose blood Pilate had mingled with their sacrifices.

And Jesus answering said unto them, Suppose ye that these Galileans were sinners above all the Galileans, because they suffered
such things?

I tell you, Nay: but, except ye repent, ye shall all likewise perish.

Or those eighteen, upon whom the tower in Siloam fell, and slew
them, think ye that they were sinners above all men that dwelt in
Jerusalem?

I tell you, Nay: but except ye repent, ye shall all likewise perish."—*Luke*, xiii, 1–5

"Therefore judge nothing before the time, until the Lord come,
who both will bring to light the hidden things of darkness, and will
make manifest the counsels of the hearts: and then shall every man
have praise of God."—*I. Cor. iv, 5.*

"Why dost thou strive against him? for he giveth not account of any of his matters."—*Job*, xxxiii, 13.

"Moreover the Lord answered Job, and said,

Shall he that contendeth with the Almighty instruct *him?* he that reproveth God, let him answer it.

Then Job answered the Lord, and said,

Behold I am vile; what shall I answer thee? I will lay mine hand upon my mouth.

Once have I spoken; but I will not answer: yea, twice; but I proceed no further."—*Job* xl, 1–5.

"Woe unto him that striveth with his Maker! Let the potsherd *strive* with the potherds of the earth. Shall the clay say to him that fashioneth it, What makest thou? or thy work, He hath no hands!" *Isaiah*, xlv, 9.

"Who hath directed the spirit of the Lord, or *being* his counsellor hath taught him?

With whom took he counsel, and *who* instructed him, and taught him in the path of judgement, and taught him knowledge, and shewed to him the way of understanding?"—*Isaiah*, xi, 13, 14.

"So then every one of us shall give account of himself to God." —*Romans*, xiv, 12.

"Peter seeing him saith to Jesus, Lord, and what *shall* this man do?

Jesus saith unto him, If I will that he tarry till I come, what *is* that to thee? follow thou me."—*John*, xxi, 21, 22.

CHAPTER XII.

Bible Views of National Trials—continued. When Prayers for Peace will prevail.

There are few persons who do not pray.

When any one desires or asks for the intervention of Deity, in any matter or cause, he prays ; and with what a variety of motives is the Divine Power daily and hourly invoked !

It will thus be seen that it is absurd to expect success in our enterprizes merely because we pray for it ; and in fact God could not respond favorably to half the petitions sent up to Him without an hourly change of all His attributes into opposite and contradictory characteristics.

Does not the profane swearer constantly call upon the Deity to damn some person or thing that is offensive to him? and will a holy and jealous Being answer such invocations merely because they are fervently uttered and frequently repeated ?

This strong but just illustration presents in a broad light the folly of expecting Divine assistance in our purposes merely because it is asked for ; and other instances equally striking and to the point could be adduced.

Every nation that goes to war commits its cause to the favor of its God ; and when two christian powers, acknowledging the same Diety, are engaged in controversy, each asks for success over the other from the same Holy Being.

Can He respond favorably to the appeals of both ?

The idea that God will be propitiated by prayer, whatever its nature, implies that He is always pleased and honored by it, whatever the motives of the petitioner ; and there can be no conclusion more unscriptural and erroneous.

Many prayers, are from the motives and feelings of the petitioner the very highest insults to the Holy Majesty of Heaven ; for they ask the aid of God in the accomplishment of objects or upon means that are wholly opposed to His righteous attributes.

Other invocations are offensive from the spirit with which they are made; for it is a melancholy fact that the prayers of nominal christians are nothing less than *instructions* to the Divine Power.

Petitions to Deity may, also, be offensive, for the reasons on which they are based, in the hearts of those who offer them : for, what-

•ver may be uttered by the lips, there is frequently an expectation of success from the merit of the petitioner or his cause.

Indeed, it is not uncommon to hear, in christian lands, such expressions as these: " God *will* help, God is *obliged* to intervene for us, for it is *His* cause, it is the cause of right and truth."

This is not the language of true christianity : for we have no right to claim the aid of the Deity in anything, but what He has promised to favor, and in the way he has appointed. He is pleased to have us plead His promises, and He encourages and commands us to do it ; but He has not bound Himself to grant us success in any worldly pursuit whatever, except in labors for our food and clothing.

His covenants are for spiritual ends; and in pursuing these He may find it best to defeat earthly purposes which we regard as of the greatest importance, and strictly just and honorable. ·

He is the best and the only true Judge of the propriety or utility of any enterprise ; and hence, an essential part of the prayer of faith is the perfect submission of the will of the petitioner to that of God.

As the kingdom, the power and the glory are His, the prevailing reason or argument for every petition must be the honor of Jehovah —and is not He the best Judge of the means which will promote that end ?

But that common errors on this subject of prayers for peace in times of national trials may be better understood, let an illustration be borrowed from the political world.

In the Confederate States of America there are many honest-minded people who think that the present exhausting struggle would soon be terminated in an honorable way, if their government would sheathe the sword and invite to negotiations.

These worthy people overlook the fact that the existing Government of the United States has declared the sword to be the sole arbiter of the conest ; and that it is upon this very point of policy that it puts itself on the country, and opposes all parties that take a different view.

There *are* parties in the United States which believe that the honor and interests of their country will be best promoted by negotiations with the people against whom they are arrayed in arms ; but the faction which now beholds the purse and wields the sword of that nation has solemnly staked everything on the issue of arms, declaring that the only voice which it will hear from those on whom it is waging cruel and bloody war, shall be that of unconditional submission to the mercy of the conquerors.   •

Of what avail, then, let it be kindly asked, are peace meetings in the Confederate States ?

With whom could commissioners open negotiations? What could they offer that would be accepted?

The authors of the war have repeatedly and plainly published the method in which they are to be influenced to grant an honorable peace to the assailed—and that is to be defeated in all their persistent efforts to subjugate the country.

Those who attend the peace meetings are mostly loyal citizens, actuated by praiseworthy motives; their end is the desire of all, but they ask for it in a way that seems likely only to prolong the contest, until there is a change of rulers and of policy in the United States.

Now, while it is blasphemy to compare God with any creature, we may illustrate the position of mortals towards Him by facts in human affairs; and in the meetings held in the Confederate States to terminate the troubles of the country, we behold the character of many well-intended but unavailing prayers for the same desirable result.

God has called for war to accomplish special ends, and we ask Him to give us peace without reference to His designs: He has furnished the sword and given it to the slaughter, and some of those concerned seem to think the surest way to have it returned to the scabbard is to appeal to the Almighty to forego the purposes which the honor of His Majesty requires Him to accomplish! Let us not be deceived: a mere prayer for peace, predicated only on the trials or merits of the sufferer, is such an appeal.

Whoever or whatever is the instrument of a people's troubles, God is the Author; and He sends wars to admonish and reform the nations, or to destroy them.

The people of the Confederate States have suffered many cruel wrongs at the hand of a remorseless human foe; but all their trials are sent of God for sin, and they are merciful admonitions to repentance and reformation.

God has purposes in permitting these calamities: are those purposes fulfilled? Was His object merely to inflict a certain amount of suffering without any reference to moral results? Any such supposition is dishonoring to the Divine Economy, and not to be tolerated for a moment.

Are His ends accomplished? are we ready to concede them?

He commands us to pray to Him in time of trouble; but we must ask for deliverance not for *our* sakes but for *His*, and this we can not honestly do without wishing to be made willing to perform His righteous will.

When His honor is vindicated, He will deliver—and His name is glorified when those whom He afflicts are ready to acknowledge His justice and their own sins, and to be turned in the way that He directs.

He tells us to make peace with Him, and we shall have peace; and He has plainly indicated the terms on which His controversy with any people shall have an end.

When He makes war, He publishes the conditions on which it shall end; He has sent all His prophets, as ambassadors to the nations, and in His Word is a widely disseminated proclamation that all can understand.

, He either has control of the American Crisis, or He has not—if He has not, why pray to Him for peace? If He has, why not honor His power and His justice in a way to secure His favor?

The prayer to Him for peace is an admission that He can end the conflict—and this admission makes Him responsible for all the calamities of the strife.

There is no escape from these conclusions; and then let it be asked, have these trials been undeserved by those who have suffered them? If they have not been merited, the sufferers have no assurance that their petitions will be heeded by a Being who afflicts without reason; if they have been deserved, then it is folly to expect their discontinuance without a removal of the cause. Who can stumble over propositions so obvious?

Let us not mock God: if He cannot stay the fiery deluge that sweeps over the land, our cries to Him are a waste of breath—if He can, He will do it only on His own conditions.

When any of the inhabitants of the Confederate States go, in their simplicity, to the earthly sovereign of the earthly instruments of their sufferings, he tells them they can have peace on absolute submission to him; if we approach the Almighty Disposer as the real Author of the convulsion, do we expect Him to be less exacting, less tenacious of His purposes than a proud, mortal tyrant? The devoted people of the Confederacy can soon terminate all their trials by unconditional submission to God or to the President of the United States: to whom will they yield? One offers the peace of death, deliverance from his wrath with the loss of honor, liberty, rights and property: the other proposes independence of the United States and of the world, on condition that the country is first willing to be freed from the bondage of destructive sins.

The Divine Sovereign has sent war as a medicine to prevent ultimate dishonor and subjugation; and to ask to be delivered from

His chastenings, with the cause remaining, is like the conduct of a sick child whose chief desire is to be relieved from the distasteful remedies with which its loving parent would save its life.

God beholds in those whom He chastens something more to be dreaded than the strokes of His rod ; and if He has taken a people in hand to heal their moral sores, it is both vain and sinful to ask Him to desist until His end is accomplished.

The time and suffering necessary to this will depend on the patients themselves ; there is an appointed way by which they may be instantly saved, and it is made plain to the dimmest vision.

God is immutable, and prayers will not change His purposes— and yet He calls on all to invoke His mercy and aid with the solemn and emphatic assurance that they shall not be disappointed. How can these two things be reconciled together ?

If a person is in a boat on the water, and holds in his hands one end of a cable, with the other fastened to the shore, he can bring himself to land : he cannot pull the earth from its place, but his efforts at the cable will drive his boat to the beach.

And thus it is with the prayers of those who rightly honor God : their faith takes hold of the immovable throne of Jehovah, and they are brought within the pale of His covenanted mercies.

There is a fixed channel for His grace, always sure ; and erring mortals, who would be saved from His justice, have only to throw themselves in this.

But what, it may be asked, is an afflicted nation to do to entitle itself to the favor and protection of God ?   How will it find the channel of His mercies ?

This whole work is intended as an answer to this question ; but in the meantime, the sum of the matter may be briefly stated here.

The people must pray for peace ; but they must, in their hearts, and with their voices, glorify God by acknowledging his power, goodness and justice.

To do this is to recognize the Almighty as the Author of their sufferings, to confess the righteousness of His proceedings, because the sufferers have sinned against Him ; and to be ready to see wherein it is that they have offended, and to amend their ways.

This is the prayer that will prevail : and when the Deity is thus invoked by a suffering people, then, and not till then, will their light break forth as the morning.

The length and number of prayers amount to nothing : it is not for their repetitions that the people are heard, but for their submission, humility, contrition and faith.

PROOFS AND ILLUSTRATIONS.

The reader is referred to the prayers of Daniel, Ezra and Nehemiah, quoted in other parts of this work, and to the remarks made upon them.

Other inspired petitions are recorded in the Sacred Oracles for the instruction of after times, and to some of these attention is now directed. In *Is.* lxiv. is a prayer of the Church in which occurs the sentence. (v. 5,) " Behold, Thou art wroth, for we have sinned "— and again (vs. 6 and 7,) it is said, " But we are all as an unclean *thing*, and all our righteousnesses *are* as filthy rags ; and we all do fade as a leaf ; and our iniquities, like the wind, have taken us away. And *there is* none that calleth upon thy name, that stirreth up himself to take hold of Thee, for Thou hast hid thy face from us, and hast consumed us because of our iniquities."

It cannot be doubted from other testimonies of the prophets that the people did pray in a certain sense, in the times of their calamity, and freely use the name of God ; but these were not accepted petitioners, because they had not stirred themselves up to take hold of Jehovah's mercies in the appointed way.

The Almighty precisely describes the true state of things Himself in *Jeremiah* viii. 6, " I hearkened and heard, *but* they spake not aright : no man repented him of his wickedness, saying, What have I done ?"

Moses informed the Jews that every fate which awaited them would come from God as the reward of their conduct ; and he directs them how to pray successfully for deliverance in time of trouble. " If they shall confess their iniquity, and the iniquity of their fathers, with their trespass which they have trespassed against Me, and that, also, they have walked contrary unto Me : and that I, also, have walked contrary unto them, and have brought them into the land of their enemies."—(*Lev.* xxvi. 40–41.)

Here God Himself expressly defines the kind of prayer from an afflicted people which He will graciously answer :

FIRST, It must confess that the sin of the sufferer has caused his trials—

SECONDLY, That God was the Author of the afflictions—

THIRDLY, That He had caused them in justice.

Again in *Deut.* iv. 29–31, Moses informs his people how to call upon God in time of trouble.

"But if from thence thou shalt seek the Lord thy God, thou shalt find *him*, if thou seek him with all thy heart, and with all thy soul.

When thou art in tribulation, and all these things are come upon thee, *even* in the latter days, if thou turn to the Lord thy God, and shall be obedient unto his voice;

(For the Lord thy God *is* a merciful God ;) he will not forsake thee, neither destroy thee, nor forget the covenant of thy fathers which he sware unto them."

In the prayer of Solomon, at the dedication of the Temple, the l-raelites and all others are taught the same doctrine in the follow-ing words:

" When thy people Israel be smitten down before the enemy, be-cause they have sinned against thee, and shall turn again to thee, and confess thy name, and pray, and make supplication unto thee in this house: .

Then hear thou in heaven, and forgive the sin of thy people Is-rael, and bring them again unto the land which thou gavest unto their fathers."—(1 *Kings* viii. 33–34.)

In Job xxxiii. 27–30, it is said, " He looketh upon men, and *if any* say, I have sinned, and perverted *that which was* right, and it profited me not :

He will deliver his soul from going into the pit, and his life shall see the light.

Lo, all these *things* worketh God oftentimes with man,

To bring back his soul from the pit, to be enlightened with the light of the living."

We are, also, taught in Proverbs xxviii. 13, that " He that cov-ereth his sins shall not prosper : but whoso confesseth and forsaketh *them* shall have mercy."

In Jeremiah xxxi. 9, God says of His people when He is ready to pour blessings upon them, "They shall come with weeping, and with supplications will I lead them."

Hear, also, other inspired teachings : " For thou desirest not sac-rifice; else would I give *it :* thou delightest not in burnt offering.

The sacrifices of God *are* a broken spirit: a broken and a contrite heart, O God, thou wilt not despise."—(*Ps.* li. 16–17.)

" Thus saith the Lord, The heaven *is* my throne, and the earth *is* my footstool : where *is* the house that ye build unto me ? and where *is* the place of my rest ?

For all those *things* hath mine hand made, and all those *things* have been, saith the Lord : but to this *man* will I look, *even* to *him that is* poor and of a contrite spirit, and trembleth at my word."— *Is.* lxvi. 1–2.)

" For my name's sake will I defer mine anger, and for my praise will I refrain for thee, that I cut thee not off."—(*Is.* xlviii. 9.)

" Therefore also now, saith the Lord, turn ye *even* to me with all your heart and with fasting, and with weeping, and with mourning :

And rend your heart, and not your garments, and turn unto the Lord your God : for he *is* gracious and merciful, slow to anger, and of great kindness, and repenteth him of the evil."—(*Joel* ii. 12–13.)

" Wherewith shall I come before the Lord, *and* bow myself before the high God ? shall I come before him with burnt offerings, with calves of a year old ?

Will the Lord be pleased with thousands of rams, *or* with ten thousands of rivers of oil ? shall I give my firstborn *for* my transgression, the fruit of my body *for* the sin of my soul ?

He hath shewed thee, O man, what *is* good ; and what doth the Lord require of thee, but to do justly, and to love mercy, and to walk humbly with thy God ?

The Lord's voice crieth unto the city, and *the man of* wisdom shall see thy name : hear ye the rod, and who hath appointed it."—(*Micah* vi. 6–9,)

" And he spake this parable unto certain which trusted in themselves that they were righteous, and despised others :

Two men went up into the temple to pray ; the one a Pharisee, and the other a publican.

The Pharisee stood and prayed thus with himself, God, I thank thee, that I am not as other men *are*, extortioners, unjust, adulterers, or even as this publican.

I fast twice in the week, I give tithes of all that I possess.

And the publican, standing afar off, would not lift up so much as his eyes unto heaven, but smote upon his breast, saying, God be merciful to me a sinner.

I tell you, this man went down to his house justified *rather* than the other : for every one that exalteth himself shall be abased ; and he that humbleth himself shall be exalted."—(*Luke* xviii. 9–14.)

" I will therefore that men pray everywhere, lifting up holy hands, without wrath and doubting."—(1 *Tim.* ii. 8.)

" Let us draw near with a true heart in full assurance of faith, having our hearts sprinkled from an evil conscience, and our bodies washed with pure water."—(*Heb.* x. 22.)

" If we say that we have no sin, we deceive ourselves, and the truth is not in us.

If we confess our sins, he is faithful and just to forgive us *our* sins, and to cleanse us from all unrighteousness.

If we say that we have not sinned, we make him a liar, and his word is not in us."—(1 *John* i. 8–10.)

" To what purpose is the multitude of your' sacrifices unto me?
saith the Lord : I am full of the burnt offerings of rams, and the
fat of fed beasts ; and I delight not in the blood of bullocks, or of
lambs, or of he goats.

When you come to appear before me, who hath required this at
your hand, to tread my courts?

Wash ye, make you clean ; put away the evil of your doings from
before mine eyes ; cease to do evil ;

Learn to do well ; seek judgment, relieve the oppressed, judge
the fatherless, plead for the widow.

Come now, and let us reason together, saith the Lord : though
your sins be as scarlet, they shall be as white as snow ; though they
be red like crimson, they shall be as wool."—(*Is.* i 11, 12, 16–18.)

" Thus saith the Lord of hosts, the God of Israel ; Put your burnt
offerings unto your sacrifices, and eat flesh.

For I spake not unto your fathers, nor commanded them in the
day that I brought them out of the land of Egypt, concerning burnt
offerings or sacrifices :

But this thing commanded I them, saying, Obey my voice, and I
will be your God, and ye shall be my people : and walk ye in all
the ways that I have commanded you, that it may be well unto
you."—(*Jer.* vii 21–23.)

" He that turneth away his ear from hearing the law, even his
prayer *shall be* abomination."—(*Prov.* xxviii. 9.)

" Though ye offer me burnt offerings and your meat offerings, I
will not accept *them ;* neither will I regard the peace offerings of
your fat beasts

Take thou away from me the noise of thy songs ; for I will not
hear the melody of thy viols.

But let judgment run down as waters, and righteousness as a
mighty stream."—(*Amos* v. 22–24.)

" But go ye and learn what *that* meaneth, I will have mercy, and
not sacrifice : for I am not come to call the righteous, but sinners
to repentance."—(*Mat.* ix. 13.)

" And Samuel said, Hath the Lord *as great* delight in burnt offerings and sacrifices, as in obeying the voice of the Lord ? Behold,
to obey *is* better than sacrifice, *and* to hearken than the fat of rams."
—(1 *Sam.* xv. 22.)

" I will not reprove thee for thy sacrifices or thy burnt offerings,
to have been continually before me.

I will take no bullock out of thy house, *nor* he goats out of thy
folds :

For every beast of the forest is mine, and the cattle upon a thou sand hills.

I know all the fowls of the mountains : and the wild beasts of the field are mine. .

If I were hungry, I would not tell thee : for the world is mine, and the fulness thereof.

Will I eat the flesh of bulls, or drink the blood of goats ?

Offer unto God thanksgiving : and pay thy vows unto the Most High :

And call upon me in the day of trouble : I will deliver thee, and thou shalt glorify me."—(Ps. L. 8–15.)

" If I regard iniquity in my heart, the Lord will not hear me."—(Ps. lxvi. 18.)

" Hast thou utterly rejected Judah ? hath thy soul loathed Zion ? why hast thou smitten us, and there is no healing for us ? we looked for peace, and there is no good ; and for the time of healing, and behold trouble !

We acknowledge, O Lord, our wickedness, and the iniquity of our fathers : for we have sinned against thee.

Do not abhor us, for thy name's sake ; do not disgrace the throne of thy glory : remember, break not thy covenant with us."—(Jer. xiv. 19–21.) .

" Behold, the Lord's hand is not shortened, that it cannot save ; neither his ear heavy, that it cannot hear :

But your iniquities have separated between you and your God, and your sins have hid his face from you, that he will not hear."—(Is. lix. 1–2.)

" Who is he that saith, and it cometh to pass, when the Lord commandeth it not ?

Out of the mouth of the Most High proceedeth not evil and good ?

Wherefore doth a living man complain, a man for the punishment of his sins ?

Let us search and try our ways, and turn again to the Lord.

Let us lift up our heart with our hands unto God in the heavens."—(Lam. iii. 37–41.)

" When he giveth quietness, who then can make trouble ? and when he hideth his face, who then can behold him ? whether it be done against a nation, or against a man only :

Surely it is meet to be said unto God, I have borne chastisement, I will not offend any more :

That which I see not teach thou me : if I have done iniquity, I will do no more."—(Job xxxiv. 29, 31–32.) .

14

SCRIPTURAL VIEWS

OF

NATIONAL TRIALS

PART II.

APPLICATION OF THE FOREGOING DOCTRINES TO THE PRESENT
CONDITION OF THE PEOPLE OF THE CONFEDERATE
STATES OF AMERICA.

CHAPTER I.

*General Summary of Doctrines of Scripture in regard to National
Trials already stated and proved.*

It has been seen,

FIRST. That, according to the Scriptures, God is almighty, ruling
every where by His own direct power, and that nothing can occur without His express permission.

SECONDLY. That this Omnipotent Being is perfectly holy, wise,
good and just: and that, therefore, the cause for every affliction
of His creatures is to be found in their violation of His righteous laws.

THIRDLY. That nations, as such, are rewarded in time for their unrepented sins; and that when they are afflicted, in any way, by
any agency, under any circumstances, the instrumentality of
their sufferings is the rod or sword of the Almighty.

FOURTHLY. That a people may be right in its issue with a national enemy, and still the latter may be used as a means for its
correction; and that whenever wars bring affliction, whatever their political origin or character, they are the chastisements of God for sin.

FIFTHLY. That when a nation suffers God may be with it in the sense of dealing mercifully for the correction of errors that may otherwise prove its ruin; but that He is not with the suffering party in the sense of trying to deliver it from the rod with which it is corrected, but does in fact Himself hold this rod.

SIXTHLY. That a people comparatively good may be smitten by the instrumentality of a more wicked nation; and that a righteous God may thus use a power of the latter kind to effect His just, wise and good ends while *its* motives are unjust and cruel, and while these motives are ripening it for future vengeance.

SEVENTHLY. That whatever the comparative merits of a nation—whatever its position, motives and attitude towards the other powers of the world, its afflictions, *in all cases*, are Divinely sent, and are a solemn admonition from God Himself of the necessity of repentance toward Him; and while it is called on to use the appliances of carnal wisdom for its defence, and is, under the Economy of God, justified and required to use such human means, and to repel arms with arms, its final success and deliverance must depend on its reconciliation to the favor of Him who smites it.

EIGHTHLY. That when a nation is assailed by another temporal power it has two issues to settle—one with its earthly enemy, and one with offended Deity; and that as all its calamities are Divinely permitted, no amount of unjust, wicked or cruel wrongs at the hands of its earthly foe will ever render it more dear to God. In all cases the issue with Heaven must be settled on the terms which the Supreme Arbiter has fixed for the deliverance of those whom He chastens; and the offence of the sufferers towards Him being a fixed and constant quantity is not mitigated or atoned for by their afflictions unless these are a means of effecting a change of disposition and action towards the Divine Author of the calamities.

These considerations do not effect the motives and conduct of those human agents whom God uses as the instruments of His corrections; these will be judged according to real character, and will in due time meet with a righteous retribution.

CHAPTER II.

General Obligations.

The conditions, efforts and prospects of the Confederate States, as viewed from a worldly stand-point, were briefly but truly presented in the first ten Chapters of the first Part of this work.

The country is engaged in a fierce and cruel war : it stands on the defensive, asking only to be let alone, and its assailants openly avow their intention to exterminate its inhabitants or reduce them to slavery.

The war has swelled to unexampled proportions, and is accompanied with atrocities without a parallel in political contests; and the assailing power, great in numbers, in wealth, and in mechanical appliances, has gathered all its resources for a life-and-death grapple, and staked its own existence on the issue of the struggle.

It has put forth the most tremendous energies, has resorted to every means of injury, and has manifested an inextinguishable hatred; and all these efforts and demonstrations have been met with corresponding union and energy in the defending party, and with a courage and determination that are plainly invincible by human power.

Patriotism, political wisdom, military strategy and ardor, loyalty and love of country, universal devotion of body and mind, of means and comfort to one end, have shone illustrious in the conduct of those who are fighting only for permission to govern themselves in their own way.

Still the horrors of a ruthless war rage through all the borders of the assailed nation; death is still offered as the result of opposition to the will of the assailants, and peace on terms worse than death. Is not the struggle an anamoly in the history of the world? The assailants are destroying their own liberties and wasting their own resources in a war to destroy those who wish to live in peace and on terms of equality with them; the defenders, by their cause, their union, their enthusiasm, their intrepidity, ought, on mere principles of human reason, to have gained their independence.

Any one, before this struggle, would have believed that such means, such endurance, such courage and devotion, would have secured to any people, so numerous, so widely scattered, and so abounding in resources, exemption from further attempts at their subjugation; but in this case every victory of the assailed is followed by a more phrenzied zeal on the part of their adversaries, every shock of arms but complicates the difficulties of a settlement, and as the storm-cloud pours out its dreadful treasures of wind and hail and lightning, it seems only to grow darker and denser with ever increasing stores of fury.

If there were but this one point of survey of these awful phenomena, the heart of the patriot and philanthropist would sicken within him, and darkly gathering himself for a last effort, he would go forth with sullen heroism unconquered but hopeless to meet the invited stroke of mysterious Fate.

But the doctrines of the succeeding Chapters carry the friend of his bleeding country to an elevation which commands a more complete and accurate view of this fearful strife; and from this unclouded height he is able to see that this wild commotion has not arisen by chance, that the storm has been launched by an unerring and almighty Hand on a certain and righteous mission, and that when it has just and fully accomplished its black and billowy masses shall vanish like the thin mists of the morning before the rising sun.

It is an infinite satisfaction to every right-thinking mind to know that afflictions have an adequate cause in the conduct of the sufferer; and that the success achieved through great sufferings is not the only reason and compensation for these trials. This revolution through which North-America is passing, entails calamities for which the future, whatever its character, cannot atone; and were the results of these troubles their only solution the sense of justice would receive a painful shock from which it could never recover.

Coming glories do not, in a proper legal view, account for past indignities which were never heeded; and the future state of the world does not furnish a satisfactory solution for the wars which its inhabitants have already endured.

If there has been a single heart-ache, in a rational creature, which had no cause in the person concerned, and which, to him, was never rewarded, it is an awful mystery; and never can any intelligent being be happy till this act of apparent injustice is fully and properly accounted for.

Nothing will satisfy the claims of inexorable justice but a cause in the sufferer himself for his trials, or a full compensation to him for his afflictions; and whatever the final results of such tragedies as those now being enacted on this continent, they would fill the whole scene with perpetual dismay and doubt if they had no solution in the conduct and character of those most immediately concerned.

For this reason, if for no other, the Scriptural views presented in this work are absolutely essential to the relief of all right-minded spectators of such scenes as those which now fill nearly half the world with morning; but these Divinely revealed solutions of the mystery of time afford another and still greater consideration to patriots and philanthropists situated. like those in the Confederate States of America.

They bring to light the glorious facts that there is not only a cause in the devoted nation for its trials, but, also, a plain, safe, and most honorable mode of deliverance : and that the Almighty Power which wields the rod of chastening says with every stroke, "I have no pleasure in the death of the wicked......turn ye, turn ye from your evil ways, for why will ye die ?"—*Ezekiel*, xxxiii, 11.

What more can be asked ? what more can be expected or wished ?

Could the Saviour of his country and the friend of justice and truth desire more than is revealed concerning the origin of his people's afflictions, and the manner and time of escape from all their dangers and sufferings ?

This is the sum of the whole matter : the nation is smitten by a righteous God for its offences towards Him, and is solemnly admonished to repent : if it humbles itself under the mighty Hand which strikes and turns from all its errors, it will be saved. The Justice that is offended can be appeased :.the Power which has raised and which directs this fearful storm, is ever ready to say to the elements, "Peace, be still !"

The method of deliverance is easy, practicable and honorable and it has been indicated in the statement and discussion of the principles which account for these national trials.

The people concerned have but to make a faithful application to themselves of the Truths of Scripture before referred to ; and that they may be the better enabled to do so,the writer proposes to make suggestions as to the duties of the different classes of Society.

From henceforth he will speak to his countrymen in the first person—and his constant prayer is that they may receive what he says in the spirit in which it is uttered.

It is of no consequence to us to enquire why others, more guilty in our estimation, are not also brought to the bar of Judgement : "The secret *things belong* unto the Lord our God ; but those *things which are* revealed *belong* unto us, and to our children forever, that we may do all the words of this law."— *Deut.* xxix, 29.

It is not for us to snatch from the Almighty's Hand

"The Sceptre and the rod,
Be judge His justice, be the God of God."

We are called to a settlement of our own accounts with Heaven; the obligations of others are the concern of creditor and debtor.

We are smitten for own transgressions; and the message to us is "Therefore amend your ways and your doings; and obey the voice of the Lord your God."—*Jer.* xxvi, 13.

If we do not harden our hearts, and stiffen our necks for destruction, we will, first of all, acknowledge that our afflictions are ordered by an almighty and holy God, for our own sins; and while the wrongs and threats of our human adversaries will only brace the sinews of our souls to a more heroic encounter with them, we will humble our hearts before Heaven, confess the justice of its dealings and submissively seek its guidance to discover our offences, and its help to forsake them.

That we may all engage the more earnestly and wisely in the work to which the lessons of the times would lead us, suggestions will now be offered as to the obligations of each class and of every individual member of Society; and to the consideration of these the succeeding chapters of this part of the work will be devoted.

The duties of the Church, as a body, will first be discussed, and next the responsibilities of each individual christian—and finally we will briefly consider what God now requires of all the members of the community whether they be professing christians or not.

The writer, as already intimated, will speak in the first person; and he will offer no other excuse than the importance of his subject for the plain manner in which he will address the people of an afflicted land. This land is the place of his birth, and it holds the ashes of his ancestors; it is dearer to him than any other abode of man under Heaven, and it is the constant desire of his soul to see it enjoying that independence, peace, and prosperity which will flow alone from the favor of Him to whom the shields of the earth belong.

CHAPTER III.

Special obligations : Duties of the Church.

The first duty of the Church in this great crisis is to impress on the public mind the fact that God reigns. In Mahommedan countries there are stationed in the minarets of all the mosques or houses of worship public criers called muezzin, whose duty it is to announce the hours for religious devotions; and at stated intervals, day and night, from year to year their deep, solemn voices are heard high and clear above the confused din of the streets below, proclaiming " God is great, God is great—come to prayer !"

There is something in this custom peculiarly suggestive; and in this as in many other things the Eternal Mind has inspired the votaries of false systems to adopt habits which testify against their own delusions, and which rebuke the corruptions, perversions and practical infidelity of the professing christian world.

The Church of God ought to be, in a spiritual sense, elevated, like these muezzins, above the cares and pursuits of the carnal world : it ought to stand perpetually on the unclouded heights of revealed Truth, and to cause the toiling millions in the dust and smoke below to hear continually the Counsel of God in all that concerns their temporal and eternal interests.

From its position, its vision can sweep the whole, horizon, while the eyes of the busy actors in the streets, and shops and fields below, can range over but a narrow scope ; and it is able, also, to survey the whole contour and every side of events that rise up like mountains before the dwellers on the earth, exposing but a section to the view of each, and causing among those who behold different and opposite fractions of their surface, diverse and hostile opinions as to their character, origin and connections. When the Church descends from these summits of perpetual day to the level of the world below, it loses itself in the errors of the nations; and the people, like travellers in the gorges of unexplored mountain ranges, wind along paths that lead them round to their starting point, and follow openings that turn in all directions, and end in impassable barriers.

The watch-tower of the christian is lifted high above every elevation of the earth, above all the mists and clouds that roll their obscuring and many-colored masses through its dense air ; and beholding all the shifting phases and eventualties of life through the cer-

15

tain and clear light of unchanging truth, he is enabled to instruct and warn his fellow-men in all the affairs of time, often to them full of painful mystery.

When the volcano pours its deluge of burning lava down the mountain' sides, or the storm bursts in fury over the plains, he knows the cavernous recesses where the fires were kindled, the nursery of clouds where the tornado was born : and more than this, he sees the direction of the scourge, he beholds the hand that hurls it, and he hears the voice that instructs it on its mission, and prescribes the bounds and conditions of its work of death.

And should he not stand in his proper place, and look and listen and cry to his people, and tell them what has befallen them, and whence it comes, and how the plague may be stayed ?

God not only reveals His secrets to His prophets, but He authorizes and commands the christians to make them known to his fellow men ; and what shall be thought of the watchman who has seen a plague commissioned against his land, and heard its charge, and who encourages his trusting and devoted countrymen to fear no evil ?

The storm of a fierce and bloody war of aggression has burst on the people of the Confederate States ; and the voice of the Church should be heard above all the fury of the elements proclaiming unceasingly that this is the work of God.

It is not sufficient at such a time merely to state, as a theory or abstract dogma, the Sovereignty of the Almighty Ruler : it is not enough to enter as saving clauses, in general prefaces, the doctrine of God's almightiness, and then devote the whole volume of its teachings to the exaltation of secondary causes. This grand fact is not to be brought on the stage, for the sake of orthodoxy, and then hid off in a corner : we cannot say that our picture is correct merely because we have given a place in it to every fact, when the most important one is so shaded off as barely to be seen, or is a mere ornamental margin to those which are its incidents.

We are not by our words, or actions or silence to have it merely inferred that the Deity is supreme, and therefore, has some vague, undefined and inscrutable connections with our calamities ; nor to console our suffering countrymen with the idea that a Good Being reigns, and that He will in the end overcome adverse circumstances whose origin is not to be understood.

But the Church should stand upon its watch and make the fact of God's certain and supreme Providence the central idea in all its teachings : should solve, resolve, and apply every event by this eternal truth, and should be the more laborious, incessant and earnest in this matter just as the people are the more inclined to give un·due prominence to secondary causes.

It should not be afraid of offending the pride or wounding the self-esteem of man : and when the righteousness of the creature and the most jealous attribute of the Creator are in conflict, the messengers of Jehovah must be the more fearless and instant in maintaining the honor of their Divine Master.

They should teach that all wars are God's wars : that this revolution is His work, His special work, and that this wicked enemy whom we abhor, is His sword.

We should give its proper place to this doctrine by faithful ·and pointed and practical illustrations and applications: should hinge upon it all our other teachings, and trace it to all its consequences, however untasteful to our carnal natures. We should refer to it all the circumstances of our position ; and we should allow no idea or fact or passion to intervene between it and the popular mind, to hide it for an instant, or to dwarf its just proportions.

Let these general remarks be illustrated by a few practical suggestions.

First. The present war, in its magnitude, continuance and bitterness, was unexpected by our people :

It is not the less the certain act of Him whom the Psalmist thus addresses " The heavens are thine, the earth also is thine : as for the world and the fulness thereof thou hast founded them. The north and the south thou hast created them "—(—*Ps.* lxxxix. 11,12.)

God was not taken by surprise, if the people were ; and though all our expectations were disappointed, there has been no uncertainty or confusion in the Divine Counsels. Whatever course the war may take, it is still under the immediate control of the Almighty ; and this the Church ought to teach, being exceedingly careful to see to it that the popular mind does not practically, if not in profession, attribute to the Deity something of the agitation, uncertainty and astonishment with which it is affected by unexpected events

Secondly. Communities in passing from one national condition to another, are often called on to encounter trials—and this is the case with the people of the Confederate States.

Now, the public are not to be permitted to infer that the principles of the Divine Economy are so defective as to render such changes necessarily afflictive : the cause of these troubles is not in the Counsels of God, but in the imperfections of man.

It was not necessary for God to place a wilderness between Egypt and Canaan : but when individuals and nations are called to higher destinies, their way is laid through trials in order to prove their dispositions, to learn them their errors and weakness, to purge out of them follies inconsistent with the more elevated position which they would occupy, to expose the rottenness of their moral state, and to lead them to the source of health.

THIRDLY. When nations are afflicted through the instrumentality of unjust and cruel men, there is a right impression that the motives of the assailants are marked and condemned by Deity ; but the carnal mind, unwilling to look to self for the cause of trouble, does not stop at this just conclusion, but forms opinions dishonoring to the Majesty of God.

It is apt to imagine that if its cause, as between it and its human adversary, is just, the Divine Power is enlisted on its side and is warring for it; and thus while it is willing to attribute every favorable turn in its affairs to the intervention of Heaven, it receives reverses as mysterious contingencies not to be accounted for by human reason.

This tendency of a people situated like those of the Confederate States, should be opposed with vigilance and care; this is a vital point and here there is danger of a breach through which the arch enemy will come like a flood.

All men have a moral sense which is often rendered more active and perceptive by heavy afflictions ; but when a nation receives gross wrongs at the hands of a temporal power, timid and weak members of the Church are afraid that a faithful declaration of the whole counsel of God will offend the glowing patriotism of the times, and bring odium on the christian name. They are disposed in this matter to adopt a method of action which is always pernicious—and that is, to wink at moral delusions which seem to have a powerful hold on the popular heart, in order to enhance the influence of the Church.

No professed disciple of Christ, in a community so well instructed as the people of this Confederacy, will openly avow the pagan doctrine that God is fighting in the conflict of nations with the passions and infirmities of mortals; but there will be some bearing the christian name who by their conduct will encourage feelings which lead to such conclusions.

When an interpreter of the living oracles indulges in those loose expressions which convey the idea that God is fighting for us, he may mean that He is chastening us for our good, but he is not so understood ; on the contrary the prejudices of the carnal heart receive such language in its literal import, and are less inclined than ever to heed the solemn admonitions of Providence.

Again: an ungarded use of popular terms by the Church may confirm the worldly element of Society in the error that the interest of Deity in a national conflict is limited to those issues which absorb the minds of the mortals concerned; and that the Almighty Dispenser takes part in the conflict solely for the sake of the temporal cause which the parties interested regard as its origin and end.

The principles already discussed show that such views are wholly unscriptural; and every one with right apprehensions of the attributes of Jehovah knows that all the revolutions of time are but incidents in the plan of His designs.

FOURTHLY. A nation situated like that of the Confederate States is apt to magnify the importance of its human adversary as an element in its own destiny; and in doing so it curtails, in its opinions, the Sovereignty of God. The purposes of the Almighty are not dependent on the favor or the enmity of His creatures; and if He designs to constitute a community a great people the malice of other human powers will not be permitted to interpose any impediments to His will. Proper conceptions of the Divine Disposer lead to the inevitable conclusion that the friendship and hatred of rivals are under His control; and hence the disposition to dwell on human opposition as *the* great hindrance to our success is a practical denial of God's Omnipotence. Let us illustrate this important matter by a common custom. We hear, on every side, various circumstances alleged as indications that the Divine Power is favoring the Confederate States—and at the same time there are references to the national enemy of a kind to lead to the impression that his designs and acts were something beyond the range of the Providences of God. *Now the truth is that the attitude and conduct of national enemies towards us are themselves a part of God's dealings with us;* and to say that He is directing all His Providences in our behalf, while a vindictive enemy is exerting his whole power for our overthrow, in act, bent on our destruction, and heaping cruel wrongs upon us, is to teach that this mortal adversary is something above or beyond the control of the Almighty.

Here again is a position to be constantly watched and defended by the Church; and here it is that short-sighted christians give another advantage to the spiritual adversary. They permit their human passions to seduce them into the habit of turning the chief attention of their hearers to the motives of the creature enemy; and by doing so they practically deny God's paramount authority by fostering the delusion that our sufferings have their origin in human malice.

FINALLY. To prevent all disastrous errors, and to be true, at such a crisis, to the best interests of the country, and to its allegiance to its Divine Head, the Church is bound to teach, in public and private, constantly and plainly, that God permits this war, and that when He is against it He can and will bring it to an instant end It is to lose no opportunity of declaring that though the Universal Sovereign may be for us, Ho is, also, for the war which afflicts us; and that to tolerate any other belief is to abridge the Sovereignty of God, and in fact to have other gods before Him.

Every day we have violations of the first Commandment; and never was it more necessary for the Church to stand in the breach and defend the most jealous attribute of its Almighty Head.

The importance of this whole subject and the lamentably loose manner in which professing christians deal with it can be best stated by an illustration : and let the Church solemnly ponder the lessons which these facts convey.

We daily hear that God is fighting for us—but this assurance is never offered as a reason for hoping for the certain termination of our country's struggle at any early period.

Parallel with this fact we have witnessed, from the first, an intense desire for the armed intervention of certain great European Powers in our behalf—and this desire is based on the firm and universal conviction that the nations in question could immediately over-power our enemy and drive him from his purpose

These two facts lie side by side before us every day : and what do they teach ? Clearly, that the favor of temporal powers is more to be desired than that of Heaven : their unequivocal language is that England and France can do in a few weeks what it may require God years to accomplish ! It is dreadful to have to write such words— but it is more awful to know that such is the ignoble estimate of the strength of the Divine Power, and of the value of its aid, practically taught in a christian land

Brethren of the Church of God, have we not added to our other sins a violation of the first and chief Commandment ?

Have we not permitted the excitement of the times to carry us from the defense of the most sensitive and vital point of revealed truth, and thus to open the way for a deluge of disastrous errors ?

Now, and always, the words below ought to ring their deep and solemn import through our souls, and to rouse us to unceasing and jealous vigilance at the first and the chief battle ground of truth and falsehood

"Thou shalt have no other gods before me."

CHAPTER IV.

Special Obligations   Duties of the Church, continued.

The Church of God is a witness on earth for His truth, and must not be deterred by any possible state of things, from the faithful utterance of its testimony.   The first element of its doctrine is the absolute and rightful supremacy of its Divine Head over all create things : the next is the holy attributes of this Almighty Disposer.

The duty of inculcating the first truth in the most practical and impressive manner has just been discussed ; and the attention of the reader is now invited to some suggestions in regard to the obligations of the Church to teach the last named doctrine above referred to

If God be almighty and holy, all men are sinners : if any man be just and offend not in heart or deed, there is a radical and deplorable defect in Divine Economy.   The ·Deity cannot be perfect in power and justice and wisdom if any of His rational creatures suffer without an adequate cause in themselves ; and as all men are born to trouble, all are sinners, or God is not what He claims to be.— Now, all know that the natural human heart, though having an inward sense of sin, is not inclined to confess its depravity ; and hence, when unconverted men meet with calamities, unless for crimes denounced by the civil authority, or condemned by the customs of society, there is a disposition to reflect on the ways of Providence.

This is especially the case when reverses overtake communities or individuals comparatively good ; and when a whole nation suffers wrong at the hands of a more offending and cruel power, this tendency to rob God of His rightful dues grows into a formidable but insidious danger.

. If the nation professes faith in the righteousness of the Supreme Arbiter, it practically curtails His Sovereignty ; and when, as in the present case of the Confederate States of America, the people are in the right as far as the issue with their creature adversaries is concerned, they are not likely to impeach the justice of the Divine Power.

When a community is standing on the defensive, fighting for existence, and for the dearest temporal interests of humanity, they desire to believe that there is justice in Heaven : it is an infinite consolation to know, when cruel wrongs are heaped upon them, that

there is a God who hears the cries of the oppressed,and who will not
acquit the guilty.   Such is the encouraging faith of the inhabitants
of the Confederate States, upon whom a proud, ambitious and remorseless foe would heap every affliction that flesh is heir to.   This
belief in the rightcousness of the Divine Power is indeed a glorious
refuge to a nation conscious of the justice of its cause, and of the
cruel malice of its invaders ; and it is precisely under such circumstances that the Divine Nature is shorn, in the carnal mind, of it-
most jealous attribute.   Nations have suffered while attacked by inferior and more profligate races : the people of the Confederate States
have been involved in sad afflictions at the hands of a Power that
would impiously assume the prerogatives of God, and that too while
they ask only to be let alone.   Is it not natural that the exiles from
homes laid in smoking ruins by bands of merciless maranders, and
the widows and orphans of heroic men who have reddened with their
hearts' blood the threshold whose sanctity they defended, should lif
up their hopes to a Tribunal whose justice never errs nor slumbers?
Are not such a people most likely to believe that God sees and marks
their wrongs, and will rise up to their defence ?   . *

It is for such reasons that the inhabitants of the Confederate States
have such a fixed impression that God is with them ; and on this
very account they are in danger of practically dishonoring the Power
in which they so confidently trust.

They are apt to think that the Divine Power sees them only as
they stand in the issue with their human enemies ; and that as they
are in the right in this controversy, Heaven will contend upon their
side.

If we so believe can we really feel that God is the Supreme, un-
controlled, and uncontrollable Disposer of events?   Do we not in-
fact limit His Power, when we claim Him as our Leader and Champion while we suffer afflictions?   How and whence come these disasters?   Was it impossible for God to prevent them ?   Does His
plan of Government involve accidents, and reverses to the innocent ?
Does He kill men in time for their good in time ?   . *

Such considerations demonstrate the necessity of that duty of the
Church discussed in the preceding chapter : they call upon the christian, at such times, to lift up his voice perpetually in the solemn utterance of God's almightiness.   To be silent in such a crisis is to
countenance an awful error ; and to proclaim the truth in regard to
Jehovah's authority alone is to leave the people to impeach another
attribute of the Divine Power.   If a nation, situated like our devoted countrymen, are faithfully instructed in regard to the *Supremu-*

ry of the Deity, they are in danger of reflecting on His *Justice ;* for with their mind entirely fixed on the iniquitous designs of their human persecutors and absorbed with the vindication of their own conduct in this struggle, they are not likely to survey all the circumstances of their position in the eye of Heaven. They consider their conduct in the struggle in which they suffer wrong as defining their character—whereas this very contest and all its results are but consequences of their true relations with the Divine Ruler.

It is not to be supposed that the world will think of this : its vision is limited to existing realities, and its judgment of actors is based only and wholly on their conduct in passing scenes.

If a people placed in the attitude of those of the Confederate States are thoroughly and properly embued with just conceptions of God's opposeless Sovereignty, they will not in heart, at least, willingly concede His perfect righteousness : and therefore if the Church has been true to its mission in regard to the first great Truth of Revelation, it has laid a foundation on which it must build another Scripture doctrine, or be a party to the dishonoring of its almighty Head.

It may preach, incessantly, and with practical emphasis, the righteousness of God ; and this it cannot effectually do except by teaching that man is an offender.

Therefore, at this great crisis, it is the solemn obligation of the christian element of Society to proclaim in the ears of the whole nation that it has committed offences for which God is correcting it.

Look at the reasons. Calamities have overtaken the country : either the honor of man or the honor of God must suffer.

If the nation is not smitten for its sins, the Divine authority is imperfect in power or justice : if God is perfect, the people are chastised for their offences.

How then can God's own appointed witness withhold its testimony at such a time ?

In periods of peace and prosperity, the principles of the Divine Economy in regard to the nations are not so likely to make the desired impression on those concerned ; but when the whole country is profoundly agitated with severe trials, men are prepared to hear " the voice of the day of the Lord," and to receive and heed the lessons which it would solemnly teach. It is the very seed time for the Truth ; and the calamities of the times will be to the efforts of the faithful laborer in God's vineyard as the early and latter rain to the wise and diligent husbandman.

It is not to be objected that the preaching of repentance to the nation will give aid and encouragement to the public enemy; nor is it to be said that patriotism requires a different course. The nation has its political ambassadors, and its public servants who represent it at the bar of the world; and it is the duty of these to defend its honor before human tribunals, and to vindicate its conduct in its issues with creature powers.

But the Christian minister, in the pulpit is an ambassador from the Court of Heaven; he stands between God and the people, and it is his sacred and perilous charge to make known to the country its position towards the Almighty Ruler.

He cannot, he dare not place the honor of God as secondary to the honor of man; and he knows, or ought to know, that the interests of the Divine Kingdom which he represents are paramount over all earthly considerations.

To speak as a man, the glory of God and the interests of His Kingdom are the special charge of the messengers of the Gospel; and in times of national trouble, these are apparently more immediately at stake than at other periods.

This is the very time that the invisible Hand is felt, and would write its great truths on the opened heart of the nation, and shall the chosen servants of this Power employ itself in efforts to efface the inscription?

This is the very day of the Lord, "a day of wrath, a day of trouble and distress, a day of wasteness and desolation, a day of darkness and gloominess, a day of clouds and thick darkness;" and when the mountains smoke with the presence of Jehovah, come to plead with the people for their sins, and to make with them a covenant of life and death, shall the very messengers of this great and terrible God, lead in the effort to drown the voice of His trumpet sounding exceeding loud and dreadful?

But this argument of patriotism is but the specious plea of selfishness: it is the momentary popularity of the individual and not the lasting good of his nation that prompts the professed Christian to ignore the controversy of the Divine Power with his nation, and to pander to the strong instincts of the carnal heart by sinking or overshadowing considerations that abase it, in giving undue prominence to those which gratify its self-esteem. The forsaking of the Divine issues at stake, in times of national trouble, for those which are discussed before the world's tribunals is exactly the opposite of that patriotic instinct which dares danger for the country's safety: it is a coward's effort to win a hero's laurels by trenching through the air where there is no enemy to encounter.

The statesman who braves the seas and encounters the cold sneers and the slanderous pens and tongues of foreign courts to uphold the honor and secure the interests of his nation—or who directs the helm at home, when the storm rages and darkness covers the face of the deep, watching when the eyes of those who are cared for are closed in sleep, beholding and avoiding a thousand dangers that others see not, gaining no credit when hidden perils are passed by the agency of his skill and daring, held responsible for contingencies that no human wisdom could avoid, calmly, intrepidly and anxiously guiding the ship of state with a forgetfulness of self and all that concerns it, in the devoted concentration of every thought and purpose to the one object, the safety of the passengers and freight, is a patriot, and will receive the award of such in history. Not less patriotic is the course of the poor woman who devotes to the public defence the strong arm on which she and her little ones trust, under God, for their daily bread—of the fathers, brothers, sisters, mothers, relatives or friends at home who ply their minds and hands to clothe or feed the poor, who submit to denials that the world knows not of, who watch and labor, devise and pray, without the expectation or hope of public honors, for the comfort and safety of the army in the field, and for the promotion and preservation of the great interests of society at home.

And the soldier who tears himself, at his country's call, from weeping wife and children, committing to the care of God his dependent ones, and going forth to meet hardships in the camp and death on the battle-field, and to fill an unknown and remote grave, without even a rudely carved memorial to preserve a name which can have no illustrious place in the annals of the great. he is a patriot, a patriot who meets danger for his country, and whose sense of duty is of that character which entitles him to the appellation of the truly brave.

These are all patriots, and worthy of the honor attached to the name ; but there is another class who can serve their country more effectually than any of these, and whose rewards in time are the least of all These are the messengers of the glorious gospel of the blessed God : the men who are dedicated and set apart to minister in Divine things, and who are the expounders of that Truth which is the light of the world, and the life of nations, as well as of individuals. They are soldiers as well as those who follow the standards of the temporal power : they have to endure hardships, to encounter perils, to war with enemies vigilant, enterprising and cruel. Their cause is the very essence of the highest, purest and noblest patriotem; and indeed it is blasphemy to pretend that God will require them to pursue a course injurious to their people or their country.

The name of Christ is forever associated with a love for man that is beyond the conception of all finite beings; and the mission of the christian is one of good will to all men, beginning with his own household, kindred and nation

And now when calamities are abroad in the land, it is the duty of these to stand continually upon their high places and proclaim to their suffering countrymen that God is almighty and just, and that therefore they are visited for their sins.

The solemn voice of their testimony should be continually heard: they should rise up early, they should cry aloud, they should weary the people with their exhortations and entreaties.

They should stand in the gates, go out into the ways, enter into the house of prayer and call to every one to hear the message of God: their souls should weep in secret places, their private conversation and their public discourses, their manners and actions should all speak the language of earnest, importunate, impressive and ceaseless warning

When they stand in the pulpit, it is not under a commission to speak to the President or Dictator of the United States, nor to his people or soldiers: they are not, in the Churches, our ministers to the powers of the world, charged with the defence of our honor before the nations.

They are to speak to the issues between God and the country—in the discharge of their spiritual vocation they are to imitate the examples of Daniel, Ezra, Nehemiah and other holy and inspired men of old, and like David, recognizing the creature enemy only as the sword of an offended Deity, lead the people to acknowledgments of God's supremacy, justice and mercy, to confessions of their sins and of the righteousness of Heaven in their correction, and to an humble and sincere penitence and reformation.

As already shown, THE HONOR OF GOD REQUIRES THIS ACTION AT THEIR HANDS; AND WHAT OTHER CONSIDERATION CAN THEY OPPOSE TO THIS?

The safety of the nation demands such action of them—and this is and ever will be the test of the true patriotism of the christian element of society.

God not only does not forbid a devotion to the authority and interests of home and country, but He exacts of His servants to be the first and best patriots of all. He gives them a light by which to distinguish the right path to national safety and greatness; and he requires them to stand in the ways, at every hazard, and exert every influence to induce the people to follow them.

And now, dear christian brethren, permit me to address you in the language of earnest and honest affection, appealing to you by common duties, common ties, and common sympathies, emotions and interests.

Are not the principles of the Divine Economy towards nations, as herein set forth, in accordance with that Infallible Word which we receive as the source and standard of all moral truth?

Is not our God an almighty God, a universal Sovereign, the King of kings and Lord of lords? Can a sparrow fall to the ground without His permission? Can a great nation bleed at every pore without His express authority? Is He not perfectly just and holy in all that He does and permits?

Does not our beloved and devoted country feel the hand of affliction laid heavily upon it?

Leaving to the worldly element of society to discuss secondary causes and results, ours is the mission to look into the true relations of things, and to make known to our dear countrymen the source and remedy of our trials as they are found in the fixed course of Divine Providence. The people expect us to lead them aright in these things—and we have in the sacred Word and the learning of our ministry the means of doing it.

Is not God in controversy with us? If so, can we succeed until we place ourselves right before the supreme Power? AND IF THESE POSITIONS BE TRUE, OUGHT NOT THE PEOPLE TO KNOW IT? If there is a difficulty in our relations with the Highest Court, with the prime source of all power, ought not this to be first adjusted? Is this matter secondary in importance to any other?

You well know, dear christian brethren, that every answer to these positions is a barrier of loose sand raised up against the resistless sweep of God's almighty truth; and you know that every veil hung before this truth is a sin against Jehovah, and treason to the nation.

The answer about the honor of the nation has been already considered; and it may be added that a people's highest honor is to honor God.

Our humiliation before Him does not humble us before our human antagonists; and so far from giving them comfort, they will gnash in unavailing fury when they see us placing ourselves in the appointed way of Heaven's blessings. They may taunt and deride; but while their lips speak high words of scorn, their hearts will wither away with impotent rage and chilling fears.

The argument against repentance that some few would put in the
mouth of an honest and enquiring nation, is the very pretext of the
Wicked One which we have so often denounced, when presenting
the gospel to individual sinners! we have told them that the plea
that the world would sneer at their humility was a cowardly fear
and the suggestion of the very enemy from whom they would escape, and who was alarmed when he saw them penitent.

How often, at such times, have we quoted the lines—

> "And Satan trembles when he sees
> The weakest saint upon his knees;"

and shall we, now that the welfare of a whole and gallant nation is
trembling in the balance, ignore our own preaching, and turn our
anxious hearers from the Living Fountain to broken cisterns?

An entire and noble nation comes to us with the anxious enquiry
"Men and brethren, what shall we do to be saved?" and shall we
pervert the inspired answer, and say, repent not, for you are holy,
and you shall be saved? Our flocks, torn and bleeding, fly to us,
their pastors, for protection; and while the great Shepherd stands
behind us, shall we turn these victims of the wolf from His fold and
His protection into wilds where the teeth of ferocious beasts will
feed upon them?

Oh dear brethren, look at the spectacle which our beloved land
presents!

Was there ever a more gallant, earnest and confiding people?—
Did a nation ever stand so firmly to-gether in its political faith, in
the midst of such dreadful trials, and meet dangers, spoliations and
death with more intrepid firmness? Were all the arts of carnal defence and warfare ever wielded with more energy, daring and courage? Look around the vast frontiers of this glorious land, and see
it girt about with a wall of heroes against which are beating the waves
of a terrible and ruthless invasion, making here and there a breach
over the dead bodies of this devoted band, and rolling in a flood of
devouring fire

Look at the battle fields, where sleep in unknown graves, myriads
of as brave men as ever confronted the storm of battle, fallen in defence of home and right: and see, still springing to the places of
the slain, the plowman from the field, the artisan from his shop, the
rich man from his palace, the peasant from his humble cot. Statesmen plan, devise, labor—soldiers endure and die—men, women and
children run to and fro in anxious efforts to aid the common cause:
still the storm of war rages on land and sea, the coasts smoke with

burning towns, the frontiers are slippery with the blood of heroes, the interior is crowded with flying exiles, homeless and houseless.

All who can do any thing for the cause are looked to with the yearning heart of a great nation ; and to us, christian brethren. more than to those strong arms which present a wall of bayonets round our borders have been turned the anxious eyes of our dear and devoted countrymen.   This honor is due, in part, to the past instructions of the Church : and how glorious is our privilege and how terrible our responsibility !

Shall we disappoint such hopes as were never before turned from the world to the Church ?   Shall we trifle alike with God, and with the victims of His displeasure ?

Shall we fail to come to the rescue girded with that invincible armor which God has provided ?   Shall we shut up Heaven that it rain not on the parched earth in the days of our prophecy ?

We have an answer of life from God : He has shown to us the thing that is good, and shall we with-hold it from our people ?

It may not be in the form that some expect—it will conflict with the carnal pride of all : but shall we shirk our duty on that account ?

Suppose that the populace whom we come to save should tear us to pieces : can we afford to conceal God's message on that account ?

Even in that extreme case, we would show no more courage than the common soldier : he goes out from dear ones, fed and clothed by the labor of his hands, to perish with disease or fall in battle, unhonored, unknown, and unlamented except by a few stricken ones in his humble home, leaving these a prey to the speculators for whose protection he offers up his life.   He knows it is his duty to obey his country's call, and he marches to danger in front, leaving trouble and anguish behind, and having no hope of any other earthly reward than the common good of all the country.

And shall the professed soldier of Heaven be less courageous than the subjects of earthly power, and when they knew that their fall shall be their eternal gain ?

But while the answer from God, and with which the true Church is charged. will not flatter the pride of the carnal heart, we have no reason to believe that the nation will not kindly receive and carefully heed it.   The people have been faithfully taught in the past— they have long had Bibles in their hands—God's witness is in their consciences, and His rod of correction has been felt and acknowledged.

The whole nation has, as it were, yearned to bear a call to repentance : it has wanted to be humbled before a just God, that it might put low humbled before proud, and cruel and wicked men

The repeated and solemn proclamations from the chosen chief of
the nation, show it: the conduct and conversation of officers and
soldiers in camp and of the people at home have displayed unmistakable indications of it

Shall we reverse the conduct of holy angels when they revealed
themselves to the bodily senses of inspired men?   When the prophet
and apostle John fell down to worship at the feet of one of these
celestial messengers, the latter said "See thou do it not:......wor-
ship God"

And when the priests of the pagan city of Lystra would have sacrificed to Paul and Barnabas, they ran among the people who would
have paid them Divine honors, rending their clothes and crying.
"Sirs, why do ye these things?   We also are men with like passions
with you, and preach unto you, that ye should turn from these van-
ities unto the living God which made heaven, and earth, and the sea,
and all things that are therein."—*Acts*, xiv, 15

And now when the people come to us to hear that they must be
humbled before Jehovah, will we arrest this good purpose to gain
for ourselves a little temporary power or notoriety?

Will we when they come into the Sanctuary, to offer sacrifices to
God, turn them from their solemn and self-abasing thoughts that
we may gain a reputation for eloquence and patriotic fervor?

When they would prostrate themselves before God, shall we lift
them up, and revive their carnal pride, that their passions may render to us the glory which their better nature was about to offer to
the Almighty?

We are not called on to tell our people they are sinners above all
men because they suffer such things: it is our business simply to
deal with the offences of our own land, leaving others to Him who
judgeth righteously.   Other nations may be viler: if so, they will
in due time receive the reward of their deeds, while our concern is
to look well to our own foundations   Suppose even that we are, as
a race, *the* chosen people of God, what says His word to those who
have enjoyed most of His instructions?

"Hear this word that the Lord hath spoken against you O children of Israel, against the whole family which I brought up from
the land of Egypt, saying, You only have I known of all the families of the earth: therefore, I will punish you for all your iniquities
Can two walk together except they be agreed?"—*Amos*, iii, 1, 2, 3.

The more generally and accurately a people is instructed in the
Divine Law, the stricter will be its accountability: "For unto
whomsoever much is given, of him shall much be required." (*Luke*,

xii, 48.) We boast with reason of our superior orthodoxy, and close adhesion, in doctrine, to the Scriptures; and let us hear the warning voice of these—" And that servant which knew his Lord's will, and prepared not himself, neither did according to his will shall be beaten with many stripes."—*Luke*, xii, 47.

Brethren, there is a sad and fearful thought connected with this matter, and the hand trembles as the pen portrays it. This is a harvest time, in the Confederate States, for those who would enrich themselves on the necessities and distresses of the public; but there is a kind of speculators who have not yet been properly classified. These are the spiritual guides who would build up their worldly renown on the ruins of a confiding nation : men who trade in the carnal passions of an excited people, and whose gains are rusted with the blood of souls.

When the vast majority of men, women and children in a great nation are earnestly laboring to prevent threatened destruction, the engrossers of the necessities of life occupy a most unenviable position; but what shall be thought of those who convert the bread of life into passional delusions which steep the soul in drunkenness that leads to both temporal and spiritual destruction ? What honest interest of this great and glorious, but bleeding and afflicted nation, is served by those who stand in the pulpits to flatter the carnal instincts of their hearers ? Who but the preachers can receive any possible benefit ?

While millions are toiling and sweating with practical aims, how disgusting is the spectacle presented by those who have refused every post of danger both in the spiritual and temporal service, and who seek the reputation of heroes by hurling anathemas at the Northern Tyrant and his bloody legions, from the secure asylum of inland Churches !

What a mockery are these idle exhibitions in this earnest and busy crisis ! What an awful trifling with infinite interests in this great day of decision !

These men lay aside the spiritual armor in the presence of the spiritual enemy, and would atone for their ignoble flight from him by assuming the weapons of the State, and furiously brandishing them in the arena where carnal powers never come in conflict !

Who and what are these ? The world does not own them as the statesmen who plead, in its forums, the causes of nations: the scarred veterans of the tented field do not recognize them as the heroes who stand in the imminent deadly breach, and turn the battle to the gate :—and we know that their ways do not belong to Zion, upon

17

whose Mount Saviours are to come, and where there are holiness
and deliverance. These are they "which have forsaken the right
way, and are gone astray, following the way of Balaam, *the son* of
Bosor, who loved the wages of unrighteousness,"—"sporting themselves with their own deceivings,"—"beguiling unstable souls,"—
"clouds *they are* without water, carried about of winds; trees whose
fruit withereth, without fruit, twice dead, plucked up by the roots;
raging waves of the sea, foaming out their own shame; wandering
-tars, to whom is reserved the blackness of darkness forever."—
Jude,—II Peter, ii.

CHAPTER V.

Special Obligations. Duties of the Church, continued.

We have just seen that the Church of the Confederate States is solemnly called on to preach repentance to the nation ; and this brings us to its next duty, which is to begin the work itself.

The lessons of the times are full of startling interest to the christian population of America : they clearly demonstrate that there is a necessity for a searching examination, on the part of the visible Church, into its own character and works.

Would this dreadful conflict have been permitted if all the nominal christians in the countries scourged by it, had been engaged in the work of their Master ?'

The nations now at war were under the influence of the religious element : they were christian nations, and all the springs of national life were under the control of the visible Church. The spiritual house-hold is, therefore, largely responsible for these calamities.

FIRST. Because if the whole, or any large part of it, had been animated with the spirit of its Head, there could not have been such a display of furious and deadly animosity.

SECONDLY. God would not have permitted calamities in which so many of His people share, and which have so interfered with the former order and work of the Church, if His professed followers had been using their vast opportunities in a way to promote His glory.

THIRDLY. The christian element of society has an instructed conscience, and ought to be well acquainted with the plan of God's dealings with His creatures ; and as it was thus its duty to warn the people of their dangers, and as its strength in numbers, learning, wealth and position gave it a predominant influence, the deplorable state of things proves that it could not have been true to this obligation.

These propositions inevitably result from the application of the doctrines of Scripture already discussed to existing facts of American Society ; nor is the force of the first weakened in the Confederate States by the consideration that the christians here were forced to fight in self-defence, by the aggressive spirit of the United States.

A cruel war for conquest and spoliation is waged against the former country, by the latter—and as far as the desires of the men interested are concerned, the people or rulers of the United States are the authors of this tragic drama.

But why was it permitted by the Almighty Disposer? And why has it been allowed to entail losses and suffering on the defending parties? All sides are punished—and this is God's own assertion of the guilt of all.

The fact that we are not responsible for the continuance of this war, does not prove our innocence in the sight of Heaven: this dreadful conflict is a solemn warning to us, not of our sin in beginning or carrying it on, but of offences for which it has been sent and continued by the Almighty.

For the reasons already given, an important part of these offences lies at the door of the visible Church; and its duty to its own character, to the country and to God, requires it to commence at once a solemn and searching inquisition into its present condition and spirit, and into its past history.

As it has clearly appeared, the christian element of society, instructed in the plans of Providence, must teach that the only way of escape from the troubles of the times, is by the general and sincere repentance of the afflicted parties; but with what grace can the Church, without a change in itself, call for reformation in the nation?

The whole public in America, has enjoyed, to some extent, the advantages of a sound religious instruction; and perhaps a majority of those who are out of the pale of the nominal Israel are aware of the nature of the vows it has made to its Divine Head.

The world always has a sharp vision for the faults of christians—and this naturally inquisitive disposition is rendered more active in America by the universal and rightfully founded impression that the Church is largely responsible for the present calamities.

With what solemn emphasis do all these facts speak to the christian public in the Confederate States! The Church knows it is commissioned to preach repentance to the nation—it knows that it is admonished to reform its own ways—and it ought to be well aware that its reproof of popular sins will be unavailing as long as it presents such glowing inconsistencies between conduct and profession.

Its own repentance is, in itself, an important element of national safety; and the reformation of people sorely scourged for sin, must also greatly depend on this example of the visible house-hold of Faith.

Christian brethren of the Confederate States! let us look to ourselves and our own house: let us awake to the awful realities of our position, and humbly, penitently and prayerfully enquire wherein it is that we have offended.

This is not the place to undertake any special enumeration of our sins as the visible Church ; but I would respectfully offer suggestions to aid in an examination which, if properly conducted, cannot but lead to the most glorious results.

1. Every inhabitant of this afflicted land who bears the name of Christ, ought to enter into a searching scrutiny of his past conduct and of his present position, as a member of the nominal Israel of God ; and he ought to contrast his whole line of conduct with the standard of religious duty plainly revealed in the Divine charter of his faith.

This work should be entered on with that sincerity and determination which ought to characterize those who are hastening to an awful account ; and it should be conducted with secret prayer, and perseveringly continued.

Every one ought to ask himself, Am I really what I profess to be ? What evidence is there in my own heart that I love God more than the world ? What do my actions prove ? What has been my ruling desire ? how have I received the countless mercies of God in the past ? Have I realized that I am not my own ? have I made any sacrifices for Christ ? has His cause been dear to me ? have I been a stumbling block to His people or the world ? have I offended any of His little ones ?

Could I have done more than I have done to arrest the course of members of my house-hold, of servants, kindred or neighbors who have perished in their sins ? Are there any now in eternity or on their way to its dread realities, without hope in Christ, who can confront me at the judgement seat and show upon my skirts the blood of their souls ?

Am I responsible for the prevalence of any vice ? have I done all I could to prevent the cold, or corrupt condition of my Church ?

Have I, as a citizen, been more influenced by party feeling, than by zeal for the interests of the Church ? have I not shown to my family and the world that I value wealth, honor or carnal enjoyment more than my heavenly inheritance ?

2. They who fear the Lord should seek out each other, and speak often one to another, of their Master's interests.

In this work, denominational prejudices should be forgotten ; and neighbors, friends and acquaintances should, without regard to sect, confess their faults to each other, commune and pray to-gether, and encourage one another in the good work of reformation.

Whenever it is possible for as many as two christians, of either sex, or any age or class, to meet to-gether, they should do so at stated and frequent intervals, to join their prayers to-gether, and to converse about the affairs of Zion. " Again I say unto you, That if two of you shall agree on earth, as touching any thing that they shall ask, it shall be done for them of my father which is in Heaven

For where two or three are gathered to-gether in my name, there am I in the midst of them." (*Math* xviii, 19, 20.) " Then they that feared the Lord, spake ofte i one to another, and the Lord hearkened and heard it : and a b k of remembrance was written before Him for them that feared the Lord, and that thought upon His name. And they shall be mine, saith the Lord of hosts, in that day when I make up my jewels ; and I will spare them as a man spareth his own son that serveth him.

Then shall ye return, and discern between the righteous and the wicked, between him that serveth God, and him that serveth Him not."—*Mal*. iii, 16, 17, 18.

This is God's covenant and He will always fulfil its glorious stipulations whenever and wherever His people perform their part of the conditions.,

3: Every congregation, or individual Church organization should, as a body, earnestly engage in the work of examination and repentance. To this end the minister should preach a series of sermons on the standard of christian character, revealed in the Scriptures, with practical and pointed reference to the condition of things in his own charge ; and the office bearers in the Church ought prayerfully to consult to gether and adopt concerted means for the warning of their people, and for the promotion of that godly sorrow which works repentance unto life. This is the first and most important business now demanding the attention of every worshiping assembly, and it cannot be neglected without a fearful risk

4. Church judicatories should, in their official capacity, take solemn notice of the tremendous responsibilities now resting on the christian public ; and they should give the weight of their public testimony against all known delinquincies and in favor of every needed reform.

5. *Now* is the time to manifest our repentance by our works ; the call of God is always for *to-day*, and when we confess that we ought to begin a required task at *some time*, we convict ourselves of sin in every hour's delay.

The time to discharge a religious duty is when it is made obvious to us ; and no doubt the trials of the period are enhanced by those public confessions which the Church is making of past derelictions and of its intention to amend its ways on some future and more fa vorable occasion.

How often have we preached to sinners of the world from this text: "And as he reasoned of righteousness, temperance, and judg-ment to come, Felix trembled, and answered, Go thy way for this time; when I have a convenient season, I will call for thee."—(*Acts* xxiv. 25.)

It is God Himself who is now reasoning to His visible Church of these things, while the whole continent quakes at the sound of His voice : shall we answer Him that His occasion does not suit us, and bid Him go His way till we shall call for Him ?

" Wherefore, when I came, *was there* no man ? when I called, *was there* none to answer ? Is my hand shortened at all, that it cannot redeem ? or have I no power to deliver ?"—(*Is.* L. 2.)

" Turn you at my reproof ; behold, I will pour out my Spirit unto you, I will make known my words unto you.

Because I have called, and you refused ; I have stretched out my hand, and no man regarded ;

But ye have set at nought all my counsel, and would none of my reproof :

I, also, will laugh at your calamity : I will mock when your fear cometh ;

When your fear cometh as desolation, and your destruction cometh as a whirlwind ; when distress and anguish cometh upon you.

Then shall they call upon me, but I will not answer ; they shall seek me early, but they shall not find me ;

For they hated knowledge, and did not choose the fear of the Lord :

They would none of my counsel : they despised all my reproof."—(*Prov.* i. 23–30.)

" Thus speaketh the Lord of hosts, saying, This people say, The time is not come, the time that the Lord's house should be built....

Now, therefore, thus saith the Lord of hosts ; consider your ways.

Ye have sown much, and bring in little ; ye eat, but ye have not enough ; ye drink, but ye are not filled with drink ; ye clothe you, but there is none warm ; and he that earneth wages, earneth wages *to put it* into a bag with holes.

Thus saith the Lord of hosts ; Consider your ways.

Go up to the mountain, and bring wood, and build the house, and I will take pleasure in it, and I will be glorified, saith the Lord.

Ye looked for much, and, lo, *it came* to little ; and when ye brought it home, I did blow upon it. Why? saith the Lord of hosts. Because of mine house that is waste, and ye run every man unto his own house

Therefore the heaven over you is stayed from dew, and the earth is stayed *from* her fruit.

And I called for a drought upon the land, and upon the mountains, and upon the corn, and upon the new wine, and upon the oil, and upon *that* which the ground bringeth forth, and upon men, and upon cattle, and upon all the labour of the hands."—(*Hag.* i. 2, 5–11.)

Thus it appears that the time to perform neglected duties of which God's judgments remind us, is when we are suffering chastisements, and that this is the only way to secure those better times to which we would adjourn our obligations.

And now, in conclusion of this subject, let us heed the solemn import of the following words:

"And when he was come near, he beheld the city, and wept over it,

Saying, If thou hadst known, even thou, at least in this thy day, the things *which belong* unto thy peace! but now they are hid from thine eyes.

For the days shall come upon thee, that thine enemies shall cast a trench about thee, and compass thee round, and keep thee in on every side,

And shall lay thee even with the ground, and thy children within thee; and they shall not leave in thee one stone upon another; because thou knewest not the time of thy visitation."—*Luke* xix. 41–44.

6. The Church ought to manifest in all its manners and actions an earnest, realizing and absorbing sense of the solemnity of the times, and of God's displeasure with itself; and in all its prayers and public deliverances it ought to make confession of its sins, and to show it is conscious there is an accursed thing in the camp of Israel, and its great anxiety to have it discovered and purged away at any expense of pride, or of consistency in injurious habits. In this matter, every sect should look for an Achan in its own tribe, for it is not a time for family jars when the safety and the honor of the whole kindred are at stake; and the Church of the Confederate States should show infinitely more concern for its own family than for that of other nations.

Every individual, every congregation, every denomination and the whole body of Christians in the Confederate States, should search at home for offences; and the godly zeal of persons and communities should turn its energies in these directions where alone it can exhort to edification, and rebuke with all authority.

Let us all, christian brethren, strive to see ourselves as others see us, as we are beheld by Him who is of purer eyes than to behold evil, and cannot look on iniquity ; let us all look on Him whom we have pierced, and mourn, and be in bitterness for Him, as those who are in bitterness for their first born.

Let there be a great mourning in all Jerusalem ; and let its sincerity and universality be demonstrated by the personal grief of every man and woman, each tribe, each family and each individual mourning apart.

When this is done, the Lord will cut off the names of the idols out of the land, and they shall not be remembered ; and " then will the Lord be jealous for His land and pity His people," and He will " remove far off the northern army," and we " shall eat in plenty, and be satisfied, and praise the name of the Lord our God that hath dealt wondrously with us."—(*Zech.* xii. *Joel* ii.)

Then shall " the Spirit be poured upon us from on high, and the wilderness be a fruitful field, and the fruitful field be counted for a forest.

Then judgment shall dwell in the wilderness, and righteousness in the fruitful field.

And the work of righteousness shall be peace ; and the effect of righteousness, quietness and assurance forever."—(*Is.* xxxii. 15–17.)

18

CHAPTER VI.

Special obligations.—Duties of Individual Christians.

There are, no doubt, many true christians in the Church of the Confederate States of America; and to each one of these who reads these pages a special appeal is now addressed.

In your hands, dear brethren, God has placed the means of your country's deliverance: upon your action, more than upon any other created agency, depends the issue of that struggle which absorbs the attention of the civilized world.

God has greatly honored His people in making them co-workers with and under Him: they have, through Christ, the power to bring down blessings on their land, and to cause "the wilderness and solitary place to be glad for them."

Wherever there is a christian heart, full of the Spirit of the Master, there is one of the nation's bulwarks; and when such are scattered among the people, and preserve and manifest the true savor of their calling, there is hope for the country, however severe its trials.

But you, dear brethren, may err in what you omit to do, as well as in what you do; and if you fail in declaring the whole counsel of God, you will share largely in the temporal afflictions of your generation.

It was not those who merely abstained from the pollutions of the times that were marked upon the forehead by the man clothed in linen, with a writer's ink-horn by his side; but the exemption from the slaughter denounced upon the inhabitants of Jerusalem was extended only to those that sighed and cried for all the abominations that were done in the midst of the city.—(*Ezek.* ix.)

Permit me then, respectfully and kindly, but with earnest and solemn emphasis to urge you to consider what has been said to the whole nominal Church; and allow me, also, to assure you that if you will faithfully pursue the course plainly marked out for you in the Divine Charter of your faith, a bright and glorious day will succeed this night of storm.

Each one of you, whatever your station or influence, is called on to testify to the sovereignty and justice of God, and to the sins of the people: each is required to afflict his soul and to be in bitterness for his own offences, and for the offences of his nation, and to exert himself to arrest the course of evil.

You very well know that the calamities of the nation are sent of God; and you know, also, that the result of these trials will glorify their Author.

His designs cannot be thwarted—neither His word nor His judgments shall return to Him void, or fail to accomplish that whereto they are sent.

If the nation amend its ways, its calamities will be the healthful chastening of a son : if it hardens its neck, it will be more sorely smitten, and will be ultimately healed or destroyed.

It is time for us all to awake to a full and practical apprehension of this great truth : we are in the midst of stern and awful realities, in the midst of one of these formative epochs, when the whole current of history depends on the action of a day.

It is a time of conflict in the spiritual, as well as in the natural world : the elements of principles always hostile are now mustered for decisive battle, and while our brethren after the flesh are doing their part so nobly, shall it be said that they failed for the want of our cooperation ?

The banners of the enemy whom we are leagued to encounter, now flaunt before us; every man is now called to assume his station for or against the cause, and there can be no neutrals in this contest. God Himself is calling the muster rolls of His nominal followers; and every one who does not respond by taking his place in line of battle, with his spiritual armor on, will be counted as a deserter from his flag, or a traitor to his cause.

If we fail to meet this crisis with the right spirit, the hopes of a gallant people will perish, our own dearest earthly interests will hasten to irretrievable ruin, and the future annals of the Church will associate our names with those who fall miserably below great occasions, or who betray their trust in the day of decision.

Upon us is devolved a responsibility which we cannot lay aside : if we meet it as we ought, our reward will be glorious—if we neglect our part, we will write ourselves ignoble for all coming time.

And now that we may, one and all, the better perform our several tasks, I venture to offer a few suggestions in regard to the special obligations of every christian.

FIRST. No one is to wait until the Church, in its organized capacity, leads the way in the work of reformation.

The Church is not a corporation, responsible to its Head only in its collective capacity ; nor is Christianity a result of associated labor, an attribute belonging only to men, in their collective capacity, when aggregated together under particular forms. Religion is a vital principle, born of Heaven, in the soul of the individual; and all who are so animated are in spiritual communion with each other and with the Divine source of their life.

The visible Church merely represents this union; but in the company of professed believers on earth, there may be, and always are many who are not in communion with God.

The soul of the true disciple is united to Christ by living joints and bands: but there is no such union between a temporal organization of men calling themselves the Church, and the Divine Power.

The Church, in its worldly form, often becomes corrupt; and reforms seldom, if ever, spring from the actions of its judicatories.

There is ever a tendency in frail, human nature to attribute to temporal organizations the power which belongs to God alone; and however pure a Church may be in doctrine, a long state of prosperity is sure to imbed its government in forms and technicalities which practically deny the power of godliness.

Machinery becomes every thing, especially to those who chiefly control it; and we have not to go far to find Church judicatories who have hedged in themselves and the energies of the bodies they represent by traditions which make the commandment of God of none effect.

To such mechanics, the manner of doing a thing is of infinitely more importance than the thing itself—and with them the whole life of the Church is preserved, diffused and transmitted through a technical routine that becomes daily more intricate, complex and cumbrous. To be experts in this Talmudical profound, and to add to its depth and opacity, are taken as signs of a promising ruler; and if the life of the Church really depended on these official tinkerings, it would be confined to such narrow and crooked channels that it could never accomplish any really useful purpose.

But whatever is commanded to the *whole* Church, is enjoined on each individual member; and while no one is to usurp places in the visible household of faith, each is to labor, in his position, and by all his means, for the results which are commanded to believers as a body.

The Church must have a government—and in this organization special parts are allotted to particular classes; but the grand duty of the christian, as such, belongs to every individual in every situation.

When, therefore, any one feels that God is calling for repentance, he is not to wait for the action of the judicatory of his church; and besides, repentance is *individual*, and not collective, and is a sacrifice which cannot be offered by any body of men in their official or organized capacity.

And let no one fear the charge of being an ambitious disturber of the peace of the Church—for the marks of a true reformer are such that they cannot be mistaken.

It is an unfavorable sign when those who profess to be called as reformers begin by separating themselves, assuming new names, and aiming at the honor of founding sects called by their own names; while the true champion of the honor of God seeks not to found or control parties but to infuse, if possible, a new and purer life into that to which he belongs.

His first effort will be to see this conformed in action to the standard of its orthodox profession; and not until he sees its principles in conflict with the doctrine of God, or its action in fixed and purposed opposition to his truth, will he forsake it for other connections.

Every one belonging to the spiritual household is required to walk according to the principles which he professes, whatever others may do—to shine as a light in the world, to hold forth the word of life to others, to mourn over his own sins, and to see and sigh for the sins of his brethren of every class and in every position. He is called on, also, to testify for the whole truth of God: to be instant and earnest in efforts to warn the world of its danger, and to point his fellow men to the only hope of safety.

Secondly. No one is to wait for a leader.

Christ is the leader of His people, and they are to call no other Lord or Master; and there is no better sign of a dead or dying Church organization than the fact that all its movements are controlled by a few notable preachers. The more there is said of Paul and Appolos, the less there is thought of Christ.

Thus saith the Lord: " Cursed *be* the man that trusteth in man, and maketh flesh his arm, and whose heart departeth from the Lord.

For he shall be like the heath in the desert, and shall not see when good cometh; but shall inhabit the parched places in the wilderness, *in* a salt land and not inhabited.

Blessed is the man that trusteth in the Lord, and whose hope the Lord is.

For he shall be as a tree planted by the waters, and *that* spreadeth out her roots by the river, and shall not see when heat cometh, but her leaf shall be green; and shall not be careful in the year of drought, neither shall cease from yielding fruit."—*Jer.* xvii, 5–8.

"Cease ye from man whose breath is in his nostrils: for wherein is he to be accounted of?"—*Isaiah* ii, 22.

Our vows, christian brethren, are to God: His Word and His Spirit are our guides, and when He calls us to a work we are not to wait until it is honored by the lead of those who are striving to make themselves the light and head of the Church.

We are to be subject to our brethren in many things, and not to take on us places in the Church, or forms of labor for which we have not been regularly set apart, according to its government; but no one is to dare to try to smother the convictions of his conscience, or to refuse a work to which God calls him merely because it has not been sanctioned by those who may be considered more learned in human knowledge, or more illustrious for eloquence or position.

THIRDLY. A man's influence with God, so to speak, and his responsibility are two different things. The latter may and does in part depend on his learning and position—the former does not

Eternity will bring to light many things which would now seem strange to us; and among these will be the relative importance to the work of Christ of the different members of His visible body on earth. It will be found that not a few who here seemed to be pillars of the Church, and who spoke with excellency of speech and enticing words of man's wisdom were builders with wood, hay and stubble—and that some who passed their lives in obscurity, or were of no reputation among the brethren, laid upon the foundation of God the gold, silver and precious stones which stand the test of that fire which shall prove every man's work of what sort it is. Famous orators and writers will suffer less in the consuming of all the shining trash with which they built monuments to their glory in time; and little ones who appeared here as babes in Christ, or passed their unhonored lives in the patient sufferance of faith shall be identified with the most illustrious works.

God sees and judges differently from men: He beholds the inner life, and His saints are great or small before Him according to the resemblance of their hearts to Christ. "The foundation of God standeth sure, having this seal, The Lord knoweth them that are His."—II *Tim.* ii, 19.

All remember what Christ said of the poor widow who cast two mites into the treasury of God; those who, like her, give all they have to the service of the Master, with a willing mind, and in the faith that the virtue of all means depends wholly on His blessing, are the great ones in the Kingdom of Heaven.

A nation may think itself much favored of God with great religious lights; and it may be possible that at the time it looks on these as the principal part of its happiness and power, the mercies of Christ are flowing down through channels that are ignoble in the sight of men.

Wherever there is a heart bearing the image of Christ, there is one of the springs of life to the state; and every one of such, whatever his or her position in the world, has power with God, through Him who has united them to Himself by living joints and bands.

Christ, in short, is the source of all good to a fallen and rebellious world; and every converted descendent of Adam is a part of the visible body of this only Medium of Divine blessings, and is encouraged and commanded freely to ask in His name for things according to His will.

FOURTHLY. It is the faith of the christian that secures efficacy to his works; and all can labor in prayer at least.

The fervent effectual prayer of the righteous man availeth much; and every servant of Christ, whatever the circumstances of his temporal condition, can wrestle in spirit with God.

We cannot estimate the importance to a community or country of a single, faithful christian in the very obscurest walk of life; and we know that God would have spared the most wicked cities on earth for the sake of ten righteous men. The truth is, the servants of Christ, as a general thing, effect more by their example than by their words; and every one who acts up to the principles of the gospel, is a living epistle to the world, written by the hand of God Himself.

Let the humble member of the Church remember this; and let him, when God's judgements are abroad in the land, manifest his sense of the solemn fact in careful and honest self-examination, in a prayerful survey of his past life, in the fasting and mourning of his spirit for his own past offences, and for the offences of his people, and in his profound and submissive anxiety to be led in the path of duty. He can at all events indicate his convictions by his own repentance and humble and contrite walk before God; and this constant attitude of fearful enquiry will be the most eloquent testimony which any can bear to the character of the Providence through which the nation is passing.

Indeed, the first appeal which all christians are to make to the conscience of the world is to be offered by their own example: their conduct is the test of the sincerity of their professions, and if their actions indicate a certain apprehension of God's displeasure for sin, their words of warning to others will come with power, while if their course displays no consciousness of offence and no fear of an angry Deity coming in the clouds of Heaven, the most eloquent and fervent rebukes and exhortations will amount to little.

The continual sound of Noah's hammer on the ark was the strongest evidence he could furnish to his cotemporaries of his convictions of God's coming judgements; and the daily and penitential confession of his own sins is the most eloquent and effective manner in which the christian can manifest his consciousness of God's displeasure with His people.

FIFTHLY. The example of the great body of the nominal Church is no excuse to any true disciple of Christ for failing to do what he feels to be the duty of all ; much less, therefore, will his neglect be justified by the eccentric conduct of a few individuals.

Whatever is commanded to the whole Church, is the special duty of each member ; and the fact that a portion of the professing christian community walk in a way unworthy of their calling only renders it the more important that others should be more diligent and faithful.

The Church of Christ, as already said, is not a corporation, acting only in its aggregate character; each individual is a responsible agent, and each is held to as strict an accountability as if he constituted the whole christian element of society. Where there are several communicants, organized into a Church, there is a subordination of parts, and to each is a special department of labor ; but each one is interested in the fidelity of every other ; and every one must aid, in his place, in the duties of the whole.

The grand duty to testify repentance towards God, and faith in the Lord Jesus Christ, is enjoined on every disciple ; and as already stated, whatever is commanded as the work of the whole Church is a responsibility resting on its component parts.

Are you ready to ask, "How are we to know that God is calling us to repentance ?"

The answer is plain : it is found in the doctrines of Scripture already discussed, applied to the circumstances of our beloved country.

We are in trouble : God sends it on us.

We are scourged with a wasting and grievous war : it is Divinely permitted.

The whole nation suffers, and the Almighty Disposer allows these calamities : are we not, therefore, sinners ?

We desire to be let alone, and yet we are persecuted with undying malice: we long for peace, and pray for it, but it does not come. Is there not a solemn lesson to us in all this?

Is not the voice of God sounding in our ears?

We have Moses and the prophets for our teachers: we have the hole testimony of God, and all the history of the past for interpreters of the severe Providences through which we are passing, and if we are not enlightened by these we would refuse to believe if one were to arise from the dead.

We walk in the light of the nineteenth century of christian progress, and all the ends of the world are met before us in solemn testimony; and from all the records of the past, from the dreadful realities of the present, and from every part of His infallible Word the v ce of Jehovah sounds perpetually in our ears, " Turn ye, turn ye, for why will ye die ?"

Oh christian brethren, let us not sleep as do those who are of the night: let us banish from our minds every seducing thought, and turn our whole souls in honest and earnest enquiry to the only source of Light and Life.

Let us judge ourselves, if we would not be judged and condemned by others, let us compare our conduct and attitude with the teachings of that Truth which we profess to honor. Let us ask ourselves, are we in the appointed way of the Divine blessing ? and let us answer this question by a faithful application of Scripture to our actions, and to the condition of our hearts.

We have no right to say we are not largely responsible for these troubles : no one of us can dare to approach the mercy seat with such a claim.

Every afflicted inhabitant of a smitten land bears part of the burden of its guilt ; and of all others, the true christian should be most ready to confess his part of the blame attaching to every class.

It does not become him, in his words or thoughts, to claim exemption from the sins which have brought judgement upon the nation ; and while it is his duty and privilege to exhort and rebuke others, his first concern should be to discover and repent of his own sins.

Let me again ask, what is our attitude before Heaven ? Are we humble ? We know if we are not, that our hearts are not right within us.

" If I shut up heaven that there be no rain, or if I command the locusts to devour the land, or if I send pestilence among the people ;

If my people, which are called by my name, shall humble themselves, and pray, and seek my face ; and turn from their wicked ways; then will I hear from heaven, and will forgive their sin, and will heal their land."—*II Chron.* vii, 13, 14.

"Behold, his soul *which* is lifted up, is not upright in him; but the just shall live by his faith."—*Hab.* ii, 4.

"Humble yourselves in the sight of the Lord, and he shall lift you up."—*James* iv, 10.

"The fear of the Lord *is* the instruction of wisdom; and before honor *is* humility."—*Prov.* xv, 33.

"Be clothed with humility: for God resisteth the proud, and giveth grace to the humble.

Humble yourselves, therefore, under the mighty hand of God, that he may exalt you in due time."—*I Peter* v, 5, 6.

"Though the Lord *be* high, yet hath he respect unto the lowly; but the proud he knoweth afar off."—*Ps.* cxxxviii, 6.

"For thus saith the high and lofty One that inhabiteth eternity, whose name *is* Holy; I dwell in the high and holy *place*, with him also *that* is of a contrite and humble spirit, to revive the spirit of the humble, and to revive the heart of the contrite ones."—*Isaiah* lviii, 15.

"Thus saith the Lord, The heaven *is* my throne, and the earth *is* my footstool: where *is* the house that ye build unto me? and where *is* the place of my rest?

For all those *things* hath mine hand made, and all those *things* have been, saith the Lord: but to this *man* will I look, *even* to *him that is* poor and of a contrite spirit, and trembleth at my word."—*Is.* lxvi. 1, 2.

This is the spirit with which, in the sight of Heaven, we are to receive calamities: this is the frame of mind with which we are to make our own confessions, and to entreat and rebuke our fellow men.

We must not only mourn over our own offences, but we must lose no opportunity for declaring the counsel of God; and we are to go forward without delay, and without waiting for any one to lead, in the path that we know to be the one of safety and of peace.

"To him that knoweth to do good, and doeth *it* not, to him it is sin." (*James* iv. 17.); and thus it is a miserable delusion in us to suppose that we shall escape merely because we abstain from what we know to be sins in others. We sin, also, if we do not warn them of the consequences of their actions; and we are especially liable to condemnation if we refuse to try to lead in the direction we know the Church ought to go.

CHAPTER VII.

Special obligations.—Duties of individual Christians, continued.

It is impossible for any christian to consider too seriously the last quotation of the previous chapter. It is the very message which I would now impress on the minds of all my brethren in the Confederate States; it is full of solemn meaning to that very class who would vainly claim exemption from the calamities of the times on the ground that they do not approve of the conduct of affairs in the religious world.

There are many individual christians, whose consciences are enlightened as to the course which the Church ought to pursue, but who believe they are too modest to thrust themselves forward as leaders; and thus they occupy the attitude of men who see their fellows about to plunge over a precipice, and who will not warn them of their danger.

Is modesty or pride the prevailing motive for silence in such cases? or is it not love of ease, and fear of trouble?

We have seen that no one, convinced of his duty, is to wait for the action of Church judicatories, or of the great body of professing believers, or for a leader, in flesh and blood; but perhaps it is proper to add a few considerations for the correction of an error which has taken strong hold of the popular mind.

In every denomination of christians, there is a body for the decision of matters connected with the Government of the Church; and whatever be the name of these assemblies, they are courts, invested with certain powers, and claiming the respect of all the members of the denomination which they represent.

It has become a habit to regard these judicatories as the eyes of the Church, and the power by which, under God, the cause of the Gospel is to be chiefly promoted; and never was there a greater mistake, or one more likely to paralyze the energies of the Church.

These bodies are all invested with certain powers which it is deemed important to lodge in the hands of appointed agents; but wherever there is power in human hands, there is a tendency to corruption.

Besides, these associations are, to a great extent, occupied with the mere *business* of the Church; and it is notorious that their members are often less anxious and earnest for spiritual things when meeting in official conclave than at any other time.

Their meetings are, in christian lands, pleasant re-unions, rendered more agreeable by the kind hospitalities of the communities in which they occur ; and it is not to be denied that these occasions are some times any thing else than edifying to the more godly persons who attend them. They furnish good opportunities for vain displays on the part of two classes of worldly-minded professors—and ambitious ministers, and fashionable families avail themselves f these occasions for seeking that kind of distinction which is dearer than the true work of the Church to carnal hearts.

It is unnecessary to dwell on this painful subject : suffice it to say, that while Conventions, Associations, Conferences, Presbyteries and Synods are bodies which subserve useful purposes, and which are essential to the well-being of the Church, they are official beings not capable, in the very nature of things, of doing, in their organized capacity, the great work of the Church.

Associated effort is very important in many things, and especially in all that pertains to worldly matters ; and it is the duty as well as the privilege of every christian to join the Church, and to act in concert with his brethren in Christ

But the Gospel is the power of God, operating on individual hearts ; and every servant of Christ owes paramount allegiance to Him, and draws from Him and from Him alone his spiritual life.

It is the individual for whose benefit Christ died : it is the individual who becomes a temple of the Holy Ghost, and who is in communion with God. Each converted soul is, therefore, as completely bound to the service of God as if there were no other christians on earth ; and the organization of believers into one body, with special departments of labor for different classes, does not relieve the humblest member of the Church of the least of his responsibilities. His relations to God as one of a large society of professed disciples are the same that they would be, if he were himself the visible Church : or rather his responsibility to his Divine Master is enhanced by the fact that others are joined with him in the visible body of Christ. He is still bound to exert himself with the same devotion of heart, body and means to the conversion of the world : and he is invested with the additional care of seeing to the purity and fidelity of his associates.

And, therefore, the delinquences of leaders in the Church, and of its judicatories, are not only no excuse for the private member, but they lay him under greater obligation to work and strive and pray for the glory of his Divine Head : in short, the progress of evil in the Church, as well as out of it, is a call on every christian, with an instructed conscience, to greater zeal, vigilance and devotion.

Now is a good time to recur to these first principles; and perhaps their neglect is one cause of the present trials.

The nominally christian public of America, and of the world, has for years past been departing in practice farther and farther from these fundamental truths; and because associated labor and capital were regarded as so important in worldly matters, the followers of Christ were more and more disposed to consider the Church as a corporation, acting and responsible only in its aggregate capacity, or being in other words but a piece of mechanism, only useful as a whole, and the component parts of which were of no value when detached.

Even a semi-infidel writer takes * notice of this fatal delusion of modern times, this attempt to affect the hearts of men by mere machinery ; and the more we study this subject in the light of Truth, the more reason have we to be surprised at the long forbearance of God with the manner in which His people were evading the responsibility with which He had invested them, and disregarding His repeated and pointed commands.

But His righteous rebuke has at last fallen upon a portion of His servants , and if they would avoid severer chastisements, they should instantly repent and do their first works over.

He is calling on the Church as a body to turn from its errors—but He is, also, with awful emphasis, proclaiming His displeasure to every individual. We are not suffering merely as members of the Church ; the scourge reaches us in all our relations, and it is the *man* and the *christian* to whom Jehovah now emphatically appeals. Every one who names the name of Christ is called on to depart from iniquity ; the axe is laid at the root of the trees, and all which do not bear good fruit will be hewn down and cast into the fire.

Every one is called on to answer for himself ; and part of the account is in relation to the manner in which he has silently suffered the errors and offences of the Church.

If the honor of God requires the christian to testify against the sins of the world, how much greater is the obligation to warn those who profane the holy name which they profess : and it is on this subject that every one is required to answer. It is no time to plead the fear of causing strife : how can there be peace when God is angry ?

---

* CARLYLE.—See his Essay on "Signs of the times."

Jeremiah, a man of most tender spirit, was made a cause of strife to his whole nation.—(*Jer.* xv. 10)—Ezekiel was commanded to cry and howl.—(*Ezek.* xxi. 12,)—and Amos was taken from a lowly pursuit, and contrary to his own wishes, to be a prophet.—(*Amos* i. 1 and vii. 14.)

Jonah, in attempting to avoid the disagreeable mission of crying in the streets of Nineveh, and of proclaiming its destruction, was overtaken in his flight by the judgment of God, and severely pun ished ; and Moses who did and suffered so much, who was such a mighty instrumentality in the hands of God, was exceedingly averse to his task, and was, by his own inspired testimony, the meekest man in all the earth.—(*Num.* xii. 3.)

When God reveals a duty to the conscience of any one, the per son so informed cannot avoid what is commanded without danger to himself and to his household ; and the very fact that he knows what ought to be done is conclusive evidence that he is called to try to see to its accomplishment. Christ himself tells us that he came not to establish peace, but a sword on earth : that he came to kindle a fire, and that his followers must not be deterred from duty by the persecutions of the visible Church, nor by the opposition and en mity of their own households The prospect of strife in the nearest and dearest relations of life, was not to deter any one from a faith ful obedience to the Master's commands ; and these teachings should now come home to the conscience of the christian with more power than at former periods.

He is always in danger when he refuses to see and obey them ; but now his true position is revealed with terrible distinctness. All his dearest temporal interests are at stake : the fate of a great and devoted nation is trembling in the balance.

Every day he is reminded of his duty by the cries of thousands made desolate by the dreadful issues of battle : every hour his senses are overwhelmed with awful evidences of the call of God upon him. His bleeding countrymen turn their yearning eyes to see how he will answer Jehovah's appeals ; and the whole land smokes and trembles while God pleads the conditions of His cove nant. Dear christian, wherever and whoever you are, arise from your fatal lethargy—behold the fearful realities which surround you, come out from your retirement of ease, and for yourself, your kindred and your country, take hold of those mercies which are as " sure as the heavens' established course."

CHAPTER VIII.

Special obligations, continued.—Duties of the whole population.

People of the Confederate States of America : I now address myself to all of you, of every class and profession.

God has cast our lot in a glorious land : we have for inheritance a country containing more natural resources than any other. under the sun.

Above all this is a land of brave men and of virtuous women : a land chiefly endeared to us for the sake of a society which has blossomed with displays of the higher attributes of man.

Until very recently the whole face of this society presented a scene of soft repose, of peace, security and comfort without a parallel in the history of the world ; but what is our condition now ?

We are begirt with fire on every side : the atmosphere is heavy with the smoke of battle, and hordes of ruthless plunderers are encamped on many of our fairest provinces.

The whole horizon is lighted up with the red glare of war, and every family and every individual is made to feel that God has laid a chastening hand upon the nation. We are indeed profoundly tried ; and only those who are mad with that wild delirium of fanaticism which now has its proper home among our enemies can lift up their heads before the Almighty, and deny that He has laid a scourge upon us.

Your first impulses in this matter were correct : the glorious Giver of our blessings is angry with us, and He is, with awful emphasis, calling us to repentance for past offences.

He has seen an accursed thing among us ; and He will refuse to settle us peaceably and securely in this delightful land until we have put away our abominations.

This was the instinctive feeling of us all when the clouds began to darken in our horizon ; and this universal sentiment was a merciful admonition from Him who now rides upon the whirlwind and directs the storm.

It was, therefore, our duty to go forward at once to the moral work required, without waiting for the whole Church to lead : to meet the machinations of the Wicked One as we met the first movement of our human assailants, by a spontaneous and a general rally in the direction of danger.

The chief part of the spiritual obligations now resting on us all does not require a leader : and that is, to humble ourselves under the mighty hand of God, and to ask to be enlightened as to our sins, with a firm purpose to forsake them at once, whatever they may be.

We have all enjoyed the advantage of faithful instruction in the past—and the voice of these lessons has been sounding in our ears. We have heard it in the morning, at evening and at night : we have heard it at our firesides, it has spoken to us in the shop and field, and cried to us from the bloody scenes of battle.

God has engraven the words on our hearts—and in every serious and honest moment we know that we are called to repentance.

We have not needed a Jonah to go through our streets and cry : we walk in the light of the nineteenth century of christian progress, and from our infancy we have enjoyed the instruction of teachers rich in all the learning of the past.

Besides, we have a better guide than even the entire Church : we have in our hands the whole counsel of God, the complete and in fallible Word, speaking to us in our own language, and in terms which we all can understand.

All the inspired prophets, historians and apostles are our teachers: God Himself, by His Scriptures of Truth. is our leader, and it is He who calls to us and to the Church alike to amend our ways

"Surely the Lord God will do nothing, but He revealeth His secret unto His servants the prophets," (Amos iii 7 :) His infallible Word will teach us all things in regard to the dispensations of His Providence which it is proper for men to know.

It has made the way of His judgments exceedingly plain ; and no man with a Bible in his hand. and which he is able to read, can for a moment be in doubt as to the origin and uses of national afflictions.

There are no cause and result in natural science more inevitably connected than those of sin and correction ; nor is there a proposition in the elementary mathematics so certain as those in regard to states which God enunciates, and which all history proves, namely : that " Righteousness exalteth a nation : but sin is a reproach to any people."—(Prov. xiv. 34)

Equally true and certain are all the teachings of that infallible Word quoted in this work ; and there is no difficulty anywhere in the universe in regard to our situation but in ourselves.

God is almighty, and He is perfectly holy ; and the whole creation is subject to His immediate, special and eternal control.

If then His power be infinite and His justice perfect, why do we suffer ? Is it not obvious that we have been and are offenders ?

If this be so, will we hesitate to turn from our errors ?

If we are, as a nation, obedient to the commands of Jehovah, who can harm us?

If God be for us, who can be against us? Can the wrath of man thwart the justice of Omnipotence? Can the elements of nature resist the will of Him who created all things by the word of His power? Can hell and earth combined mar the plans of Him who has determined the bounds of all animate and inanimate agencies?

Suppose our creature foes do rage and imagine a vain thing: can they injure those whom Jehovah would hide under the covert of His wings?

What has been the invariable result when God has arisen, in the past, to save the meek of the earth? What is the testimony of the Psalmist?

"The stout-hearted are spoiled, they have slept their sleep: and none of the men of might have found their hands.

At thy rebuke, O God of Jacob, both the chariot and horse are cast into a dead sleep.

Thou, *even* thou, *art* to be feared: and who may stand in thy sight when once thou art angry?......Surely the wrath of man shall praise thee: the remainder of wrath shalt thou restrain."—(*Ps.* lxxvi. 5–7, 10.)

Such ever have been and ever will be the thoughts of all who see in their true light, the ways of Divine Providence—and such shall be our rejoicing if we will but heed lessons that are as plain as the sun in the Heavens.

God is unchangeable: He is the same Being to-day that He was when the prophets spake His Word.

He lives and reigns: He is at this moment governing, by His opposeless power, the whole creation that has sprung from His will.

Every event that is now transpiring, from the motions of the myriads of shining worlds that revolve through the amplitude of space, to the actions of the smallest insect that crawls in the dust of the earth, is the subject of his special notice and care; and the great revolution in human affairs in which we are actors is as directly under His management as if it were the sole subject of His government.

His eye is on us every moment: and in all the countless eventualties of this terrible upheaving there is not an incident, from the silent tear-drops of the poor and obscure widow, to the battle that shakes the continent and fills ten thousand breasts with anguish, but is watched and controlled by the Infinite Mind.

He is able, ready, and willing to cause these troubles to end; and the instant we place ourselves right before Him, and take hold of His strength in the way of His own appointment, He will say to the stormy elements, "Peace, be still!"

Friends, countrymen, will you not be healed ?

"Come, and let us return unto the Lord : for He hath torn, and He will heal us; He hath smitten, and He will bind us up."

We have not to wait for a leader; our Bibles will direct us in the way we should go.

1. We must humble ourselves under the mighty Hand of God— and confess that we have fallen by our own iniquities.

2. We must, with continued and earnest prayer, seek for the cause of our calamities, in our past sins, and in the present condition of our hearts; and be ready to give ourselves freely to any reformation demanded by the Word of God.

3. We must not dictate the mode and time of our deliverance; and we must be ready to sacrifice all pride, all predilection, all cherished sins at the Divine Command.

4. We must repudiate all hope of gaining the favor of Heaven by any mere work of our hands while our hearts are evil.

The chosen Chief of the Nation, in the faithful exercise of his functions, calls on us, from time to time, to devote special days to fasting, humiliation and prayer; but we totally misapprehend the meaning and spirit of these solemn appeals when we suppose that we are expected to humble ourselves only on the appointed days.

These recommendations constitute all that can be done by the political head of the people, to direct in their spiritual exercises; they are intended to foster proper habits, and special days and special acts are suggested that their public, universal, and solemn observance may have the more influence in fixing upon the minds of all, the great religious truths bearing on our condition.

The high and just object of these calls is defeated when we undertake to conciliate Heaven by mere abstinence from food on stated occasions; and certainly, we act with supreme folly when we suppose that by refusing to eat for one day, we lay God under obligations. It is equally a perversion of these recommendations, to humble or try to humble ourselves on one day, and then to return with renewed energy to all our sinful ways: and all such conduct is contrary to the spirit of the President's proclamations, and an insult to that Holy God, whose intervention in our behalf we would secure.

We cannot fast always in body—nor can we observe every day as one of public humiliation and social prayer; but we ought to do what it is in the heart or our chief magistrate to see us engaged in, to clothe our spirits in humility before God, to bear about in our hearts a continual sense of our unworthiness in the sight of Heaven, and to turn with persistent strivings from all our errors.

The bodily fasting is intended to be a sign and promoter of inward grief for sin; and the devotion of certain days to public manifestations of repentance to impress forcibly on the public mind the necessity of a general reformation.

It is expected by those who proclaim these fasts that they will be a means of commencing a permanent work of good : that they will, in fact, but be a means to an end, and not the end itself. Therefore, they who content themselves with a mere outward observance of the appointed days, have in reality added to their former sins—just as those who try to be religious on the sabbath, and are openly wicked on every other day, are the farthest off from the true kingdom of Heaven.

5. God says, " *At what* instant I shall speak concerning a nation, and concerning a kingdom, to pluck up, and to pull down, and to destroy it:

If that nation, against whom I have pronounced, turn from their evil, I will repent of the evil that I thought to do unto them."—(*Jer.* xviii. 7–8.)

This truth is as certain as the existence of Him who spake it ; and it affords a sure, unfailing hope to every afflicted people.

There never was an exception to this rule since the world began, and there never will be while nations exist ; and God will begin to be merciful at the very *instant* that the nation turns from its evil way.

* The almighty Sovereign is unchangeable ; and the rules of His gracious dealings are as fixed as His own eternal existence.

With Him is no variableness, neither shadow of turning; and the course of His judgments and mercies is established on the immovable foundations of His own being.

All the attributes of His nature forbid that He should be angry, for a moment, with those who have placed themselves in the appointed channel of His favor; He cannot do otherwise than heal all who take hold of His strength.

In one direction, His look is fixed with an eternal smile—in another He is always a consuming fire.

But poor, erring mortals are very likely to stumble at the word "instant"—for they are apt to think that God will and must help them when they begin to wish He would.

Let me admonish you, my countrymen, of the vanity of such

hopes : permit me earnestly to call your attention to a vital consideration in this matter. A people may be for months and years crying to Heaven without securing its aid ; and it is not because God
'does not hear, but because they have not, in fact, turned in heart
and action, from the errors which have brought down His displeasure.

Hear what He Himself says of a people who thought they had afflicted their souls before Him ; " I hearkened and heard, *but* they
spake not aright. · No man repented him of his wickedness, saying,
What have I done ? every one turned to his course, as the horse
rusheth into the battle.

Yea, the stork in the heaven knoweth her appointed times ; and
the turtle, and the crane and the swallow observe the time of their
coming ; but my people know not the judgment of the Lord.

How do ye say, We *are* wise, and the law of the Lord *is* with us ?
Lo, certainly in vain made he *it ;* the pen of the scribes *is* in vain.

The wise *men* are ashamed, they are dismayed and taken : lo, they
have rejected the word of the Lord ; and what wisdom *is* in them ?

Therefore, will I give their wives to others, *and* their fields to
them that shall inherit *them :* for every one from the least even
unto the greatest is given to covetousness, from the prophet even
unto the priest every one dealeth falsely.

For they have healed the hurt of the daughter of my people
slightly, saying, Peace, peace ; when *there is* no peace."—(*Jer.* viii.
6-11.)

Here we are made plainly to understand, *First*, that God hears
and hearkens, listens attentively when any one cries to Him, and
never fails to mark the purport of his words and thoughts.

Secondly, That words avail nothing, when the fixed purposes, the
secret leanings of the heart, and their corresponding actions speak
a different language.

Thirdly, That the rule of God's judgments is as certain as the
laws of Nature, and that they who are instructed by His word ought
to be led as surely and as invariably by it to their own best interests as irrational animals are carried, by infallible instinct, to fulfil the law of their being.

Fourthly, In every case of national calamity, the people suffer,
because the law of God speaks in vain : it opens a plain way of
safety, but it is rejected by those who profess to heed it.

Fifthly, The hurt of the country will not be healed merely because it cries for peace—and it will not be cured until there is a
real reformation of the errors which caused it.

This is eternal and immutable truth, whether we receive it or not; and though we have prayed long and earnestly to God, He has not yet heard, in the thoughts of our hearts and the course of our actions, the petitions which He has sworn by Himself, shall secure His favor.

Let me, then, implore you to heed the solemn lessons which our unavailing prayers teach us: let me remind you that every whisper has been heard, but that every secret instinct and every action have, also, been seen and marked.

The simple but great fact is that God has not failed to hear, but we have not spoken aright; and we are, therefore, the more impressively called on to look into our hearts, to ask for light, to pray first of all and most of all to be instructed as to our sins, and to be able to forsake them.

This is a call made upon all: it sounds loudly from the scenes of carnage where the chivalry of our land lies in gory beds, it whispers to our hearts through the thousand trials and sorrows that invade every circle, and it speaks with a tongue of fire from the living Word to which we turn our hopes.

Every fact of our situation admonishes us that we have not yet spoken to God aright; and in such a case it is the plain dictate of reason to enquire what it is that we should do that we have not done, and what actions we should forsake. In this primary and absolutely essential work every one should engage: there is one word of instruction open to all, one source of light and life accessible to high and low, to the ignorant and the learned.

When God created the world, light was the first day's work; and now, if we would save our country, let us pray for Divine guidance in the task.

We have all approached the mercy seat with too much confidence in ourselves; we have not only come to the throne of grace without true repentance in our hearts, but we have never felt as we ought, our need of Divine direction. If we have undertaken to repent, it has been with the belief that we knew what it was that we had to turn from.

WE HAVE NOT ASKED THE DIVINE AID IN SELECTING SINS FOR SACRIFICE: WE HAVE GONE INTO OUR FOLDS, AND TAKEN WHAT WE COULD BEST AFFORD TO SPARE.'

Professing to know that Jehovah has called on us for a burnt offering, we have not sought his directions as to the victims: but we ourselves have chosen such as we thought would be pleasing, as a burnt offering to God, and when men so act they are sure to flatter themselves that Heaven is best satisfied with what they can most easily give.

Hence, each one has taken the sin he is least inclined to or feels least interest in, and has lashed it and branded it with great parade before God and man; and each one has hidden away in his heart and actions the very offence that the Divine justice is demanding.

Dear countrymen and friends, permit me to speak plainly to you, for I speak in the name of your best interests: if God demands a sacrifice of us, it is *His* place and not *ours* to designate the victim.

We must go up to the mount where we are called to devotion as Abraham went into the land of Moriah: we must go prepared to offer up what is as dear to us as was Isaac, the heir of promise, to the father of the faithful.

Let us all, then, begin our religious work anew: let us, every one, put the knife to our pride, acknowledge our first error, and come to God with an humble and honest desire to be taught by Him in regard to our offences, and with a firm reliance on His aid to enable us to devote to the slaughter whatever He may direct. Let us ask His aid in setting forth a catalogue of our sins: let us ask for help to see wherein it is that we need repentance, and for grace to do and suffer whatever is required.

This is the first step to safety; it is the foundation of all true reformation.

Will not every one enter on it without delay?

It is not to be undertaken in any formal way: it is to be accomplished through prayer, self-examination, and the study of the Divine Oracles. All can read, all can hear when the Word is read: all can meditate, all can pray.

O that there was a heart for this in every inhabitant of this devoted land! that from the Potomac to the Rio-Grande, the great absorbing thought of all would be, "Why is the Almighty displeased with this people? what are *my* sins? what is demanded of *me?* what can *I* do to appease the Divine wrath?"

When such reflections fill the breast of the soldier on his mid night watch, in camp, on the march, and in the shock of battle when they occupy the minds alike of the farmer in his fields, the mechanic in his shop, the statesman in his cabinet, and the minister in the sacred desk—when all the people of this great and suffering nation, prompted by such reflections, turn anxiously to the Source of Truth, to the Infallible Word, and to secret, earnest and importunate prayer, then will be the beginning of the end, then shall the long looked for morning dawn brightly and sweetly on this dark night of horrors!

"Then," oh dear Confederacy, "shall thy light break forth as the morning, and thine health shall spring forth speedily: and thy righteousness shall go before thee : the glory of the Lord shall be thy rearward.

Then shalt thou call, and the Lord shall answer : thou shalt cry, and he shall say, Here I am."—*Is.* lviii, 8, 9.

6. We are a christian nation : that is, we have been instructed by the Word of God, and we profess to receive it as the only source of Truth.

We invoke the aid of the God of the Bible ; and we rely on it for our defence in regard to the charges brought against us by those who, on these grounds, would exterminate us from the earth.

The Holy Scriptures are, therefore, our witness, and we cannot receive and reject their testimony to suit our pleasure.

If we invoke what they say in one place, for our defence, we must receive and be judged by all their evidence : and hence we are bound by our own conduct, more than any other people on earth, to honor the whole Word of God, and to live as individuals and as a nation according to its precepts.

We lay the corner stone of our social system on this Word : we are, therefore, bound to construct the whole edifice according to its directions.

It is in one cardinal point, our only political text-book—and this being so, we trifle with Jehovah if we reject its authority in those matters which we think do not suit us.

In our controversy with the nations about slavery we summon the Word of God to the witness stand ; and thus, like the Jews of old, we have as a nation, solemnly bound ourselves to take this as our national chart and covenant.

The people of the Confederate States are, therefore, each and all pledged even in a way different from all other political communities, to see the Bible disseminated, studied, reverenced and obeyed.

This is, also, a work in which all can engage ; and more than any other people, each individual of the nation is required to see the spirit of Divine Truth reflected in the laws of the land.

Every one is bound to " search the Scriptures;" and every one is under obligations which none can throw off, to judge himself, to judge others and to judge society by the whole counsel of God.

If we are, as individuals or as an organized society, living in open violation of any of the teachings of the Divine Word, we are more guilty than any other people : we have literally chosen God for our King, and if we disobey any of His commands we are traitors to our own elected Government.

It is of the first importance that we should all, immediately and practically, realize this great fact of our position ; and whether we are willing to receive it or not, it still remains and will enter as a ponderous element into the balances which weigh our national character.

And it must be remembered that no individual can say that he has been true in his allegiance to Divine Truth if he has not made any effort to restrain others from treason : for every one is called on to see the law obeyed, and to tolerate its infraction is to be a party to it.

Laws, or at all events, their execution, will generally be but the outward reflection of the inward character of the people ; and if this is so of civil Government, it will certainly be true of social manners and customs.

The people of the Confederate States thus occupy, by their own choice, a high but fearfully responsible position ; they have, in their political capacity, chosen the Word of God for their judge, and they must stand or fall by its decisions.

Those who feel a license to sin in all other respects because they have selected God as their arbiter in one particular, mock the high and holy Majesty of Heaven ; while it is equally impious to excuse the evil practices of society because the theory of its organization is in accordance with the teachings of Divine Truth.

Every one of us is called on to examine his past conduct and his present course, as a citizen and as a man, by the whole revealed will of God—and, also, to exert himself to see that the conduct of others conforms to the same standard.

We have voluntarily elevated the Scriptures in judgement over us : in how many respects do we, as individuals and as a nation, disregard their injunctions and their warning !

We cannot continue to do so and expect prosperity ; the very charter of our hopes denounces such expectations as supreme and wicked folly.

Let me then speak to my countrymen in the language of Moses when he made an end of speaking all the words concerning the principles and facts of the Divine Economy towards nations which God inspired him to teach the Israelites in a song that they might not forget them :

" Set your hearts unto all the words which I testify among you this day, ' (to wit, the whole revealed of God—) " which ye shall command your children to observe to do, all the words of this law.

For it *is* not a vain thing for you : because it is your life."—*Deut.* xxxii, 46, 47.

By building our national system on the Divine Word as the highest political as well as moral authority, we have avouched the Lord to be our God, and promised by our conduct to walk in His ways, and to keep His statutes, and His commandments, and His judgements, and to hearken unto His voice: if we do so He will make us high above all nations in praise, in name and in honor, but if we do not, then shall fall upon us the fearful curses denounced in our covenant of life.

7. When is the time to turn from the offences for which the nation is chastised? Now, *right now*, is the proper time. There can be no better opportunity: possibly no other occasion will ever be offered.

We trifle with God when we promise future reformation; we impeach His character when we contend that when He corrects us He places us in such circumstances that we cannot amend our ways.

We are indeed in the midst of terrible events; but can any exigency in human affairs suspend the Government of God, or elevate any duty above the obligation to serve and obey Him?

We often hear the remark that when the war is over and better times have come, we will, as men and as christians, as a Church and as a people, give ourselves to needed reforms; and no doubt there is a general promise, in the popular heart, to see to various moral improvements when once we have gained our national independence.

Friends, countrymen, it is fearful to scrutinize this attitude in its true light before a Holy God: if we really knew it, the language which it utters impugns the wisdom and righteousness of God, elevates the necessities and will of the creature above the Providences of the creator, and is in fact one of our greatest sins.

When God, by His judgments, says *now* is the time to repent. we reply that the occasion does not suit, for we have more important work on hand: and when He says, "Do this and you shall live and prosper," we answer that *we* will first secure our life and prosperity and then attend to His injunction.

He says, "Repent and you shall have my favor:" we reply,— "grant us thy forgiveness and we will repent."

He commands us to bring forth fruits meet for repentance, to show that we are in earnest by our works: we claim to have become sorry for our sins, but insist that we cannot reform our errors until the Almighty has ceased to plague us for them!

Is not this the true interpretation of all our promises of future reformation?.

And is it not in itself a sufficient cause for the continuance of all our trials?

21

If we will not turn from our offences while adversity brings them to mind, will we be likely to do it when prosperity has hardened our hearts?

Besides, if we would but reflect, we would plainly see that our circumstances are now more favorable to reforms than they will probably ever be again : ideed, no people ever had better opportunities for modeling the whole machinery of Society according to the Standard of Divine Truth.

Our young Republic has been born of the convulsions occasioned by a question which its founders refer wholly to the teachings of Holy Scripture as the only binding authority ; and thus the state is solemnly pledged to accept the whole Word of God as its rule of action.

We are cut off from intercourse with all foreign influences ; and never again can we legislate or labor in Society with such perfect exemption from the out side pressure exerted on all the States of the world.

Our government owes no obligations to any temporal power on earth : we are trammeled by no treaties or commercial regulations or necessities, by no intrigues of foreign courts, and are free from the seductions of foreign thought penetrating the national heart and coloring its sentiments through books, periodicals and the intercourse of trade.

The great tragedy in which we are acting has stimulated the national mind to unwonted energy, and prepared it to take earnest and practical hold of great and salutary truths : sectarian, party and sectional barriers are borne down by the pressure of the grand events of the times, and there is less internal strife in the nation than there probably ever will be again in our history as a free and independent people

The fierce, incendiary assaults upon our city, has, as it were, brought all the inhabitants together, high and low, bond and free, in one house : all former prejudices are now forgotten, and every mind is exercised with the one mastering thought for the common safety.

If we cannot now make our laws, our literature, our course of justice, our educational systems, our social institutions and habits, and our religious exertions reflect more purely the spirit of the Gospel, then we never can by the mere aid of opportunities : and it is time for every one to wake up to this solemn truth.

Minister of the Gospel, statesman, writer, teacher, citizen of the country, whoever you are that intend to exert yourself in a good work to put your country right before God, now, *now*, NOW, is the time for you to act: this is God's time and, therefore, the best that will ever again occur.

It is not only unsafe to delay, it is sinful: this is the day, this the hour when every one who intends to serve God in the promotion of reforms in society, is called by the voice of Heaven, and by the wail of a bleeding nation to come forward to the work.

Now is the time to preach the glorious gospel to full audiences of earnest men and women who come together to hear what God says, and not the discussions of jarring sectaries: now is the time to write good books which all will read who can lay their hands upon them, now is the time by systems of schools, common as the dews of Heaven, to prepare against popular ignorance, vice and beggary, now is the time to banish infidel literature from the schools, to expunge unjust laws from the statute book, to denounce oppression and robbery, to hunt up and expose moral abuses, to apply the knife to every sore of society.

And now, my dear countrymen, will you go forward in the path of duty, of safety, and of glory?

SCRIPTURAL VIEWS

OF

NATIONAL TRIALS

PART III.

SUGGESTIONS IN REGARD TO THE SINS FOR WHICH THE PEOPLE
OF THE CONFEDERATE STATES ARE SUFFERING.

CHAPTER II.

General reflections.

An important element in the work of reformation is the knowledge of sins to be repented of ; and whatever tends to lead to such discovery on the part of an afflicted people is an aid to their deliverance.

How is a nation to be made aware of the offences for which it is scourged ?

The first step in this direction is that general consciousness of sin which all who are smitten of God ought to feel ; and when the mind of a chastened creature is brought to this condition, and is prepared to ask for light in an humble, submissive and penitential mood, it will not fail to discover the errors from which the leadings of Providence would turn it.

This first step is the most difficult of all : indeed, when it is taken the work of reformation and deliverance is more than half accomplished.

It is very hard for the carnal heart to say with David, " I was dumb, I opened not my mouth ; because Thou didst *it*.

Remove Thy stroke away from me : I am consumed by the blow of Thy hand."—(*Ps.* xxxix. 9–10.)

Still the answer of those who are to be healed of God when He
smites them is that of the Psalmist, and of Job, when the Almighty
rebuked him: " Behold, I am vile; what shall I answer Thee? I
will lay my hand upon my mouth."—(*Job* xl 4.)

" I have heard of Thee by the hearing of the ear; but now mine
eye hath seen Thee

Wherefore I abhor *myself*, and repent in dust and ashes."—(*Job*
xlii. 5–6.)

All the inhabitants of a christian land, like that of the Confederate States, have heard of God by the hearing of the ear; for the
benefit of such all the prophets and inspired men of old have written, and before them all the centuries of the past recite their instructive lessons.

They have had in their hands the whole counsel of God; and now
this great Being speaks to them by the audible and awful voice of
His Providence.

Their eyes now see His ways in the paths of His judgments—and
if they are prepared to be healed, they will feel and confess their
vileness, and in a spirit of perfect submission and honesty, listen to
hear what is commanded.

There is no need of a new prophet; we, my beloved countrymen,
have a sure word of prophecy amply sufficient; we are not of the
night, but of the day, and should not sleep or be drunken as those
who have no light.

If we receive our afflictions with the right spirit, we will know
and confess that we are sinners, and that God is correcting us for
our offences; and when we are brought to this frame of mind, we
will at once begin to search our hearts and our past lives for the
causes of our calamities.

We are all solemnly called to make this examination: we are required to test our dispositions and conduct as professed christians,
as jurors and judges, as citizens of a republic controlled by the
people, as masters and as members of society, by that standard of truth and righteousness which has been in our hands
from the beginning, which has been faithfully expounded among us
from the first settlement of the country.

We are to take into our review everything for which we are responsible as a people and as individuals—the character of our laws
and the manner of their execution, the conduct and spirit of Church
organizations, the general management of that class of persons whom
we hold in bondage, and our individual actions and tempers,
and the frame of mind with which we have received the countless
blessings of Providence in the past.

If the whole population, feeling that the stroke of God is on it for sin, will humbly, honestly and earnestly turn its thoughts in this way, submissively and pentiently seeking Divine direction, then will the end of these afflictions be near at hand.

All inspiration tells us this : every prophet that God has sent 'o the nations proclaims this truth for our special benefit, and all the promises and attributes of Jehovah are bound for its fulfilment

Will we not remember the days of old, the works of the Lord and His wonders in the past, the displays of the power, truth, justice and mercy of God from the beginning of the world ? will we not hear His own voice speaking to us from two mountains on either side of us, from the one denouncing curses and from the other blessings?

It is both the duty and the interest of the afflicted nation to begin this work at once—and it is not to be deferred for the fear of the world's ridicule or taunts. Enemies may rage and jeer—but it will be with the inward sinking of those who know that the prey has escaped from the snare, which they had laid.

In making this examination we ought to talk freely with each other : " Then they that feared the Lord spake often one to another : and the Lord hearkened, and heard it: and a book of remembrance was written before Him for them that feared the Lord, and that thought upon His name.

And they shall be mine, saith the Lord of hosts, in the day when I make up my jewels ; and I will spare them, as a man spareth his own son that serveth him.

Then shall ye return and discern between the righteous and the wicked, between him that serveth God and him that serveth Him not."—(Mal iii. 16-18.)

Here is a clear test of those who serve the Lord, especially in times of degeneracy and trouble : the interests of their Heavenly Kingdom, the honor of God, and the promotion of His work occupy the first place in their thoughts, and this common bond draws them often together to talk of the matters nearest to their hearts.

No doubt, one cause of the continuance and complication of our troubles is the failure of the christian element of society to seek out each other, and to talk together of the condition and prospects of the Church ; for this failure indicates that there are feelings in professors stronger than the love of Christ, while it has a bad effect on the world, and prevents those discoveries and that hopeful and energetic action which follow from free communion, and mutual counsels and encouragements on the part of those engaged in a common enterprise.

According to the theory of the Church, its members are strangers and pilgrims on earth, citizens of a foreign or Heavenly kingdom: and if their feelings and actions corresponded with this theory, they would, when convulsions occurred in the land of their sojourn, draw instinctively together, and their first thoughts being of the country which they represented, they would try to shape a common course, and one most conducive to its honor and interests.

Sudden revolutions are most likely to display our strongest instincts: when our house is unexpectedly wrapt in flames, our first thoughts are for those things which we value most. At such times common interests and common sympathies overmaster all minor differences, and the ruling sentiment creates a brotherhood of feeling and a cooperation of action ; and such a spontaneous movement towards a central and common object of most tender solicitude, ought to have been witnessed among all the nominal followers of Christ, when the American troubles began. .

It is not too late to talk together of His kingdom ; there is and has been in many a heart a yearning to unfold itself to others of kindred sympathies.

To aid in right reflections and actions, I venture, in the spirit of christian love, to suggest topics for consideration ; and I do it not as one commissioned to tell my countrymen what their offences are, but from those motives with which we are commanded to confess our faults one to another, and to aid each other, and our kindred and people to escape from the revealed wrath of God, in the way of His own appointment.

THE OLD UNITED STATES.—*The discovery of the Continent and the settlement and unparalleled prosperity of North America, due alone to the Providence of God, universally treated in a way to encourage practical infidelity.*

It is more than possible that the people of the Confederate States indulge in a radical error in regard to their responsibility for the sins of the country of which they once formed a part.

When they severed their connection with the political organism known as the United States, they did not thereby become discharged from moral penalties previously incurred by the population of that country.

If God was displeased with the whole nation for its moral character, His righteous displeasure will not be appeased by a mere change of political relations; and the consequences of their sins will pursue the guilty parties into every new form of Government which they may adopt, until they manifest a sincere repentance.

Political mutations do not discharge moral obligations: if they did, then the justice of Heaven would depend on the will of its creatures.

The Southern part of the old United States exercised a very important influence on the policy and character of the whole country; from the slave States came a very large majority of the Presidents of the Republic: they furnished a large portion of the leading executive officers, and their representatives had great influence, for many years, in shaping the action of Congress.

The States of the new Confederacy must, therefore, share in the guilt of the old government of which they were integral members; and the very manner in which these constituent parts with-drew their connection from the United States, proves this proposition.

Individual men did not, in heart or word, protest against the iniquities of the land, and absolve themselves from the consequences by forsaking the country; but *political communities, in their organized capacity, and for political reasons, were the actors in the revolution which occurred.* It was not a forsaking of the whole country and of its responsibilities, by citizens, who are moral agents; but it was a dissolution of the country by a withdrawal of a portion of those political units which composed the Government, each political

22

unit consisting of large masses of men who, as individuals, were not purging their consciences of the former sins of the land, but were acting on their obligations to State Sovereignties, and aiming at the protection of their temporal interests from the usurpations, fanaticism and injustice of their former political brethren.

The people of the seceding States are, therefore, not absolved from the moral penalties incurred by the whole public of which they were formerly a part, and while they were a consenting part; and it thence becomes a matter of vital interest to them to examine carefully the past career of that country which is now arrayed in hostility against them.

They justly claim a share in all the glories of the old Union with equal justice they are partly responsible for all its crimes.

And it is more incumbent on them than on those whom they have left to make this examination: for they are now in a position to do it with more freedom and under, and are in no danger of incurring thereby the displeasure of the powers that be. They are, it is to be hoped, beyond the power of the United States: let them then, if they would escape the retributions in store for that country, purge themselves of its sins by a full and free confession, and by a sincere and humble repentance.

The intelligent and honest reader will easily recall many of these ins to mind—and to aid him in the task the following hints are submitted to his consideration.

First. The unparalleled prosperity of the country was wholly attributed to the wisdom and virtue of man. The discovery, history and settlement of America were themes which called forth feelings and ideas which were leading to practical infidelity; and indeed the whole outpouring of the American heart and mind on the subject of its own existence and condition was a loud and persistent contradiction of the testimony of God.

The great, underlying truth of human depravity and helplessness was more and more ignored; and the errors of principle and feeling fostered by unexampled prosperity to a monstrous growth had led to the perverting of all the facts of history to sustain them.

The manner in which the Continent was discovered reflects any thing else than honor on the human race: it is in fact a matter of great surprise that the existence of an immense part of the earth's surface was not dreamed of by its most intelligent inhabitants for thousands of years, and plainly indicates the impossibility of man's stumbling on the most obvious facts until God is ready to use them for the fulfilment of His wise designs. America was held back from the thoughts of philosophy until God was ready to open it up as an Asylum for the advocates of a free Bible, and the christianization of a large portion of the darkest region of the earth; and when the discovery was made it was by a person who received no countenance from the philosophy and enterprize of a learned and commercial age, and who was indebted for the means of his voyage, not to the sagacity of man, but to the simple faith of woman.

Even the discoverer had little idea of what was before him: he was not seeking a new Continent but a short passage to an old one, and thus, as it has been well said, "the pursuit of error was leading him on to truth."

The permanent settlement of a large portion of the new region was contrary to all human foresight and arrangement; the first explorers and proprietors of North America were in vain pursuit of the precious minerals and the aromatics of "the gorgeous east," and were utterly blind to what after circumstances proved to be the real advantages of the country.

The most famous statesmen and scholars of Europe, men whose names are illustrious in history, devised political, moral and municipal systems for the new settlements, all of which proved utter and ruinous failures; and the permanent institutions of the country were born of the nursing Providences of God, called accidents and circumstances, and not of the learning and foresight of men.

When the British Colonies first resisted the Mother Country, they had no idea of throwing off their allegiance; and when they did proclaim themselves a free and independent nationality, they went through a seven years' struggle without having the remotest idea that it would end in the establishment of a democratic republic. If there were any such views they are not to be found in the public deliverances of a long period of great mental activity; and the probability is that the English political system was the model before the eyes of those who were the heroes and sages of the first great American Revolution.

Here again the character of one man turns the whole tide of human expectations; and it is a fair inference from facts that a limited Monarchy was not established because he alone whom the people would have for king would not occupy such a position. It is not an honor to the human race that its deliverance from its own tendencies is made to depend on a single member of it; and the fact that there has been but one Washington in all the family of Adam, is in reality their shame and not their glory.

When the Constitution of the United States was devised, it was

most bitterly denounced and opposed by many of those who had taken the lead in the revolution from which it resulted : and among
these were the great names of Samuel Adams and Hancock in Massachusetts, of Clinton in New York, and of Henry in Virginia.

After one of the hardest struggles known in political warfare the
Constitution was adopted : unexampled prosperity followed, and for
more than half a century the teeming heart and intellect of a great,
intelligent and active nation filled the world with the written and
spoken praises of man.

Churchmen and laymen lent their influence to doctrines which
glorify man, and as a natural consequence, discredit God ; and the
whole Literature of America bore this universal burden, " The United States are the hope of the World." This infidel idea had pene
trated the hearts of the people to the remotest ends of the earth ;
and the founders of the western Republic were regarded as having
achieved a new era in the history of the human race.

Even among the most orthodox christians there was a strong disposition to put results before causes : and the christianization and
reformation of the world were made to depend on the progress of
good government, of commerce, arts and learning, while in fact these
are themselves the product of gospel influences.

No one but the Omniscient can know the extent of the evils which
the state of things briefly adverted to, was likely to entail upon the
world ; but the proud arch that lifted itself up as a new gospel to
the nations, is struck by the lightning of Heaven, and falls a hopeless ruin on the heads of those who would have elevated it above the
Power which reared it.

This disastrous overthrow seems now to fill the earth with dark
ness ; but the people had turned from the true sun, and were walking in the light of sparks of their own kindling.

The real hope of the world, the Author of our past blessings still
remains ; and now that vain illusions are extinguished, the nations
will be in better condition to turn to Him, and to the conditions of
His mercies.

There has been, indeed, a woful destruction on this once happy
and peaceful continent ; but in these vast ruins a pernicious error
has found a grave, and from the smouldering heap a glorious and
healthful Truth will spring.

The moral of all the facts adverted to is this : to the wisdom and
providence and mercy of God alone are due the discovery of America, and all the good laws, good government, peace and security and
happiness of the people.

The depravity of man was ever in the way of all the good results that have occurred; but the All-wise Disposer was continually directing circumstances, contrary to all human foresight, to the beneficent ends which filled the world with light and hope.

But all this teaching was perverted—American history was a great Pantheistic Temple where incense was daily burned at a thousand idol shrines—the American idea was a grand falsehood, attributing to the theories and forms of government the virtues of the causes from which these forms and systems sprang, claiming for the civilization of the times the power to foster and sustain the very Truths from which all the good characteristics of that civilization flowed.

Therefore, in mercy to the world, God left man for a moment to himself, and at that period in history when he could profit most by the experience of the past, by the universal diffusion of learning, by the most useful and beneficent arts, and by the most perfect forms, systems and laws; and the Truth of Revelation receives another awful and impressive demonstration in the instant fall of the creature from his lofty heights, with irretreivable ruin and combustion down to a horrid abyss of strife, carnage, slavery, want and wretchedness.

His mad passions pervert the very institutions to which he attributed all his prosperity, to purposes of oppression and robbery; and when his victims would escape from his political connection, he instantly revolutionizes the theory and spirit of his government to adapt it to his own passion for conquest, spoliation, murder and rapine.

And thus, the continent but a few days ago, smiling like the garden of Eden, is now one wide scene of smoking desolation—and a people looked to over the whole earth as godlike, with every advantage of education and experience, the freest, the most prosperous, the most wealthy, the most abounding in every material and mental resource, in all useful arts, in all moral agencies, of any race ever sprung from the loins of Adams, are, in the very proudest day of their strength, suddenly transformed into besotted mad-men, putting forth the most phrensied energies for the immediate destruction of all they once held dear, and hurrying themselves with amazing velocity from the proudest heights of christian civilization to the lowest depths of savage brutality.

Thus, the world is made, in this dreadful manner, to unlearn the false philosophy which all America was diligently teaching; and the people of the States receding from the old Confederacy are caused to suffer from the insanity of those whom they have left, because they were guilty with them in encouraging the practical infidelity before referred to.

They never repudiated—indeed, they ardently believed in the great American delusion of man's perfectibility by human agencies; and in all their movements since the disruption, they indicate the existence of the old leaven.

They based the former glory of the American people on political agencies; they display the same principle in tracing the degeneracy of this age to similar causes.

When the Confederates desire to be unlike their enemies merely in civil institutions, they thereby manifest a participation in the grand ideas of the North; and that is, in the belief, that the character of a people depends on forms of Government, that justice and injustice, virtue and vice have their origin in political or municipal regulations.

Good government results from private and public virtue—and all virtue is the offspring of gospel influences.

This is the whole philosophy of political progress and degeneracy; and this is the lesson the people of the Confederate States must learn before their troubles will prepare them for greatness.

They must cease from man—they must mourn over their former idolatries, must feel and confess that their former glorying in man and in man's inventions was their shame, must tear from their hearts that proud philosophy which has become a part of their nature, and with humility confess that their past history, like the history of every race, only illustrates the wisdom and goodness of God and the depravity and folly of man.

The palmy days of the old Republic must not be allowed to inspire any feeling of self-sufficiency: that bright and glorious era which now seems like a dream of the past, must not be permitted to countenance, for a moment, the fallacious idea of the inherent virtue of any race of fallen men.

We must surrender the glories of the past as not our own: when we claimed them as man's proud inheritance, we robbed God and made Him a liar.

Man in his natural state, is the same depraved creature everywhere, with evil and downward instincts; and when he is lifted to a high elevation in the scale of being, and made the instrument of illustrious actions, it is through the refining and ennobling influences of the Gospel to whose beneficent power he is everywhere naturally hostile.

It is a hard lesson for mortals, raised up under the traditions of America, to learn that the glory of their past history is God's; but it must be taught or the people concerned will be hopelessly ruined.

The repudiation of God and confidence in man is the cause of the awful tragedy now being enacted : the abasing of the creature, and the just exaltation of the source of every good and perfect gift, will lead all concerned to even a more happy state than any condition of the past.

If men, and forms of Government, are the sole reliance of a people, they will become the victims of a cruel and unjust tyranny, whether they adopt a republican, monarchical or imperial system: if the heart of the nation is, to any large extent, purified by the gospel of Christ, the condition of the masses will be upward and onward whatever the nominal character of their political system.

And the doctrine of human depravity must be practically felt, and carried to all its legitimate results ; it must be applied to nations as well as to individuals, to our own people as well as to foreigners, to our fathers and to our children, to men in republics and men in monarchies, to the voters in a free democracy, to the electors in an oligarchy, to the dictators or kings, or emperors in absolute powers.

We must expect error, frailty, passion, prejudice and folly to be innate characteristics of unconverted men in all social conditions, and in every political system : to be ruling elements in savage and civilized nature, in every unsanctified depository of human power, whether it be an individual, a select few, or the whole body of citizens.

These tendencies will, of course, be greatly modified by circumstances ; but after all, the controlling power of even circumstances will depend on the amount of vital godliness in the heart of the nation.

It is to be expected that where the power of a state really reposes in the entire mass of citizens, there will be a more equitable administration, and more respect for the rights and welfare of all : self-interest, in such a community, is the interest of the whole state, and the greater the number of persons there are concerned in carrying on a system of policy, the greater the conflict of passion and prejudice, and the less probability there is that any individual or clique will be able to level every interest to its own narrow views. In addition to all this, where the sovereignty of the country is in all its people, each individual is a sort of mirror to every other, and there is a free uncovering of each other's vices and errors, while every one's selfish propensities meet a strong check in the rival tendencies of all others.

But such freedom cannot long exist without a pure religious sentiment of controlling power ; and all the world now sees, in the

... of the United States, a solemn, and painful but wholesome ... of the eternal truths of God.

A self-interest as obvious as the day, ought to restrain that peo... attempt to conquer the Confederate States; the very desire to subjugate another people is an ignoring of the spirit of their own institutions, and the efforts put forth must, in their nature, extinguish the last spark of popular rights

What will the *people* of the United States gain even if the *Government* succeeds in subjugating a brave and determined nation, inhabiting a vast extent of territory?

They will be burdened with enormous taxes—they will be subjects of a power which must be imperial to preserve itself, which must keep in service immense armies and navies, and which must have unlimited authority over the men and means of its own country.

Its power to make and hold conquests will be utterly inconsistent with republican ideas: and while its own people must thus become slaves to the central and colossal despotism which they would build up to enslave others, inequalities in society will rapidly supervene, the rich few will become richer, the many poor will become poorer, and the chance of losing its foreign conquests will be a never-failing excuse for domination, exaction, corruption, injustice and cruelty at home

It would seem that any rational mind can understand all this, but are such views, so obvious and so convincing, of any force among the maddened populace of the United States?

What then is the moral? Are these people the most ignoble or the most ignorant of the earth? They have been famous for their knowledge of their own interests, they are undoubtedly an enlightened people, and the masses have been, heretofore, comparatively sober, industrious and self relying.

Has republicanism proved a failure?

To account for this course on this ground is to be guilty of a supreme absurdity: for the very essence of the charge against them is that they have surrendered their rights as freemen and are the willing and ready vassals of a fierce, cruel and treacherous despotism.

Shall we say that republicanism is not a good form of government because it is overthrown by other forms not so desirable?

If the objection to a republic is that a one man power follows it, how can a one man power be more desirable? Is it not the height of folly to say a one man power is the better form of Government because when the chief authority is vested in the body of the people they will afterwards choose a single ruler?

This is equivalent to arguing that it is better to be sick than well, as health, if abused, leads to sickness: better never to live at all than to enjoy life, as death will follow life.

It is time for the people of the Confederate States to discard all this reasoning in a circle, all those transparent subterfuges of an infidelity, which would account for the painful phenomena of human existence by any absurdity rather than by the Truth : and to receive in all their length and breadth the infallible teachings of inspired Writ.

Man is depraved—and in his natural state he is capable of any folly, of any crime, of any abomination. If left to himself he will act on the law of his nature as an individual, and in masses : he will do so in the savage and in the civilized state, and his own passions would make for him a hell in any region. The unconverted, individual heart, is, under Satan, the source, the primary fountain of all the abominations that vex the earth : here, in the bosoms of kings, of oligarchs, of democrats, of philosophers, of the sons of saints, martyrs, prophets and apostles, in every soul of man born into the world, in whatever condition, of whatever parentage, however polished by learning and art, there are the seeds which, if left to themselves, if not eradicated by the power of the Gospel, will ripen into those curses which fill the earth with fraud, violence and mourning.

It is not the form of Government that produces a great race of men : it is a race of godly men that establishes wise, just and beneficent systems.

The glorious days of the old Republic of the United States were but a natural part of the fruit of those causes which raised up the men of '76—and the spirit of the age of '76, as far as it was good, and wise, and self-denying and far-sighted, was an out-growth that had its living roots in a soil not seen by the common observer, in a former, vivifying christianity now forgotten.

The elevated and truly heroic spirit of that first revolution, the constitution and laws which followed, and all the subsequent happiness and prosperity of the Continent of North America, are the growth of one seminal principal, sown broad-cast upon the land long before : and that was the vital godliness of the mass of that sturdy race who settled the country and whose Text-book, in all things, was the Word of God.

And all the evils of this Second Revolution—the fanaticism which first kindled the fires of sectional hate, the perversity which violated solemn national compacts and trampled under feet the guarantees of a wise and just Constitution—the madness which drove a numerical majority to attempted spoliation of the rights of their brethren, and the subsequent disruption of the Union of the States, with a fierce and unrighteous war entailing untold calamities on aggressors and defendants, and the blind infatuation which still hurls the vindictive assailants upon greater and greater atrocities, all these are the bitter fruits of seeds that have long been growing in the furrows of the field.

When we began to celebrate the praises of man as the founder of American prosperity, we commenced to plant for the harvest of death; and at last these doctrines reached, in one end of the land, their natural culmination in that monstrous self-esteem which is a wild delirium, an intense idolatry of self, inconsistent with peace, freedom or justice.

Let the people of the Confederate States then beware: let them truly repent of former sins in this matter, and let them, by their actions, bring forth the fruits of repentance.

Let them take down the idol shrines that crowd their history—let them cut down their groves, and demolish their high places, and let them write in every niche, once dedicated to the image of creatures, "God only is great—man is vile." Let the christian element of society display its faith in the gospel it preaches by relying on that for the reformation of the world: by setting itself to the work of human progress by directing all its energies to the conversion of individual souls, and the purification of the primary springs of national life by the means of God's appointment.

CHAPTER III.

Sins of the old United States, continued.—Aggressive character of the country towards weaker powers, and its demoralizing tendency at home.—Ingratitude of the people for the peculiar blessings of Divine Providence.—Failure of the Church to discharge the obligations imposed by its great opportunities.

Another sin of the people of the United States before the dissolution of the old Union was there aggressive character towards other communities. God had bestowed on them nearly a whole continent for a possession; and they had no neighbors sufficiently strong to excite any apprehensions. They were separated by oceans from the great powers of the world, and were less exposed to injury from without than any nation that ever existed; their resources were comparatively unlimited, their public burdens were very light; and they produced within themselves nearly everything important to their prosperity, and furnished to the world the staple which was deemed most essential for its clothing, and large quantities of food, fuel and timber.

The people felt the advantage of their position; and the country bore itself in a proud, insolent and defiant manner towards other powers.

It was a great, swaggering bully in the streets of the world, ready to take offence on the slightest grounds, and seeking pretexts for quarrels with those of inferior strength: it was a giant which knew its superior power, and was disposed to use it unjustly, because it could do it with impunity.

It advanced claims inconsistent with the rights and honor of others; and it was always over sensitive and ready for a quarrel with those whose territories lay contiguous, and which it knew, in case of a fight, could be appropriated.

To cover its greedy aims, it sanctified its lust under the blasphemous assumption of a manifest destiny to live, extend and rule: thus claiming that the Providence of God was but the nurse and prop of its ambition, and that the Divine counsels could not do otherwise than bend to its interests.

In short, this doctrine of manifest destiny meant simply that the ambitious purposes of the United States were the highest law of the universe; and that the Moral Economy of God, hitherto pro-

ceeding on immutable principles, was now to adopt itself to the interests, whims and wishes of a people who could not injure others
nor destroy themselves by any violation of the eternal laws of right.

Acting on these views the government respected its plighted faith
only when it seemed to be its interest to do so ; and it was its fixed
policy to endeavor to strengthen itself with its own people and to
excite their enthusiasm by appeals to the worst passions of fallen
Nature.

It acted on that most abominable maxim that the end justifies the
means ; and having the power, it would not scruple to infringe on
the rights of others, and justify itself before its own public on the
plea that their interest required it, and that this apparent interest
was the supreme law of Heaven and earth.

The people became accustomed to the idea that when the glory
and power of the country seemed to demand it, the claims of absolute justice were synonymous with disloyalty ; and when gain
was made by foreign aggression, it was patriotic and becoming to
applaud the measure, however accomplished. He was a foe to the
country, and an adherent of its enemies who ever questioned the
propriety of its encroachments ; and a government founded on the
principle of the inherent and inalienable right of every community
to choose its own political system, acted on the idea that the forci-
ble extension of its institutions among others was the greatest blessing that could be bestowed upon them.

These open and persistent perversities of sacred principles by the
whole nation in its organized capacity, soon manifested their inevitable fruits ; and the economy which controlled the Government in
its exterior relations exerted a poisonous influence on the internal
condition of things.

The nation or community which uses the principles of the Evil
One as allies in foreign contests, must expect them to remain as mis-
chievous guests ; and the principles which controlled the foreign
policy of the United States became the code or standard for domestic communities in their conduct to each other.

The action of the Government in seeking to strengthen itself at
home by a constantly aggressive attitude abroad, did much to unsettle, in the popular mind, the sacredness of public compacts ; and
as the Federal Sovereignty pandered to the depraved instincts of
the whole populace to that extent that it became a test of patriotism to sustain every movement which encroached upon exterior
powers, so the states were encouraged to put a loose construction on
their compacts with each other.

If a politician, aspiring to national eminence, found the shortest and surest road to power in advocating national aggrandizement at the expense of other nations, was it not natural that demagogues aspiring to rule the States, should make their way through local prejudices, and by claiming that their own communities were interested in aggressions on the rights of others?

The Federal Government was the mirror and glass of fashion to the state authorities; and as it became the settled policy of the former to sustain itself at home by a bullying attitude to its equals, or other national sovereignties, so the latter were disposed to exalt themselves in popular estimation by a disregard of their obligations to each other.

In the central capitol the national politicians competed with each other for national preeminence in violent efforts to inflame the passions of the citizens of the United States against the rights and interests of other powers; and so the capitols of Massachusetts and Vermont became theatres in which rival demagogues vied for the applause of their home audiences by incendiary appeals to their prejudices against Virginia and South Carolina.

The disregard for constitutional guaranties manifested by state authorities, and their violation of their compacts with each other, was but a development of the national policy, the home application of a principle practised in foreign affairs; and when it was claimed that the will of numerical majorities was the supreme law, above all written stipulations, what was it but the logical application to the internal or domestic economy of the Government of that principle, held sacred in its foreign policy, that it had a right to do whatever its interests demanded, and it had the power to accomplish?

If its manifest destiny had placed the whole country above all systems of ethics and above those inexorable rules of moral right by which all other nations had to stand or fall, on the same ground the decision of the majority of voters of the country was the fiat of fate, and the standard of all political justice.

Therefore, the claim of the free-soilers that they had the right to do whatever they had the physical power to effect, was the legitimate fruit of a tree which the whole nation had planted, nourished and declared to be sacred; and the declaration that minorities of states, in the Federal system, had no rights, was nothing more nor less than the home application of the doctrine of the Confederacy that the United States, because it was the strongest power in America, was the sole arbiter of its destinies.

Thus, the unrighteous ethics of our foreign code were a two-edged sword that cut both ways; and the unjust and unholy ambition which sanctified the lust of foreign domination as the law of God, war, by the righteous retributions of the Divine Arbiter, made an effectual instrument for the eternal dismemberment of the power which would have used the doctrine for the extension of its dominion over a large portion of the globe.

It was said by Shakespeare that our pleasant sins (those to which we are most fondly attached) are made whips for our chastisement; and this was but a poetical rendering of the great principle of Divine Truth, " Whoso diggeth a pit shall fall therein ; and he that rolleth a stone, it will return upon him."—(*Prov.* xxvi. 27.)

The people of the Confederate States can easily see that the conduct of that party which caused a dismemberment of the old Union is abominable; but let them remember with humiliation and penitence that they helped to nourish into life and vigor the doctrine which fanaticism has borrowed to work their destruction. They did not make the fanatics; but they assisted in urging the weapons with which these incendiaries destroyed the most glorious political fabric known in history.

We helped to feed, to pet and ready reared a fierce beast dangerous to the peace and integrity of other nations, and we hissed on when it terrified and tore the weak wayfarers beyond our camp; and if now its whelps have followed their native instincts in biting and tearing us, wherein are they more odious than the parent which we assisted in raising?   •

And when we ask to be delivered from the power of a fierce and cruel assailant, why should we not first desire to have washed out from our souls the guilt of a principle on which he acts ? We must not only repudiate and detest this doctrine as used by our enemies for our destruction—but we must sincerely confess and repent of our offences when hugging it to our hearts for our own aggrandizement.

If it is wicked when turned against us, it was unrighteous when used for our advancement : and as we can see how hateful it is in the conduct of the present United States, we have an opportunity of judging the character of our conduct when we were a responsible part of the same nation and aided in fostering its aggressive spirit towards all the American world.

We shared in the abomination that it was the manifest destiny of this one power to swallow the continent ; and we stood stoutly for that Monroe doctrine that Europe had no right to interfere in any way with the international affairs of the new world.

When we maintained this principle, we were part of a Confederacy which was more than a match for all its neighbors on the Continent; and when we thought that if the strong powers of the old world could be kept aloof, we could give the law to America, and extend ourselves over it at our leisure, or control it to our purposes.

Now, the Confederate States, in the infancy of their existence, and without a navy, belong, temporarily, to the weaker powers, that is weaker in numbers and in means of national defence, other than the heroic hearts and strong arms of its people; and in this condition, the aggressive nation of which this was once a part, would strike it to the earth and grind it to powder, by opposing, in its attempt at separate nationality, those wicked traditions of "the manifest destiny of the United States," which it helped to foster.

The people of the Confederate States can, also, see how heartless is the course of Europe in refusing by legitimate means to give moral aid to a nation struggling for existence and liberty against a proud, ambitious and cruel power which would exterminate them solely because their destruction would enhance its greatness; and yet is not Europe, from what motives it is not for the writer to say, acting strictly on that Monroe doctrine for which we were extremely jealous?

The "United States," as a power, though impaired in strength, still remains; and upon the Confederate States it is warring with the traditions of national policy which the Confederates helped to foster when a part of the Government.

It becomes them then to repent of doctrines from whose results they would be delivered: to deplore the part they took in casting into the national heart the intolerance of a rival and the lust for dominion from which they now so cruelly suffer. If it was ever right in the United States to over-run all neighboring American communities against their will, it is still right: it is not wrong in that country to seek to abate as a nuisance an adjoining power merely because we have left it. *It was never right:* and while it is to us Confederates a sacrifice of pride to acknowledge this, we have no reason to claim Divine intervention till we do so. Our request for the aid of God against our ambitious assailants is an appeal to Him to condemn and defeat doctrines which we once cherished: and is it not a mockery of the Divine justice to expect it to oppose principles when they work against us, and to favor them when they can be used for our aggrandizement? Let us see, in part of the conduct of the United States, the development of our own doctrines; and let us, with this horrid picture before us, throw dust on our heads, and coarse ourselves for the part we took in creating and fostering that insatiate greediness, that wicked assumption of an inherent, Divine right to domineer over all America which has culminated in one of the most terrible wars in history.

It is not to be denied that the people of the United States are greatly encouraged to the immense sacrifices they are making by the delusive hope of having a continent under the control of one power; and before the disruption of the old Union the population of the Confederate States helped to foster this idea of a single dominion for America.

We must, therefore, repudiate the doctrine of one dominion for America, not simply because we are no longer interested in it. We must repent of the sin of having aided in nourishing this unholy lust of universal control, and must see, with humiliation, in the present unrighteous conduct of the United States the bitter fruits of a principle for which we are, in part, responsible.

THIRDLY. The population of the old United States were the most ungrateful on earth; and from this sin no section was exempt.

The people of the Southern States long had reason to complain of their Northern neighbors; and the discontents growing out of the aggressive and constitution-despising spirit of Abolitionism are not referred to here as part of the evidence of the charge preferred above.

It was a characteristic of the whole population to murmur at every thing; and so far from cherishing a lively sense of their infinite and peculiar blessings the people were continually complaining of the ways of Providence.

The seasons, in their estimation, were always too wet or too dry, too cold or too hot: their State taxes, light as the webs of the gossamer compared with the public burdens of other nations, and always levied for the good of the masses, and returned to them with a thousand fold interest, often excited the most scandalous complaints.

It is not necessary to dwell on this subject: the public mind will itself recall recollections whose force words cannot enhance.

The language of America was one of complaint, of reproaches, of bitter murmurings: every little disappointment or cross was greatly magnified, a spirit of restless discontent pervaded the whole population, and there was hardly any disposition to see and know and confess with gratitude their peculiar obligations to God.

The beneficent Being, who in infinite Mercy to us, brought us to these shores, remote from the corruptions, trials and wars of the old world, and planted and nourished us here, is now giving us an opportunity to survey the past and to see how shamefully we requited His goodness ; and if these troubles should produce only such fruits as these the result will be good.

FOURTHLY. The professed christianity of the old United States did not discharge the one hundredth part of its obligations to its chosen Master.

It is not pretended that the nominal Church does any where receive in their obvious spirit the injunctions of its Divine Head ; it is admitted that the great body of professed believers has generally failed and most lamentably failed to manifest by its acts any just appreciation of the purposes of God in making man a co-worker with Him in the building up of His Kingdom on earth.

The purposes are too plain to be mistaken ; and no part of the Holy Scriptures is more explicit and emphatic than those passages which define the position and duties of the professed believer.

The christian is not his own, he is bought with a price—he is a soldier of the cross—he is a missionary sent into all the world to preach the Gospel to every creature.

In short, to give himself and all he has, to the edification and extension of the Church ; and however the carnal mind may theorize, refine and act, the passages which teach this doctrine are as plain as language can be made, and they recognize no exceptions of persons, of places or of periods.

Judged by the unmistakable standard revealed in the Word of God, the Church in modern times would not be recognized but for its name ; the picture is so unlike the original that it can be known only by its label.

But the faults of one part of the believing world do not excuse those of another : and, in fact, the circumstances under which America was colonized, and the opportunities which its people have had of learning lessons from the history of their mother countries, constitute them debtors to the failings of others.

They have been instructed by the sins of other nations and by their consequences ; and the christian public of the United States have enjoyed, in knowledge and in means, such opportunities of doing good as were never before vouchsafed to any people.

The political power never pretended to interfere with spiritual affairs : the Church, in a worldly sense, enjoyed unexampled prosperity, commanding the respect of the whole community, and embracing a very large proportion of the wealth, learning, enterprise and influence of the country.

The nation was respected and feared in every part of the earth—

ts commerce reached every part of the globe, and its citizens were found prosecuting, in safety, the pursuits of pleasure and gain wherever men, civilized or savage, existed.

The people were not, as in other places, monopolized by the struggle for the mere means of existence; and the nominal Church of the United States, if it had been actuated, by the spirit of the apostolic age, could have evangelized the whole known world.

It is unnecessary to dwell on the subject; the facts of the Church's condition and operations placed in connection with the injunctions of Scripture would present to the mind of the earnest christian a most deplorable picture.

It seemed that Americans were destined to enjoy an exemption from the original discipline of constitution imposed on the Church militant; and action everywhere indicated the belief that the self-denials, the toils, the self-dedication demanded in Holy Writ of the disciples of Christ were intended only for the earlier and darker ages. The army of the cross, as it increased in numbers and worldly equipment, became more and more inert, luxurious and effeminate; and the vast legions enlisted under the Saviour's banners were quartered in easy barracks, were mustered only for holyday review, and never seemed to dream that they had been recruited for actual service in the field. The soldiers of the kingdom were distinguished from the world only by a uniform or badge; and with the exception of a little band of volunteers, did nothing for the service but inscribe their names on the muster rolls, and lived and acted as if there was profound peace between their Master and his enemy.

Their officers seemed to indicate, by their conduct, the belief that they were placed in command only for the purpose of recruiting and of carrying their troops through an easy drill; and thus a great and well-appointed army was employing itself only with idle evolutions while the adversary was everywhere filling the world with desolations.

CHAPTER IV.

SINS OF THE CONFEDERATE STATES.

Negro Slavery, and the position of the Government in regard to it, offers to the Church immense advantages which have been only partially used for the propagation of the gospel.

While the people of the Confederate States are required to answer for offences of which they are guilty in common with the other populations of what was once the United States, they are also called to an account for sins which belong more peculiarly to themselves.

And first among these will be mentioned the action of the christian public towards that race who are apparently one of the leading causes of the present terrible struggle.

Undoubtedly, the whole continent has offended against the justice of Heaven in its conduct towards the African element of society and not the least fearful of the accounts is that which is owed by those who profess to be the peculiar friends of the negro.

But the sins of abolitionists do not justify those of masters; and in fact, the responsibility of the latter class is enhanced by the conduct of the former.

The fanatical agitators of the North have been a means of placing the christian public of the South in the most advantageous position for usefulness ever enjoyed by the Church; and to this subject the special and earnest attention of the reader is directed.

There has been an exhausting discussion in regard to the rightfulness of slavery as it exists in America, in both its political and moral aspects; and the result has been the general repudiation, at the South, of all mere human authority on the subject.

All classes of the community, in the Confederate States, have agreed that the Word of God is the only Source of Truth on the subjects which have most agitated society in America; and thus, by universal consent and choice, the Bible has been adopted, in slaveholding states, as the only Text Book in regard to those great social and political questions which distinguish them from the rest of the world.

It was said by the old reformers that the Bible is the religion of Protestants; and now, in the latter ages, these inspired Oracles have been adopted by a whole nation as its political creed.

On one subject at least—in regard to the fundamental principle of their existence, the slaveholding states of Protestant America have long occupied the position once held by the Jews: they have as people, as political organism, chosen God for their Lawgiver, and agreed to be governed by His Word.

And, thus, has the Almighty Arbiter turned the wicked agitations of infidel reformers to the glory of His own name; and those who have endeavored to pervert His Word have succeeded only in giving it greater power.

Have christians of the slaveholding states availed themselves of his grand result of a controversy begun for very different purposes?

Have they been quick to perceive the breach made for them, and to enter with all the reforming power of Divine Truth, into the very heart of the state?

The law-makers of their country have said to the Church, "We build our institutions on the authority of that Word on which you are founded: we discard all other teaching, and on this alone we will stand or fall. Tell us what the Scriptures teach in regard to the lawfulness of slavery—and make known this doctrine and our position in regard to it to all the people."

What a glorious opportunity was here presented to christians!—And what have they done?

Did they reply to the State, that it must receive and abide by the *whole* testimony of its own witness—and did they exert themselves to enforce what the Scriptures command in regard to the duties of Masters? Did they say to the politicians, "As you have agreed to take the Word of God for the corner stone of your political structure, you must build according to this foundation: if you base the *rights of Masters* on this authority alone, you are bound by your own acts, to be guided solely by it in the *regulation of their duties?*"

This was the plain course for the Church—but has it not failed to see and pursue it?

When the *rightfulness* of slavery was discussed, christians have been bold to reject all human teaching, were not ashamed, as they ought not to have been, to repudiate the authority of some of their own political fathers, and of the most eminent names of men; but when they came to the *obligations* of those owning slaves, they have indicated a subjection to the influence of human opinion, infirmity and passion.

When vindicating the *claims* of the governing class, the disputants had the courage to rise above all the actions, teachings, denunciations and taunts of men in every walk, of communities, of nations

and of the world, and to repose on the unclouded summits of Divine
Truth; but in the treatment of the *obligations* of this class, even
christians yielded to the force of habit and of prejudice, and what
was worst of all, allowed the actions and opinions of vile and atheis-
tic abolitionists to determine their line of duty !

Reforms which the conscience of the whole Church felt were demanded, sternly demanded by the immutable Law of God, were ad-
journed for the reason that an attempt to effect them would be considered as a triumph to the free-soilers; and thus while we could
face the sneers of the whole world in defending our *interests*, we
could not endure the gibes of fanatics in the prosecution of our *duties* !

The Church confined itself almost wholly to one view of the Bible
doctrine in regard to slavery; and although its own States offered
to it the most glorious opportunity of declaring and enforcing the
whole counsel of God, it permitted a foreign faction of bigoted tra-
ducers of itself and perverters of Divine Truth, to control its action !

The uniform plea for not urging reforms demanded by the very
authority on which the institution of slavery was sustained, was that
it might increase the influence and power of the opposers of Truth :
a reason which carried absurdity on its very face. The slavery defended by the Scriptures is the slavery conducted according to their
injunctions; and as the abolitionists were very generally infidels,
and the Southern Church regarded itself as the Champion of Divine
Truth, it was certainly a very false inference to suppose that the full
enforcement of Bible doctrines would be a triumph to the enemies
of the Bible.

Will God permit the faithful teaching of His own Truth to weaken
its power ?

Will He permit its just application to strengthen His enemies ?

The truth is, and it is a melancholy one, while the State was open
and ready for just reforms, the Church was afraid to advocate them :
afraid, in fact, not of God, nor of the triumph of His enemies, but
of the taunts and ridicule of His and of its enemies, and of the passions of man at home.

But, in the Providence of God, the reason alleged for inaction in
matters confessed to be of vital moment, has now passed away : abolitionists have done their utmost, and the State has openly defied
their efforts.

The Confederate States of America is a Government composed of
States which have forever severed their political connection with

be fanatics who have disturbed their peace in the old Union of the
United States; and this struggle which now shakes the world speaks
a voice which it is impossible to mistake.

The people of the new Government have formed themselves into
this relation for the protection of their rights; and they are now
shut out from the world, and thrown wholly on their own resources,
and are contending against the most enormous military armament
ever raised on earth.

They are submitting to sacrifices such as were never before made
by a nation for other than a religious cause: they are united to a
man, and are doing and enduring what will entitle them to the de-
signation of heroic, in all coming history.

To these toils and privations they are encouraged by the Church:
they are exhorted to stand thus, released from the nations, and to
venture their lives on every earthly occasion in defense of their
cause. And what is the cause?

It is one of human rights: it is, in truth, the cause merely of
the rights, the temporal rights of the enslavers.

And can the Church thus encourage the State to encounter the treason of a foreign nation, and to submit to every
affliction that a life can sustain, for political rights, and still refuse
to contend for what is inculcated by the command of God Almighty, under the plea that a defence of the whole Truth might lead
to trouble from abroad? It tells its people to stand up for their
temporal privileges, and to meet every danger which a world in arms
can bring upon them; it justly bids them not to heed or care for the
opinion, the threats or the denunciations of their fellow men,
but heroically to stand by their cause as long as there is an arm to
wield a weapon. All this the christian element of society rightly
feels that it can afford to do, and in acting thus, it discharges its
duty to the State; and why cannot it be equally bold in its advocacy
of the interests of its spiritual kingdom?

Had it, long ago, attempted the reforms which the Law of God
demands, it could not have encouraged the fanatics of the North to
do more than they have already attempted ———. All the non-
slaveholding States are banded together now in a fierce, cruel and
savage attempt to exterminate the ruling race of the Confederate
States—and what more can they do? They can laugh at us if we
attempt reforms: and a Church that can stimulate its people to the
most tremendous sacrifices in defence of their civil rights, cannot
afford to encourage them to the performance of moral obligations
for fear of the ridicule of those enemies whose devilish hatred is already pouring on them all the vials of its wrath!

The more we consider the plea under which the criminal christianity of the Confederate States has sheltered itself from the performance of its obvious duties in regard to slavery, the more ridiculous and shameful it seems; but whatever the nature of this excuse before the present revolution, it no longer exists at all.

The hard logic of events has removed all cause for this shallow pretext; and now that there can be no longer any fears about encouraging the abolitionists, why does not the christian public call for those reforms whose importance it has always admitted?

Why does not the Church bear its testimony in favor of the sacredness of the marriage relation, even in slaves, and in favor of ameliorations of the whole system of servitude which the Law of God and the spirit of christianity require?

The answer now is, that the time is inconvenient; in other words, the Church seems to say, " We are too busy now in maintaining the rights of masters to attend to considerations growing out of their duties."

What is the nature of *this* plea?

We all appeal to God to aid us in the defence of our *rights* as the proprietors of slaves, and defend ourselves before Him and the world by His Word: and yet when called on to perform the *obligations* which those rights entail, and which that Word inseparably couples with them, we ask to be excused to a more convenient time! Will God trust us?

Will the world believe us in earnest when we profess to place ourselves on the Divine Law?

And what is infinitely more important, will God regard us as sincere in our expressed determination to make the whole subject of slavery hereafter conform to His requirements?

The truth is—(and it is said with diffidence of it)—the Church, as a body, is not as ripe for improvements in our slave codes, the State; and while the latter has furnished to it the most glorious opportunities for usefulness, it has so far failed to enter on a mission commanded to it by its Divine Head, and to which it has been encouraged by the circumstances and the disposition of the country.

It is extremely probable that God is now chastising the country for its sins in connection with the subject of slavery—and that the author may not be misunderstood he will venture to suggest, in a brief form, what in his estimation, these offences are:

First, In the neglect, on the part of the Church, as a body, to exert itself, according to its knowledge and opportunities, for the enlightenment of the public mind as to the whole counsel of God on the subject of slavery.

No one can deny that christians have permitted themselves to be too much monopolized with one question connected with the institution of slavery, and that is its lawful use according to Scripture; while, under any circumstances, they ought to have been equally jealous in inculcating what the infallible Word teaches in regard to the obligations of masters and servants.

No condition of things is ever an excuse for the silence of the Church as to the command of God; but in the region now constituting the Confederate States, the public authorities interposed no difficulties in the way of a faithful exposition of the Divine Law in relation to the duties of every class of society. And not only was there no danger of persecution or commotion from the promulgation of the doctrines of the whole Divine Code, but the political world assumed a position directly inviting to such a course. As already stated, the discussion of the subject of slavery compelled its advocates to repudiate all human authority, and to rely on the Bible as their only defence; and when they were shut up to this Book, they had to claim for it that it was the Word of God, and the infallible standard of right. Now, the Church is supposed to be versed in all the requirements of this Word—and the world naturally looks to christians for expositions of its teachings.

And whether the world depends on the church or not, for information as to what is commanded in these Sacred Oracles, it, the world, in the Confederate States, has chosen them as its political text-book—and thus it was compelled, by its own agreement, to receive and obey all its injunctions. It could not call a witness and receive and reject its testimony according to its own views of its interests; it was bound to abide by all that was said in the writing which it introduced as evidence in its behalf.

Thus, the christian public was literally invited to come forward and enforce the whole teaching of this Word in regard to every relation of life; and at any time it could have done so, and commanded the respectful attention of the State.

And what are the facts?

Where are the solemn deliverances of the Church in regard to the sacredness of the marriage relation, in every class of society? What has it done for parent and child? Where are the evidences of its efforts to secure a more complete observance of the sabbath, by warning masters that they who cause others to violate the law are themselves participators in the crime?

When and where has it taught, with the weight of a public and solemn deliverance, that if the management of masters was such as to compel their slaves to use the sabbath for their own secular work, the proprietors were responsible?

All confess that our slave code is not what it ought to be—and do not all know that this has resulted more from the want of just information on the part of legislators and the world, than from any feelings of cruelty towards the slave? All the world knows, or ought to know, how kindly masters, in America, are inclined towards their servants: why has not advantage been taken of this position of things, to have a slave code, wise and just, based on the teachings of eternal Truth?

" The priest's lips should keep knowledge, and they should seek the law at his mouth: for he is the messenger of the Lord of hosts," (*Mal.* ii. 7;) and among all the discussions of slavery by our learned and orthodox ministry, how little has been said or written on that branch of the subject which really most concerns us!

It is not the duty of the slaveholding States to convince the outside world that they are right—but it is a duty, a solemn obligation of christians there, to endeavor to see to it that the institution of slavery conducted on Bible principles. Yet what a waste of learning there has been on the former subject!—an expenditure of argument ending only in the more bitter opposition of those outside enemies, and in their open attempt by violence, fraud and savage cruelty to change the state of things among us to their own notions.

And how little has been said or written on the latter branch of the matter, and the one only in which it would have been profitable to engage in discussion! The enemies of our State did not want to know the truth, and the spirit which animated them plainly showed that if they were beaten in argument, they intended to resort to brute force; while masters at home were open to conviction, and ready to follow what was plainly demonstrated to be the path of duty and, therefore, of interest.

There has undoubtedly been a great offence here; and if the Church permits *any* excuse to prevent it from entering *at once, right now,* on its proper work, it must not dare to ask the indulgence of Heaven.

Suppose our national enemies do jeer us: shall we cower before the words of those whose swords we defy?

Suppose the world taunts us: why should we dread its ridicule? Are we depending on it? Is it doing anything for us? But such arguments, even if true, are unworthy of those who profess to look to God for instructions as to their duties; and yet, they are not even founded on just conclusions as to the state of things in the world. We tell all nations that we defend our institutions, because they are founded on God's Word: we refuse the advice of foreign intermeddlers, because, as we allege, their views of philanthropy are not based on Scriptural Truth.

If, then, we begin to conduct the whole system of slavery on Bible principles, we will demonstrate our consistency and sincerity: and so far from making ourselves liable to criticism we will stop the mouths of all who pretend to believe in the Sacred Oracles.

Secondly, The christian element of society, at the South, has failed in its collective capacity to organize such systematic, efficient and thorough means for the instruction of the heathen brought to its doors, as were easily in its power—and individual and believing masters have not properly appreciated and acted on their opportunities for the same great work.

This is a most important subject, and a whole book might be profitably devoted to it; but the limits and purposes of this work will permit only a bare allusion to some leading thoughts

The Church was organized to go into all the world and preach the gospel to every creature; and every individual christian is under orders to labor unceasingly for the extension of the Redeemer's Kingdom on earth.

In obedience to this command, the messenger of Christ is to brave the perils of the sea and of the wilderness—to endure hunger and thirst, heat and cold, to face persecutions, and to submit, if necessary, to the deprivation of every earthly source of enjoyment.

Some few missionaries, with the spirit of the Master, are now laboring in inhospitable regions among idolaters who fear and hate them, and whose speech they can understand with difficulty: they have gone to their work at heavy expense, they are deprived of the comforts of home and of civilized and christian society, and they know they must spend their lives with the hope, at best, of gathering only a handful of converts to the Cross of Christ.

The christian master can be a missionary to the people of the most ignorant and savage continent of the globe, without any of these hardships. Africa, from the beginning, has been a benighted region; but in these latter ages, multitudes of its teeming population have been brought to the christians of America, to the people who are the freest and happiest in their homes of any in the world, and placed under their care and protection.

Ethiopia has come to America; and not only so, but the missionary, in his home here of abundance, ease and comfort, in his home of perfect liberty of conscience, is clothed, fed and nursed by the heathen whom he is to instruct.

His hearer speaks his own language, shares in all his cares and sympathies, is docile and teachable, and looks up to him as his philosopher, guide and friend, in every affair of life. He is in his house : the instructor sees his pupil, without sacrifice of time, every day and night, and every day in the whole year has opportunities of preaching to him, effectually, the glorious gospel of the blessed God. And to add to all this, the worldly interest of the missionary is promoted by his faithful religious teachings : his hearer is his slave, and rendered more diligent, faithful and thrifty, more peaceable and obedient by his moral training.

Here, on this wonderful theatre, God would demonstrate, in the most obvious manner, what is really true in all cases—and that is, that the christian portion of the world has a direct temporal interest in faithfully performing the work of the Church.

Causes and results are here brought into immediate and visible contact : and christian masters and negro slaves are in a position to illustrate how believers are rendered more prosperous, secure and happy on earth by extending the influences of the gospel in the world.

If the christian slave can be a means of converting his owner, he is sure of better treatment—if the christian master is true to the spiritual interests of his slave, he will be more faithfully served.

The Church, in the slave States, is *immediately* paid, in temporal benefits, for its services to the heathen : it receives an instant reward, even in worldly blessings ; and its individual members are enriched, and made more secure in their homes, while their business is rendered less vexatious. And then, here is much of Africa, that land of a long, long night of death : here are the means of reaching soon, with the healing influences of the gospel, the very heart of the most savage and dreary portion of the earth.

Oh what glorious privileges have been enjoyed by the christian masters of America ! how great have been their inducements to use them to the utmost !

And what has been done ?

Much, indeed, has been accomplished—but it was not the result of direct effort, and of general desire and system. Perhaps, more of Africa's benighted race have been brought to a knowledge of the truth in the slave States of America, than in all the world besides : but this is due to circumstances, to the Providence of God, more than to the concerted and persevering efforts of the Church.

The Church has no right to point with pride to the thousands of its faithful members, gathered from the dusky sons of Canaan; it is either called on to weep that it has been so blind and cold and negligent.

It is the solemn duty of every christian master to consider himself as a missionary to his slaves—and the Church in its collective capacity is unfaithful to its Lord when it neglects to cultivate the African field with ceaseless care and diligence.

These hints are sufficient: let christian masters study their duties in the light of Scripture and of the great facts of their position, and let them look back and contrast with this standard, their actual conduct.

THIRDLY. Conscientious and christian masters have not exerted that influence on the conduct of hard and cruel proprietors which they might have done. In many places the public has to a certain extent understood its duties in this respect, and has, by voluntary exertions, restrained individuals from the inhuman treatment of their servants; but it is as incumbent on the community as a body politic to exercise its power in preventing abuses by masters as in the cases of husband and wife, and parent and child. The most sacred of all the relations is that of husband and wife; but in christian lands the law-making power considers it to be its privilege and its duty to protect the weaker party from cruel treatment by the stronger.

The interest of the master in his slave is clearly not inconsistent with the existence of such an authority in the State; for if the supreme power cannot prevent the inhumanity of its subjects towards their servants, then it is unable to perform the chief function of all authority, the repression of crime and the promotion of justice.

It is not necessary to discuss here the limits of such an authority in slave-holding communities; all right-thinking persons can draw the line for themselves, for it is as easy to prevent the injustice of masters without impairing their rightful authority as it is that of husbands and parents without violating their God-given rights. Besides, in our form of Government, the sovereignty reposes in the people—and in every State of the Confederacy the owners of slaves will control the Government.

Man, under all circumstances, may abuse his privileges—and it is no argument against slavery to say that the law has to protect the slave against the violence of the master. The argument might lie more plainly the other way—that slavery is an evil when there is no human power to regulate the conduct of the proprietor.

We do not conclude that civil Goverament is a sin because it is liable to abuse from the depraved passions of those who administer it : and it is no argument against the lawfulness of magistrates, and of the claims of husbands, parents and guardians that they have thrown around their evil tendencies the restraints of Constitution and laws.

There ever will be men who will be prompted by their passions to abuse any and every trust ; and for this reason it is that the Government was ordained of God, that it might repress the development of such passions into acts of injustice and cruelty. On this ground it is that slavery is justified : it subjects the passions of an inferior or more brutal race to the controlling influence of a superior

And now, since the Confederate States have severed their connection with abolition communities, there is no longer the semblance of a reason why the State should not represent the sentiment of the majority of its citizens in preventing the perversion of their authority on the part of individual proprietors of slaves.

This whole matter always belonged to the State and not to the general Government ; and hence the attempt at such an exercise of power never could have strengthened the hands of the enemies of the South.

But arguments derived from the conduct of abolition fanatics are now at an end ;—and the whole country being under the undisputed control of owners of slaves, it is the duty of the governing class at once to see that justice is done to its christian sentiment and character in such civil regulations as will tend effectually to prevent a cruel or brutal master from those acts which all condemn, and which are a reflection on the dignity and justice of the State.

This is an obligation which the whole community owes to God, the Supreme Arbiter and Judge ; for He represents Himself as being especially the guardian and defender of the poor, the helpless and the stranger, and if they cry in vain to the State for justice,He will depose the earthly Sovereign from his place. A. in all cases, interest is here combined with duty ; for by such repression of crimes by masters toward their slaves, the opposition to the institution of slavery is weakened, the slaves are made more contented, and there is much less danger of resistance and rebellion.

FOURTHLY. Since this revolution commenced, there has been a disposition manifested under great excitement, and seeming provocation, to take revenge on these poor deluded negroes who have been induced by severe temptations to quit the service of their masters, and withdraw to the lines of the public enemy. Those who have has-by instilled such ideas, must, on reflection, see their error, for their conclusions strike at the very root of the argument in favor of African slavery. The negro is supposed to be wholly incapable of self-government, and such indeed, is the fact; and for this reason, because he cannot know and choose what is for his own good, he is held in bondage, as a minor, who cannot safely be clothed with legal responsibility.

How then can he be an offender worthy of the vengeance of the State for being deceived and carried off by the flattering lies of those who promise him a better condition.

Is not the desire of change natural to all men? and how can the poor negro know but by actual experience, the vanity of those delusive hopes which his and his master's enemies present in such glowing colors before his imagination?

The truth is, the developments of this tremendous revolution have only placed masters under additional obligations to deal kindly with their servants, and to make every allowance for their ignorance and errors.

The disposition and conduct of the slaves of the Confederate States during this crisis are among the most remarkable phenomena of history; and no generous and discriminating mind can contemplate this picture without profound emotion.

The time was when it was considered dangerous to permit the slaves of America to hear of the discussions growing out of their condition; and the intrigues, designs and views of the abolitionists were, as far as possible, kept from their knowledge.

But the convulsion which has shaken the Continent has advertized itself, and all its issues to the feeblest intellects—and every inhabitant of the United States and of the Confederate States knows that the two nations are grappled in a life and death struggle over the existence of slavery.

The negroes are all aware that the whole of the resources of an immense power are put under contribution to change their condition: they see the country of their masters sealed up from the world by a navy which cannot be resisted, and their territories desolated by vast armies on whose banners is emblazoned freedom to the slave and death to his master.

They behold their owners driven from their homes in distress and poverty—they see the whole country drained of its men and arms, and having to exert every nerve and energy to ward off the fierce, terrible and thick-falling blows aimed at its destruction.

The whole white population of the Continent is tossed with furious passion—and there is a continual display of scenes calculated to harden the heart and chill, if not blast, all the charities, sympa-thies and sensibilities of nature.

Even the christian element is sorely tried by the furious tempest, and a deluge of selfishness sweeps away every restraint which law and public opinion had thrown round the avarice and ambition of depraved nature : and everywhere the eye rests on one wide scene of dreary desolation, man preying on his fellow, and seeking to devour him by open arms or by fraud and cunning.

And during all this long night of horrors the slave population, heretofore erroneously supposed to be the most dangerous part of society, has proved to be the most quiet and conservative ; and under temptations which have rarely assailed infirm nature, the negroes are generally found at their accustomed posts, diligently laboring for the sustenance of those whom they hear denounced as their enemies, contented, cheerful, docile and affectionate.

The Sirocco of selfishness which has dried up the tender charities of nature in all other races of the Continent, has made little impres-sion on their hearts ; and though, like their owners, they have been put to many inconveniences, their pliant natures have readily adapt-ed themselves to the change of circumstances, and they cling to the fortunes of their distressed proprietors with a constancy and unfail-ing devotion which are among the most shining displays of this fear-ful crisis.

Shall these things make no impression ? shall they be forgotten ? Will.the ruling . e fail to learn the lessons which they so impres-sively teach ?

There have been, of course, exceptions to the conduct herein des-cribed ; but could any have expected the infirmities of depraved na-ture, in an ignorant and half-barbarous race, to have given way in fewer instances to the powerfully seductive influence. brought to bear upon them ?

The slaves, by a general rebellion, could have added serious com-plications to the horrors of this revolution : but so far from striking against their masters, they have been a great source of strength, and have vastly added to the means of defence against their professed liberators.

The conduct of the faithful majority has more than atoned for the errors of those who have been seduced, bribed or driven to disaffec-tion ; and this fidelity under fiery trials is not to be a reason for a treatment hereafter based on the supposition that they have no feel-ings or aspirations, but for a course of management which shall ir-al... a just appreciation of their loyalty, and a true regard for their wants.

Their conduct seems to be a clear indication that God does not disapprove of their condition as slaves: it seems to settle, in the most conclusive manner, the question as to the abstract right of their masters to hold them in bondage.

If God had been moving for a general change of their condition, there would have been, everywhere, unmistakable sings of this in their own disposition—for when a race is about to be conducted to a new destiny, its whole nature begins to bud with signs of the coming revolution. On the other hand, while the conduct of the slaves settles the lawfulness of their position, it, also, as clearly demonstrates the obligations of their masters; and if these latter fail to see and appreciate their duties, let them beware lest the next revolution begins in a different place.

And FINALLY, as the poor negro has proved his fidelity to his master under the greatest temptations that could assail him, let not the latter excuse himself from his duties on the ground that the times interpose difficulties in his way.

Did the slave say he would serve and labor for his master when the country was settled, and he could not pursue any other course? Did he adjourn his obedience until the armies which promised him liberation, were removed, and until the independence of the country having been acquired, he would have to make a virtue of necessity, and would then be an obedient servant because he had no other safe course to pursue?

Shall not the master vindicate the justice of his claims by a moral courage as honorable to him as that which has been displayed by his servant?

Will he not now, in this very day of trial, courageously dare the taunts of his enemies in purging his statute-book of every injustice to the devoted slave who has so nobly stood by him in his hour of need?

This is the kind of retaliation that will make both races glorious; this is the work now needed to crown the heroism of the nation and to give consistency and enduring lustre to this grand revolution.

The fidelity of the slave makes it a debt of honor which cannot be delayed—the courage and devotion of the ruling race, in the face of a frowning world, require it as the crowning act of greatness, and the justice of God demands it.

Noble Confederate brethren! you are meeting with steadfast courage many dangers which might appal less constant and heroic spirits: let us crown our deeds *by conquering our own prejudices*, BY DARING TO DO WHAT IS RIGHT, and our triumph will be certain and our history glorious!

CHAPTER V.

Sins of the Confederate States, continued.—The people enter on a new national career, and accept the awful issue of civil war, forced upon them, without that humble and reverent desire to secure the favor of God becoming in a christian community placed in such solemn circumstances.—Neglect of gospel agencies at the commencement of the war.

It is respectfully suggested that all of us have offended in the spirit with which we have received the chastisements of Heaven during the present war.

As it was remarked in a former part of this work, God often corrects nations and individuals for what He sees in them, as well as for the development of these dispositions in outward acts; and in His sight the people of the Confederate States must have appeared entirely confident and secure in a sense of their own righteousness.

There is a great deal of intelligence among the people of the Confederate States; and they were sufficiently taught by history to know that civil wars are always terrible and afflictive.

When the President of the United States made a wicked appeal to the arbitrament of the sword, thus committing a flagrant outrage on the letter and spirit of the institutions he was called to preserve, every educated man could see that an awful conflagration had commenced; and while it was incumbent on all to enter on this new and most momentous crisis in American history with humiliation and prayer, the whole continent was in a blaze with the jubilant manifestations of an opposite disposition.

It is not necessary to refer to the wild exultation of hate, malice and unholy ambition which characterized the aggressors in this fearful strife—the purpose of this work is to deal only with the sins of the people of the Confederate States.

It becomes this nation to meet the bloody issue forced upon it with unanimity, with energy and fortitude; but all those, and an enthusiastic patriotism, always a virtue, are entirely consistent with humility towards God, confession of sins, and sincere repentance for them.

But because we were right in our controversy with our human adversary, we seemed to take it for granted that we stood justified in the sight of Heaven; and it must be confessed that while the acts

26

and proclamations of the highest political authorities were intended to remind the people of the duty and necessity of humiliation, the indiscreet course f certain spiritual guides often had an opposite effect.

It was a fiery trial—and in the first excitement, christians did not distinguish between sins towa l ir enemies and sins in the sight of God.

There was a failure to apply justly to self the principles of the Divine Economy often before expounded correctly in theory; and there were implied reflections on the supremacy of the great Arbiter, when we constantly assumed that He was wholly with us, in the sense of aiding us with all His power to resist our adversaries.

God being the absolute Disposer, we could not suffer without His direct permission ; and if He did permit us to be afflicted without sin, then His justice was imperfect.

If He was infinitely holy, and was trying to deliver us, His power was not supreme—for the war continued, and its afflictions multiplied.

Besides, it is always irreverent in frail creatures to presume on the favor of Heaven without a sincere, humble and prayerful searching of their dispositions and previous conduct; nor is it at all honoring to God to note only those providences which favor us and to ignore all those which have borne heavily upon us. Such a disposition often leads us away from the appointed channels of the Divine essing—it blinds us to the lessons that are intended to admonish us of errors that may prove fatal, and confirms us in sins of which God would heal us.

The writer desires to deal with his countrymen, on this subject, with great tenderness and charity ; but his sense of duty to their best interests, and to the universal Judge, compels him to say that the whole Church did not seem to be fully alive, at first, to the true character and meaning of our national trials ; it was not universally taught that those troubles were permitted by a Holy and Almighty God, and were, in fact, His direct chastisements for the sins of the land.

Perhaps, this is enough on this topic—especially as a more healthy spirit, and one much more honoring to God, is now generally exhibited.

It must, however, be added, by way of warning, that often when persons think they are honoring the Deity by giving glory to Him, they are only flattering themselves ; for, in such cases, only the victories which advance their cause are ascribed to Him, while there is no recognition of His Hand or His Justice in adverse or discouraging events.

It is extremely gratifying to our self-esteem to believe that the Sovereign of the universe takes our part, and works for our deliverance—but if we attribute only successes to Him, it is ourselves that we honor and not Him. The Mahommedan, the Inquisitor and the Hindoo all alike ascribe glory to the Deity when their hopes are gratified; and a spirit that goes no farther, however much it may use the great name of Jehovah, is not the piety of the true believer in the Lord Jesus Christ.

The christian beholds the rod, and who hath appointed it;—He hears the Lord's voice crying to the city in every calamity, and always when smitten as well as when lifted up, he is ready to say, "Thou didst it," and Thou art "justified when Thou speakest, and clear when Thou judgest," for I acknowledge my transgressions, and my sin is ever before me."

AGAIN: At the commencement of hostilities, there was a disposition on the part of some of those to whose keeping, under God, is committed the honor and prosperity of His spiritual Kingdom on earth, to regard the work of the Church as of secondary importance for the time at least.

Perhaps, this did not result so much from a desire to ignore the paramount claims of the appointed means of grace and of blessing to individuals and nations, as from a confused but most unscriptural idea that the great Adversary of God and man had radically changed his policy, and the seat of his machinations.

It was forgotten, in the whirl of things, that the human heart, everywhere on earth, is the field of Satan's operations; and the country, seeing so much of the Devil's work in the conduct of its carnal foes, was inclined to regard this contest of nations as being an issue between the powers of light and darkness.

The Church did not take the pains it might and ought to have assumed to correct this radical and fatal error, and yet one natural to the carnal mind; and so, those agencies on which the happiness of society always depends, were greatly neglected, while those whose business it is to work them with ceaseless devotion and faith in their efficacy and in their's alone, seemed to encourage the idea that the kingdom and power of Satan would be most effectually curtailed by those material weapons which would kill the bodies of men under his influence.

Nothing can be more opposite to the whole theory of the Scriptures—yet general action seemed to indicate general acquiescence in this fatal delusion.

The result is an impressive and most just display of Divine justice. The Church was permitted to see that which it deemed most essential—the State was united, as one man, in its political faith, and the whole population has been ready to give itself, and all it has to increase the military strength of the country.

Such loyalty to government, under the most searching trials, such a spirit of self-sacrifice and heroism to lend energy to the military arm have never been witnessed before in any people : but right here this union, liberality and courage cease.

The Union asked for was granted : the machinations of the Evil One in the points dreaded were prevented or defeated.

This work, dealing with and for the life of a nation, of a people the dearest to the writer of all others, must speak honestly ; and it must be stated that there was a general impression that the assaults of the Devil were to be feared only through the United States and the sympathizers with that power.

Such views were natural to those who are without the spiritual discernment of true christianity.

The government of the nation referred to, had declared an unprovoked war on the rights, liberties and very existence of the people of the Confederate States—and its subjects seemed united and enthusiastic, and ready to sacrifice themselves in a phrenzied effort to destroy those who simply desired to be left alone.

It was excusable in men of the world—it was even an indication of a generous nature in such, to suppose that these apparently Satanic movements would be resisted, by those who were so cruelly threatened, with united hands and brotherly hearts. Such persons naturally supposed that opposition to the political movements instigated by the Arch-Fiend, was opposition, out-and-out, to his whole character and aims ; and that none of those who were arrayed against the work he was seemingly instigating through national agencies were liable to his deceptions or likely to serve under his banners.

But it was the duty of the Church to see and instantly to correct this great mistake ; and it ought to have known that the Prince of of darkness makes his most fatal attacks on man not by the carnal weapons of their human foes, but through the evil impulses of their own fallen natures.

Unhappily, these sure approaches to the very citadel of the nation's life were left unguarded by those who, under God, can alone contend successfully at these vital points—and the Father of lies, exceeding in his bold and profound strategy, entered through the defenceless breaches, and gained one of his grandest apparent triumphs.

While the Church was busy in the work of others, and for which it was little qualified, it left the important domain committed to its special care, to the ravages of the enemy; and now, when it is too late, we see that the Devil can most successfully serve our national foes not by striking through their fleshly arms, or working in their hearts, but by corrupting our own natures, and causing our own hands to inflict on ourselves those deadly blows which always come from home.

Behold to-day the results of a practical disbelief in the doctrines of human depravity with respect to our own people! Look at the wide-spread moral desolations of the country, and say if a learned and orthodox Church was ever more emphatically and suddenly reminded of a neglect of duty!

And see how society has suffered, not by the desertion of their posts by all or any large part of the spiritual guides of the country, but by the merely temporary relaxation of the energies of the Church in their appropriate sphere.

Would the loss of half a score of great battles have entailed so many disasters, and so seriously threatened the subjugation of the country?

Have we not already partially surrendered our independence?—Freedom begins in the soul, and while this is virtuous and heroic it cannot be destroyed by killing mortal bodies—when this is corrupted and demoralized, it is ready for submission and chains.

Has not the heart of the nation been nearly paralyzed with selfishness, intense, inordinate and insatiate?

Behold the swarm of extortioners, speculators, gamblers, house-burners, and robbers who are preying with voracious appetite upon the carcass of the body-politic, and say if the life of independence can long survive! See the horde of hungry camp-followers of the Devil gathering spoils in the heart of every society, and deny, if we can, the necessity of preaching repentance to our own people as well as to others!

It is unnecessary to try to enumerate the victims that have fallen here under the power of the wicked one; their bodies lie festering in corruption in every neighborhood from the Potomac to the Rio Grande.

Every where human depravity asserts its existence and its power in our fallen countrymen: the slain cannot be buried from our sight or smell, and we look on appalled at the dreadful slaughter.

It is not intended, in the remarks above, to reflect on those individual ministers who supposed that from education and the bent of

their genius they had peculiar qualifications needed in other departments in the infancy of our national existence; but to show the fatal character of the impression that the gospel is less important at
one time than another.

The error with which this work would deal was that disposition
to consider the preaching of the Gospel and the proper work of the
Church, a thing, for the time, not so essential as other matters; an
error which does not appear so much in doctrinal expositions as in
the actions of those who ought to know that Christ is always and every where the light and the life of the world.

The true Gospel is based on the idea that all men are by nature
depraved—and that every family of the race of Adam is capable, if
not restrained by the grace of God, of any wickedness or enormity
ever committed by mortals. It implies that Christianity is the salt
of the earth—and that but for it there is no society that would no.
rot in its own filth, or call down by its abominations the vengeance
of Heaven. The work of the Church is to preach these things to
all men, at all times, "beginning at Jerusalem," or its own home,
among its own kindred, and those who from their intimate connection with true believers may be outwardly, nationally or ceremo-
niously, most moral, to declare to the world that it lies in wickedness, that it is alienated from the life of God, and liable to any abomination, and to eternal wrath, and to present a crucified Redeemer
the only hope of individuals and of nations; to labor for the conversion of individuals from death to life, from the bondage and darkness of nature to the glorious life, light and liberty of the gospel of
peace, as the only means of reforming society, of blessing our country or of doing good to the world. This is the work of the Church
—the work of God, the only work that promises any good to men
or nations: it cannot be suspended for any human contingency, and
if there is any time when it is more important than others, any cri
sis when the welfare of individuals and States demands a more faithful
earnest and constant exposition of the great truths of Scripture, and
a solemn application to the hearts and consciences of our own people
of their dreadful state by nature, and of their need of regeneration
through the power of the Holy Spirit, it is when they are entering
on the awful drama of revolution and civil war.

We could have known this without the sad lessons with which a
holy and merciful God has reproved our errors; but it is not yet
too late to retrace our ways, and the nation may be saved, though
society must long suffer from the deplorable wounds which the Adversary has made upon it.

Let us confess our sins and turn from them ; and if we love our own country more than other lands, and prize the welfare of our own people above that of other nations, let us stand in the gaps here, and girded with the whole armor of God, be as zealous and courageous to fight His battles on our own soil as in the distant regions of our human foes.

We cannot now reform our national enemies if we would, and our exhortations and rebukes to him being so connected with political excitements, would be anything else but profitable : but we have at home a wide and glorious field, and one in which we can successfully labor without complicating the work of the Church, in the minds of those to be benefited, with the passions of the world or the issues of political parties. We are called to it by the voice of patriotism, by the instincts of self-interest, and by the command of God ; and if we are wise and destined to be saviours coming up on Mount Zion for the rescue of a bleeding land, to be repairers of the breach, and to make the wilderness and solitary place glad for us, and to rejoice in fruitfulness and beauty, we will go forward to its culture without delay.

"Come, and let us return unto the Lord : for He hath torn, and he will heal us; he hath smitten, and he will bind us up......

Then shall we know, if we follow on to know the Lord : his going forth is prepared as the morning ; and He shall come unto us as the rain, as the latter *and* former rain unto the earth."---(*Hosea* vi. 1-3.)

CONCLUSION.

The writer of this work entertains an abiding hope that God is with the people of the Confederate States in the best and highest sense.

He has laid upon them the rod of affliction : and when He smites it is always for sin, and with the purpose of correcting or destroying.

It is as certain as the existence of a righteous and almighty Deity that the country is suffering for its offences towards Him : it is equally certain that the Author of these afflictions will make them effectual for His purposes. If He intends only to correct, He will not withhold His hand until there is repentance and reformation : if He designs to destroy, all the creature power of the universe cannot prevent the accomplishment of His will.

The earth is His, and He made it—and His opposeless will must be carried out upon it, and in all its deep places.

From the whole tenor of the Divine Word, and from the manner in which the people of the Confederate States are suffering, it is evident that the result of their chastisement is to depend on themselves. Though sorely afflicted, they have over and over again been delivered in a way that clearly indicates the mercy of Heaven ; and there can be no doubt that if they will make the right use of their troubles, these fiery trials will be made to inure to their lasting advantage. In this way the Lord is with the country ; but if it, from pride, will not accept of its judgments as of Divine origin, and will not, therefore, enquire for and remove the offending cause, these troubles will not be stayed.

It is not reverence for God, but respect for their own righteousness that induces individuals and nations to consider their sufferings as wholly the work of the Devil or of the creature agents employed : it is not because they really think God too good and just to punish them so cruelly, but because, in fact, they esteem themselves too good and just to merit the displeasure of Heaven.

This is a most unhealthy disposition, and it is infinitely more dangerous to a people than all the fleets and armies of a hostile world.

If such is our temper, it must be purged out of us as an absolutely necessary step to our deliverance—and if we refuse to be healed of this disposition, we never can be saved from the judgments it has brought upon us.

It is not necessary to enquire why this Confederacy is more afflicted than other nations; if the most righteous people were to be dealt with according to their own merits, they would instantly be destroyed.

The fact, therefore, that more corrupt communities are now suffering less than we are, is no argument against the Divine origin of our calamities; it is indeed one great reason to demonstrate the mercy that sends our trials.

"Whom the Lord loveth he chasteneth;" and they who receive such chastening with the repentance and submission of children, will be greatly benefited by it.

To receive punishment as a child is to *receive it as the work of our Father, to acknowledge its justice, to find in our own conduct the causes, and thus to honor the afflicting Parent and to abase ourselves.*

God's honor and our humility are essentially connected: and if, under His rod, we act as dutiful children, we will confess our faults, approve our stripes, and try to amend our ways.

God is evidently dealing with us as a just and merciful Father: He sees in us errors that would lead to our ruin, and He smites us to turn us from these sins whose wages will be death.

The whole inspired Word is full of such teaching—and the doctrine is illustrated with force and tenderness in the 2nd chapter of the prophecy of Hosea.

The nation of the Jews, the nominal and visible Church, is represented as a beloved and erring wife, seduced from her duty and affection to her faithful husband; and the Lord, speaking in the character of the latter, reminds her of her poor and despised condition before she was honored by his love, and tells her that he will take from her the wealth and luxuries, the jewels and fine apparel which He had bestowed upon her, and leave her in the squalid and destitute condition in which He found her.

Yet though she has grievously injured Him, He will not finally repudiate her from His care and affections; and in His apparently harsh treatment He is adopting means to recover her from her follies, and to restore her again to her right position of a virtuous, loved and honored wife.

The Divine speaker thus concludes His account of the means by which He will accomplish His just and benevolent ends:

"Therefore, behold, I will allure her, and bring her into the wilderness, and speak comfortably unto her.

• And I will give her her vineyards from thence, and the valley of Achor for a door of hope: and she shall sing there, as in the days of her youth, and as in the day when she came up out of the land of Egypt."—*Hosea*, ii, 14, 15.

The force and beauty of this passage have no parallel in uninspired writings.

The Bible reader will remember that the valley of Achor, means the valley of trouble: it is the name of the place where Achan and his house-hold were stoned for causing trouble to Israel by taking of the accursed thing.

An expedition of Joshua against the men of Ai was defeated—and in answer to the prayers of the leader of Israel, God informed him why this disaster had overtaken his arms and why the Divine Power was against him even while he was attempting to execute its express command. (See *Joshua* chap. viii—and Part first of this work.)

The first step in the reformation of the frail and sinning wife was to strip her of her ornaments and to reduce her to poverty; and while this seemed harsh, it was a mercy, for it turned from her the affections of her seducers, humbled her vain pride, and brought to her mind the true source of her comforts.

Then her faithful and loving Lord *allures* her into the wilderness: takes her into a desert place—the verb of action indicating, with great pathos and force, the kindness of the motive and the manner of this action.

To "take into the wilderness" is a very expressive figure often used in Scripture to indicate the apparently severe trials by which individuals and especially communities, and the Church are to be reformed.

Thus it was a great mercy to be carried into the wilderness, to be cut off from human society, from human philosophy, and from human aid: it was a sure indication of a purpose to prepare the subject of these trials by such an education as their blind and corrupt natures demanded, for a high and illustrious destiny.

In this state—in the solitary desert, where the voice of seduction cannot be heard, and where the luxuries and society that corrupt the soul, cannot be found, the erring wife is not left to desolation and despair. When she is humbled, and thoughtful, filled with sorrow for her vain and sinful life, her True Lord comes to her and "speaks comfortably to her:" He tenderly indicates His abiding care, and His unchanged affection, He wins her back to her first love.

and loyalty, and finding in Him and in His love and in her own now virtuous affections, in her self-respect and elevating society a new life that renews her virtuous and happy youth, she sings as in the sinless and joyful days of her first espousals. Yea, from thence, through this wilderness lies the road to her vineyards, to her comforts and wealth—and the valley of Achor, the low vale of trouble and trial is the very door of a new and blessed hope which never could have dawned upon her in her former courses.

How instructive and how full of encouragement is this passage of the Sacred Oracles, to the people of the Confederate States!

We are, dear friends, in a howling wilderness; and we came into these desert wastes as soon as we started from our old country to the new one which we would build up for ourselves.

It was the mercy of the Supreme Ruler which caused our road to through these dreary wastes: for here we can remember and repent of our former ingratitude, infidelity and idolatry, here we are compelled to feel our dependence on that Divine Power which bore and nourished us all the days of old, which by a series of amazing Providences, brought our fathers to the wilds of America, settled and protected them here, and from a poor, despised and ignoble condition, lifted them to the highest places of the earth, clothed them with rich apparel, fed them with the finest of the wheat, and with milk and honey and butter of kine, and poured upon them every comfort and luxury. Our prosperity hardened our hearts, we forgot the hand that brought us forth from Egypt, from the house of bondage; and our corrupt affections went a whoring after the gods and the abominations of the nations.

But we were not left to perish in our corruptions: we are allured from our seductive associations, from the society of men, from the enjoyments and philosophy that made our souls to stray, and in these desolate wastes God comes to us with awful displays, and pleads with us face to face.

We are shut up to the guidance and protection of the Sole Arbiter: we are brought back to the true Source of all national and individual life and happiness.

God has come to us to talk with us and teach us; He has brought us out here to expose to us our diseased condition, to bring all our pernicious ways to our minds, to learn us anew our dependence on Him, to wean us from our idolatrous and our pernicious ways, and to make with us anew the covenant of life and peace which was solemnly signed when we were espoused to Him and brought poor and naked to this western world.

If we are teachable—if we will turn to the counsels of Him who would wind us to Himself, this wilderness will lead us to our vineyards: this valley of trouble shall be the door of hope, because it is the way to God!

"Who is wise, and he shall understand these *things?* prudent and he shall know them? For the ways of the Lord *are* right, and the just shall walk in them: but the transgressors shall fall therein."—*Hosea*, xiv. 9.